DEAD LUCKY

DEAD LUCKY

LIFE AFTER DEATH ON MOUNT EVEREST

Lincoln Hall

JEREMY P. TARCHER/PENGUIN
a member of Penguin Group (USA) Inc.
New York

JEREMY P. TARCHER/PENGUIN
Published by the Penguin Group
Penguin Group (USA) Inc., 375 Hudson Street, New York, New York 10014, USA •
Penguin Group (Canada), 90 Eglinton Avenue East, Suite 700, Toronto, Ontario M4P 2Y3, Canada
(a division of Pearson Canada Inc.) • Penguin Books Ltd, 80 Strand, London WC2R 0RL, England •
Penguin Ireland, 25 St Stephen's Green, Dublin 2, Ireland (a division of Penguin Books Ltd) •
Penguin Group (Australia), 250 Camberwell Road, Camberwell, Victoria 3124, Australia
(a division of Pearson Australia Group Pty Ltd) • Penguin Books India Pvt Ltd, 11 Community Centre,
Panchsheel Park, New Delhi–110 017, India • Penguin Group (NZ), 67 Apollo Drive, Rosedale,
North Shore 0632, New Zealand (a division of Pearson New Zealand Ltd) • Penguin Books
(South Africa) (Pty) Ltd, 24 Sturdee Avenue, Rosebank Johannesburg 2196, South Africa

Penguin Books Ltd, Registered Offices:
80 Strand, London WC2R 0RL, England

Originally published in Australia by Random House 2007
First trade paperback edition 2009
Copyright © 2007, 2009 by Lincoln Hall
Interior illustrations © 2007 by Ken Beatty

Most Tarcher/Penguin books are available at special quantity discounts for bulk purchase for sales pro-
motions, premiums, fund-raising, and educational needs. Special books or book excerpts also can be created
to fit specific needs. For details, write Penguin Group (USA) Inc. Special Markets, 375 Hudson Street, New
York, NY 10014.

The Library of Congress catalogued the hardcover as follows:

Hall, Lincoln.
Dead lucky : life after death on Mount Everest / Lincoln Hall.
p.   cm.
Originally published in Australia by Random House in 2007;
published simultaneously in Canada.
Includes index.
ISBN 978-1-58542-646-1
1. Hall, Lincoln, date.   2. Mountaineers—Australia—Biography.
3. Mountaineering accidents—Everest, Mount (China and Nepal).
4. Mountaineering—Everest, Mount (China and Nepal).   I. Title.
GV199.92.H3235A3   2008   2008006676
796.522092—dc22
[B]

ISBN 978-1-58542-719-2 (paperback edition)

Printed in the United States of America
3   5   7   9   10   8   6   4   2

BOOK DESIGN BY AMANDA DEWEY

While the author has made every effort to provide accurate telephone numbers and Internet addresses at the
time of publication, neither the publisher nor the author assumes any responsibility for errors, or for changes
that occur after publication. Further, the publisher does not have any control over and does not assume any
responsibility for author or third-party websites or their content.

TO MY FAMILY,

Barbara, Dylan, Dorje,
Al, Julia, and Michele

CONTENTS

FOREWORD

by Lachlan Murdoch

ON THE MORNING OF Saturday, May 27, 2006, the world's newspapers had an obvious splash. Lincoln Hall, one of Australia's most accomplished mountaineers, had survived a night near the summit of Mount Everest after having been declared dead by his fellow climbers. "Back from the dead," "Lazarus," and "Miracle climber" were all words employed by zealous editors as they tried to convey what none of us could really imagine: a night spent alone in the thin air of 28,000 feet, balanced precipitously between the mountain and a great void below, between hallucinatory visions and terrifying reality, between life and death.

Having met Lincoln many years ago, I would not have been shocked to hear of his death on the world's highest mountain. I would probably have been more shocked to read that he had died in a car accident or crossing the road. That's not because I thought he was some thrill seeker, some adrenaline junkie with a death wish. Actually, I knew Lincoln to be an excellent and very accomplished climber. The fact is, several great climbers I had either met as a youth or bumped into at climbing campgrounds or parking lots have since prematurely met their end. The headlines that morning in May 2006 were so shocking, not because Lincoln died on Everest that night but because he did not.

An extremely experienced mountaineer, who had both the good sense and great discipline to turn back shy of Everest's summit in 1984, Lincoln wrote of that decision in his book *White Limbo* that "The summit was not everything. Survival was," and of the disappointment he would later feel for having lost what he then believed was his one chance to stand for a few moments upon the top of the world. Knowing that had he pushed on to the summit he would likely have died, he wrote: "Although I will never see the summit panorama other than through the eyes of Tim and Greg [his fellow climbers], I know no view is worth that price."

Unexpectedly, twenty-two years later, Lincoln had a second chance to summit Everest. He climbed strongly to the mountain's apex, where he did indeed enjoy the rarest of views. It was a perfect day. With only a few clouds in the sky and with the lightest wind, Lincoln was feeling good. He would not, it appeared, have to pay that ultimate price. Critically, he was focused on the dangers of the descent ahead.

Next time you look at a summit picture, try to look beyond the tired faces allowing quick, compulsory smiles framed by panoramic views. Often you will see something else. Sometimes, below the surface, you will see the summiteers' weariness, their knowledge that the climb is only half complete. Perhaps an eye askew on the weather, or on the time, or on a struggling climbing partner, or an ear picking up the muffled sound of a distant avalanche. Adrenaline and fear are both characters in the background, along with the ever-present danger of acute altitude sickness at the most extreme heights.

Lincoln did not linger on the summit and started down the mountain after allowing himself the briefest of rests. It was then disaster struck. The day and night that followed were extraordinary by any measure and comprise a story that is certain to become a classic of mountaineering literature. The narrative tells us not only of Lincoln's journey back from the dead but also of his family's and colleagues' struggle to come to terms with the loss of a husband, father, and friend before learning of his miraculous survival. Why do some of us climb mountains while others are happy with a comfortable job and a decent retirement plan? Why do some need to find their limit, step right up to it, peer over the edge, and step gingerly back? The question has been asked so many times it is now a sort of cliché, although at its heart it is really a riddle. Readers searching for a simple answer to such a question will not find it within *Dead Lucky,* as no book or essay or lecture can expose an answer to something that cannot be taught or learned. It must be felt. What Lincoln Hall does so effectively in *Dead Lucky* is allow the reader into the most private thoughts and feelings of a man who must climb mountains; and in doing so, gives us some hints to perhaps allow us to unravel the riddle for ourselves.

A keen reader of mountaineering literature will immediately recognize *Dead Lucky* as among the very best of its genre. It is a top-shelf book and a great read. Those familiar with his earlier books will notice a slightly older, more mature Lincoln in these pages. He is a very human character, with strongly felt responsibilities to his family, which at times he struggles to reconcile with his climbing. He is also a character who knows his own limitations and frailties, and understands that sometimes on a mountain, as in life, events can happen that are unexpected and out of your control. In effect, he is more like the rest of us, which makes his story all the more remarkable.

AUTHOR'S NOTE

DEAD LUCKY HAS BEEN the most difficult of the eight books I have written, which hardly seems fair because it was an intense adventure that only needed to be written down. But the issue of writing was where my problems began—frostbite to my hands made it hard enough for me to hold up my trousers, let alone write a book. The benefit of an adventure that kills you and then brings you back to life is that the key scenes are unforgettable. Unable to write or type, I made use of the dictaphone that I had taken on the expedition. I have found that the best way for me to add conversations to a book is to repeat them into a recording device as soon as possible after they have been spoken. Luckily, my almost-undamaged left thumb was all I needed to operate the dictaphone, and instead of just conversations, I was constantly recording thoughts, relating incidents, and describing scenes.

My efforts to gather the building blocks for my book received a giant boost when Brent Waters offered to help me recall those parts of my adventure that remained unclear to me. His method was to ask me to relate in detail the events of the expedition—which I willingly did, for up to five hours at a time. Brent sometimes asked for more detail and sometimes identified gaps in my story. In this way, he managed to prompt me to recall vividly much of what had happened. All of this was recorded on Brent's dictaphone. As well as prompting memories to surface, the process also helped me understand my part in the broader narrative of the pre-monsoon Everest climbing season of 2006. What was omitted from this narrative were the colors and the sounds and the shapes that help paint a big picture. As soon as I was able to write, I began to build upon the framework by adding people, places, moods, emotions, and conversations.

During my twenties, mountaineering expeditions were a regular part of my life, but the past two decades have been quite different. My focus has been on my family, and major expeditions have been few and far between. More commonly, I have led simpler climbing trips as a guide, which allowed me to stay in touch with the mountains without being away for more than three or four weeks. But the true connection with a mountain can happen only during a major mountaineering expedition. From the moment I commit to an expedition, my life becomes more intense. Success can only come with proper planning from the beginning, so immediately there is attention to detail. What was different about my 2006 visit to Mount Everest was that the attention to detail continued after the expedition was over. My frostbitten extremities and my weakened body meant that every act had to be taken with great care. My book was constantly in my mind and my dictaphone was constantly nearby. The sense of commitment that began when I decided to go to Everest continued until I completed the very last page of this book.

There are particular barriers to writing a firsthand account of a high-altitude mountaineering expedition. Physical exhaustion and oxygen deprivation threaten the mind as much as the body. In everyday life, one's memory is compromised by omission or misinterpretation, but at high altitude the effect is much greater, and precise recall is very difficult. After a major summit is achieved, the broad picture may be shared by everyone who was there, but individual details will be different. Accordingly, some of what I have written here may differ from the accounts of others who were on Mount Everest at the same time. For example, the demise of Jacques-Hugues Letrange, as reported on the Internet, differed greatly from the version of events related to me by Caroline Letrange on the day she returned to Advance Base Camp from her high point of 27,000 feet.

Apart from such irregularities, which are to be expected, I had the different languages of cerebral edema and hallucinations to translate for my readers. Both these influences gave me a very different take on reality. My approach was to immerse myself in these altered states so that I could convey the experiences. My last three books have been about other people, so it is refreshing to write a story of my own again. One of the great satisfactions of writing is that in order to convey a feeling or a concept in my writing I am first forced to understand it myself; only then can it ring true for my readers. In the same vein, when I succeed in describing the nature of a landscape—as opposed to just throwing a few adjectives at it—I feel more connected to that place, to the point where the writing becomes a silent dialogue with the natural world.

This book is not a comprehensive account of what happened on the Tibetan side of Mount Everest in April and May 2006. It is my personal story. The conversations related here, if not always verbatim, are true in essence. Many are based upon recordings made on video cameras, iPods, and dictaphones, as well as transcripts of radio and television interviews. Several members of our expedition have been able to confirm details with me. Their contributions were particularly useful because I left my diary in a tent at 27,000 feet, and I was not able to retrieve it during the difficult descent that followed two days later. Perhaps, one day, a high-altitude archaeologist will stumble across my diary and will ratify the events contained in *Dead Lucky*. Far more likely, however, is that the tent where I left my black notebook will be destroyed by the wind, with the disintegration of the notebook itself following not long afterward. Pages will take off in the breeze like errant Buddhist prayer flags. But instead of holy messages, those fluttering pages will carry only jottings of homesickness, friendship, and the fulfillment of dreams.

LUKLA

AMA DABLAM

LHOTSE

MT. EVEREST   NUPTSE

CAMP3
27,200 feet
            CAMP 2 25,300 feet
      NORTH COL X
      23,200 feet CAMP 1
                                              2006
ABC X   CHANGTSE   NEPALESE BASE
21,000 feet   X CAMP
                        LHO LA
                        19,800 feet

                                    X ABC 1984
                                      18,000 feet

INTERMEDIATE CAMP X
      19,000 feet   2006

                                          2006, 1984
                                          X BASE CAMP
                                            17,000 feet

N

EVEREST 1984

A DEEP RUMBLE SHATTERED the peace of the mountainscape—the familiar, gut-wrenching roar of an avalanche. Alone and 3,000 feet above the Rongbuk Glacier, I felt safe, huddled in the embryonic hollow that was the beginnings of our snow-cave. Every avalanche of the last few weeks had taken one of two courses. Either they plummeted down the Great Couloir—a wide ice gully immediately to the east of me that split Mount Everest's North Face from its summit pyramid to the bottom of the mountain—or they peeled away from the slab that spread westward across the entire expanse of the North Face.

My bolt-hole in the mountainside was at this stage so small that I had to twist and wriggle to escape onto the three-foot-wide ledge I had dug along the slope outside. Within fifteen seconds I was on the ledge, a frozen porch set in the heavens. The tiny snow-cave, destined to become our Camp Two—our first camp on the mountain itself—was in the side of a spur that rose above the surrounding slopes like a shark's fin above the waves. I envisioned that any avalanche coming my way would be parted by the spur, just as the fin would cut through water.

Most of the avalanches occurred to the west of me, so I looked in that direction, across the vast snow-covered slab I had named White Limbo. My eyes were hungry for the unmatchable display of power that is a Himalayan avalanche. Still, I heard the roar, but there was nothing to be seen. I looked to the east, but the snow slopes of the North Ridge were frozen and motionless. The sound grew louder, the thunder bearing down. I lifted my head and gasped in horror.

The snow-load from the entire upper section of the Great Couloir had cut loose, creating a monster avalanche. Huge clouds of it fanned outward, too much to be funneled down the couloir. Within moments, the overflow would wipe me and my invincible spur off the mountain, like hairs shaved from an upper lip, such was the scale of this awesome place.

But I wasn't interested in the scale of things. I seized my only hope—there must always be hope—and groveled back into the snow-cave. Already claustrophobic, I peered anxiously through the low entrance, my heart furiously thumping. Within seconds the avalanche hit. A blast of air blew spindrift through the entrance, then hundreds of tons of snow roared by with the speed and momentum of an express train. More snow swirled into the cave and still more thundered past in a constant blur of white. Instinct drove me to wriggle out, away from the threat of being buried alive inside the slope. But as soon as I dragged myself out onto the ledge, I thought the avalanche would now crush me. It was too late to do anything but lie low on the ledge, facedown, my hands over my nose and mouth to keep out the snow. Time seemed to freeze, but the snow kept coming. I wanted it to be over, but also I wanted time to remain frozen so I could stay alive.

Then suddenly the whiteness vanished, and with it the noise. In its place was an incredibly bright sky, not yet blue but filled with millions of crushed snowflakes, particles sparkling as if the world's entire supply of glitter had been thrown into the sky above me. I lay on my back, laughing with delight and trembling uncontrollably. Our special spur had, in fact, proved to be invincible.

Suddenly I remembered my friends. I wanted to stand but did not trust my trembling legs. I crawled along the ledge and peered over the lip. Greg was only 150 feet below, his harness clipped loosely to the rope.

"You okay?" I shouted.

"Yeah," he called, barely audible, his breath stolen by the avalanche. "But bloody cold. My clothing's filled with snow."

"And Tim?"

"He's fine. Below me. Just out of sight."

It was unbelievable that each of us was still alive. The rope, which Tim had tied to an aluminum picket hammered into the firm snow, had withstood the huge forces of the avalanche. If the picket had given way, Greg and Tim would have been killed. Instead, both men had not only survived but also continued on to the summit together one month later, achieving our expedition's goal of climbing a new route without supplementary oxygen.

THE HUGE AVALANCHE had come very close to killing the three of us, and the slope was still exposed to danger. Luck had come into play, and if luck is allowed to intrude into the dangerous sport of mountain climbing, sooner or later there will be bad luck and people will die.

The first time I had allowed luck to enter the arena of my mountaineering had been in 1983, during our climb of Annapurna II. The mountain seemed to single me out. I was battered and bruised by a rock avalanche that cracked my protective helmet like an eggshell. In a separate incident I was struck by an ice block the size of a television and narrowly avoided being knocked off a cliff. After becoming the first climbers to reach Annapurna II's summit via the mountain's huge South Face, we were trapped in a snowstorm during our descent. The previous storm had lasted nine days, so we could not risk sitting this one out. For each of the next three days we battled our way down the mountain, not knowing if we would be alive at the end of the day, so great were the dangers from snow and ice avalanches and chest-deep snow. Luck had definitely come into play. When we were safely off the mountain, I declared that I would never again let myself be trapped by such dangerous circumstances.

However, only ten months later I found myself on the Central Rongbuk Glacier, two miles away from the base of the North Face of Everest, with a huge avalanche bearing down on us. It had looked as though the avalanche would hit us, but by the time the clouds of snow reached us, they had lost all momentum and the snowflakes fluttered down around us. That was our introduction to the dangers of the North Face, dangers we had to face for the next two months.

By the time we retreated from our highest camp at 26,700 feet, we had absolutely no resources left, not even the shortest piece of rope. It was a perilous descent, and if the weather had turned bad, it would have been the end of us.

At the end of that expedition, with a new route, without oxygen in the bag, and despite gaining my credentials as a high-altitude mountaineer, I vowed that it was time to give up big mountains. I had managed to climb within a few hours of the summit without oxygen, but if I continued to climb at this level, where we pushed the boundaries of what was possible, I would find myself relying on luck yet again. After a year of narrow escapes, I decided to call it quits and to focus my energy on the safer and less uncomfortable sport of rock climbing.

ONCE A CLIMBER, always a climber—or so it seemed. After becoming a father, I found that a day of rock climbing once or twice a month was enough to stop me getting restless. As my sons grew older and more independent, I became able to take a few weeks away to work as a guide on easier mountains in the Himalaya, the Andes, and Antarctica. The climbing of smaller Himalayan peaks nestled among the giants seemed like the perfect compromise—not too great a demand on my family, not too low-key for me. But there were times when I found myself looking up at the highest of all mountains, remembering how close I had come and what a great experience even retreating without the summit had been.

PART ONE

—◄—◆—►—

DREAM CATCHER

One

SINGAPORE 2004

W E HAD BEEN LIVING in Singapore for almost two years when the phone call came. I was dripping with sweat, as I had not long returned from my evening run beside the canal behind our condominium complex. This evening I was content with my usual six miles, which came in at just under an hour's worth of jogging, door to door. Not superfast times, but I was in my late forties and had only just discovered the joys of running. It might seem strange to take up such a sport while living one degree north of the equator in the perpetually sticky heat of Singapore. I had not planned it that way; the catalyst was our younger son, Dorje, developing a sudden passion for roller hockey.

Dorje took to the game not long after we arrived. Already a keen inline skater, he picked up the new skills quickly and suddenly found himself in the selection squad for a hockey tournament in Canada. For a twelve-year-old, Dorje's skills and game sense were good, but his fitness was lacking. My wife, Barbara, suggested he skate back and forth along the exercise track beside the canal, with me by his side offering moral support. My lack of enthusiasm for this idea carried no weight. Three times a week I found myself running along the canal, oozing sweat while my son skated. Of course, Dorje skated in the bike lane at three times my speed, creating his own cooling breeze. Soon I began to enjoy the exercise and took to running the same distance he skated, which meant he was showered and watching television by the time I got home.

After the tournament in Canada, Dorje let his training go. By that stage I was hooked on jogging, having learned how to manage exercise in the tropics. I chose to run after dark, when much of the sun's heat had radiated from the tarmac path up into the sky. The hillside above the path was dense with jungle. The patches of yellow light that encircled the well-spaced street-lamps were flooded with moths and other insects. Every evening, not far above my head, bats made high-speed raids between the lamps, hunting their favorite moths and other strange equatorial insects. In such a setting it was impossible to forget the fertility of the tropics.

I finished my run, returned to our apartment, and stood in front of the slowly rotating wall fan near the dining table. I jerked the string-switch twice to bring it to full speed and fed on the cooling blast of air. The refrigerator was five steps away in the kitchen, and after two minutes in front of the fan, I darted in there, grabbed a low-sugar, low-fizz isotonic drink, and returned to the fan. It generally took twenty minutes for me to stop sweating, but tonight, after ten minutes, the phone rang.

It was Michael Dillon calling from Sydney. He was a good friend I hadn't heard from since we had moved to Singapore in 2002. In 1984 we had been on Mount Everest together, with Mike as cameraman and me as expedition organizer and climber; in 1993 we had the same roles in the Indonesian province of Irian Jaya. In Irian, our small team made the first-ever film of climbing Carstensz Pyramid, the highest peak in Australasia. That was an amazing expedition, involving Dani locals as guides, thick jungle, jagged limestone peaks, and glaciers only three degrees south of the equator. Mike was the ideal adventure cameraman. He had made several films with Sir Edmund Hillary, and almost a hundred other documentaries, many of them his own projects. Softspoken and terminally polite, Mike carried a camera at all times when he was working on a film, but he was as unobtrusive as a black dog on a dark night, which made him a great filmmaker—that and his superb ability to visualize exactly how each scene should be shot.

I was delighted to hear from him. Mike is not one for small talk. At school he would have been one of those children who speaks only when spoken to. This evening he had something to say. He wanted to talk to me about a documentary he was working on about a teenager from the Blue Mountains, west of Sydney. At the age of fourteen, Christopher

Harris wanted to climb the highest mountain on each of the continents, a quest known as the Seven Summits. Of course, the most difficult of these is Mount Everest. Mike did not exactly invite me to get involved with Christopher's upcoming Everest climb, but he made it clear he needed a high-altitude cameraman, a role I had performed on several mountains.

When the call was over, I went down the few steps to our bedroom and onto the balcony, which overlooked the pool. My sweat had cooled me by now. Our eldest son was noisily completing twenty laps. Dylan was a naturally strong swimmer, but he disliked the idea of doing laps. Much of his non-school time was spent at his computer, managing a gaming clan on the Internet. While in Singapore, he had begun to play *Battlefield 1942,* a game that is at its most exciting when two teams of twenty or thirty players battle it out across the Internet. Dylan realized that this particular game had much more to offer than the popular shoot-'em-up games. It became such a favorite that he set up a website and began to recruit a clan of gamers. There was something about Dylan's site that hit buttons around the world, and from a few dozen players he soon had hundreds. Within a year there were eight thousand members in his clan, and his site hosted forums covering half a dozen different online games. Management of the clan threatened to overwhelm his life, but at age fifteen Dylan was still young enough for us to enforce some rules—namely, that he not forsake his natural athletic skills for a life in front of his computer.

Dylan dragged himself out of the pool and headed toward the balcony. Our building was on a slope, so although I had jogged up two flights of stairs to get to our front door, the balconies at the rear were only ten feet above ground level. A change in levels between the living room and the bedroom allowed an acrobatic shortcut into our apartment, thanks to the railing beside the steps that led down to the pool. Dylan clambered onto the handrail, carefully stood up, then stretched a hand out to the wall for balance. Next he stepped across to the top railing of our balcony and hopped down beside me. It was the kind of technique you developed when you had a mountaineer as a father. The alternative was to walk around to the front entrance of our apartment and up the stairs.

"Not too bad, was it?" I asked, a reference to his reluctance to go swimming.

"Nah, it was good."

It was classic Dylan—he enjoyed whatever he did once he got into the rhythm of it. A typical teenager, he shook his head in order to shower me with the water from his hair. He stepped into our bedroom and left a line of wet footprints across the tiles as he left the room.

I turned back to the pool and watched the water settle until it became as still as glass in the breathless tropical air. In the background I could hear the *pok-pok* of tennis being played under lights at the back of our condominium.

It was time to talk with Barbara. I found her standing in the kitchen, a cookbook open on the counter in front of her, checking the details of a recipe. I slipped my arms around her waist from behind, and being considerably taller, I was able to look over her shoulder. The book was open at a picture of stir-fried Asian greens with cubes of tofu, bright red slivers of capsicum, and slices of strange-looking mushrooms. My head was next to hers and I could smell Givenchy perfume on her neck. I had bought if for her about a year ago, choosing the largest bottle in the range because it came with a free shoulder bag. Barbara had been pleased but had asked if I wanted her to smell the same for the next three years. I didn't answer at the time—I tickled her instead—but a year down the track the bottle was a third empty; I knew this because she kept it in the fridge door, next to the sports drinks. Silently I sniffed her neck again, and it smelled as good as ever.

"That was Mike Dillon on the phone," I said, releasing her from my arms. "In Sydney. He was telling me about a fourteen-year-old Blue Mountains boy who wants to climb Mount Everest."

She turned around to listen, engaging me with her spectacular blue eyes, the kind of eyes that stun everyone who sees them.

"Fourteen's very young," she said.

"Yeah, but he's climbed quite a few mountains, including Mount Cook when he was twelve, and that's no easy climb."

"But still no comparison with Everest."

"No."

I hesitated. "Mike's planning to make a doco about it and wants to know whether I am interested in being the high-altitude cameraman."

"When would this happen?"

"Next season, which is April and May next year."

"And you'd like to go, obviously."

"If it happens, yeah."

I played it down, wanting to get her opinion, uncolored by any enthusiasm I might show.

Barbara said nothing for a moment, and then, "That would be okay. I know you're always careful."

"But what do you really think?"

"That you'll make the right decisions. And I guess I'm happy to support you in achieving a dream you've had for such a long time."

I kissed her and gave her a big hug. As I pulled away, I said, "It's only an idea at this stage, so we'll just see how it pans out."

With a touch of a smile she held my eyes, and I could tell she knew I was not as casual about it as I pretended to be. Those extraordinary eyes—I could never escape them. Then she cut me free by turning back to her recipe book.

I walked out to the balcony that opened off our living room and leaned on the railing next to my sweat-sodden T-shirt. The view at this level was across a wide lawn with huge condominium towers silhouetted by the lights from the freeway across the canal. The blackness between the canal and the freeway signified jungle.

I thought about the richness of the life in that jungle, and it reminded me of the incredible rainforests of Borneo. A few months earlier we had enjoyed a great family holiday climbing Mount Kinabalu with Margaret Werner, one of our closest friends. Although not a technical climb, Kinabalu is one of the highlights of my thirty-year climbing career, largely because I shared it with my family. Each of them experienced the gamut of feelings that comes with a major climb—initial intimidation, growing confidence, patches of fear on the tricky sections, and the huge feeling of achievement upon reaching the summit.

Mike's phone call had triggered some of these emotions in me, so it was not surprising that I should think of my most recent climb. Then my thoughts returned to the mountain of mountains. As I had said to Barbara, the Everest expedition was no more than an idea at this stage, but I had not added that it was an idea that excited me greatly. Why had I played down my excitement and talked to her about it so casually? I had some unfinished business with Mount Everest, but I also had a wife whom I loved passionately and two amazing sons. How could I consider leaving them for two months while I returned to the dangerous, inhospitable environment of the world's highest mountain?

The answer could be found in the way that, decades ago, climbing had captured my soul.

Two

RETURN TO EVEREST

WITH OUR THREE-YEAR STAY in Singapore coming to a close, I decided it was the perfect time to act on a long-term dream. For years I had thought about a trek to Everest Base Camp. Now, with the possibility of a full-scale climbing expedition the following year, I was even keener to visit the region with Barbara and the boys. I wanted them to see Everest close up so they could appreciate its impossible enormity, while breathing for themselves the oxygen-starved air at Base Camp. I wanted them to understand how Mount Everest had been such a powerful force in my past, how it shaped my present, and how it might soon shape my future. But, of course, the boys were more interested to visit the world's most famous landmark, which happened to be loosely linked to my name, along with those of many other climbers.

My link to Everest came from my role in establishing only the second new route on the mountain to be climbed without the use of supplementary oxygen. The first such ascent had been accomplished by Reinhold Messner, the most influential mountaineer of modern times, who at the same time became the first person to climb the mountain solo. Our ascent had been an extraordinary team effort, achieved without Sherpa support, but because I did not reach the summit myself, I burned with disappointment immediately after the climb.

Three years later I was the first person ever to stand on the summit ridge of Mount Minto. My five friends were climbing the final steep slope, but I waited for them so that we could trudge up together to the tip of the highest peak in Antarctica's deserted Victoria Land. While I waited, I stared out over range after range of mountains, almost all of them untouched, our peak the centerpiece. Between us and the coast, the only signs of human presence were our camp on the far side of a high pass and one hundred miles of ski tracks and caches that led to our small yacht anchored against the sea ice in vast Moubray Bay. My disappointment at not reaching the summit of Everest seemed immaterial. The issue became an item of unfinished business, just a candle in the twilight. Nevertheless, Everest remained a special presence in my life. My family did not know that on any day since October 1984 I could have closed my eyes and seen the summit pyramid as clearly as if I were back in Tibet, at the spot near our Advance Base Camp where I spent hours alone with my yoga, alone with my thoughts, staring upward.

I could not expect Dylan or Dorje to grasp even a hint of what the mountain meant to me. Barbara understood at a spiritual level my connection but could not relate to my willingness to embrace such great dangers. She knew that climbing had shaped my character, and she wasn't about to undermine the catalyst that had delivered to her the man with whom she chose to spend her life.

IN LATE DECEMBER 2004 we caught an early morning taxi to Singapore's Changi Airport, en route to Nepal. The flight to Bangkok was uneventful, and we were in luck on the next leg to Kathmandu. The high peaks of the Himalaya rose above a sea of clouds. First we saw Kanchenjunga, the world's third-highest peak, and its outliers. The clouds maintained a level horizon obscuring all the ranges until we approached the Everest region, where the next cluster of giant mountains broke through. There was Makalu at number five, Lhotse at number four, the mighty Everest itself, and then Cho Oyu at number six. The mountains stood proud until we dropped into the clouds, the beginning of our landing in Kathmandu.

My good friend Ang Karma Sherpa was waiting for us at the doors to the airport terminal. Eager porters wheeled our carts down the middle of the road to the carpark with taxis honking and minibuses spewing out black smoke. Chaos and confusion is a standard welcome to Kathmandu, but there was something different about the journey back to Karma's house.

"Where's all the traffic?" I asked.

"The Maoists have declared a strike," Karma explained. "They threaten that anyone still doing business will get their shop blown up. And they bombed some stores. The only vehicles they let on the road in a strike are tourist vehicles. That is why we have the sign."

He gestured to a large piece of paper taped to the windshield. From inside I could make out the word *Tourist*. The sign obscured some of the driver's vision, but because of the minimal traffic on the roads today it was not an issue.

We went directly to Ang Karma's house on the outskirts of Kathmandu, not far from the airport and the Tibetan Buddhist epicenter of Boudhanath. We were warmly greeted in excellent English by Karma's wife, Kunga. I cast my mind back to when Barbara and I first met Kunga. Dylan was a baby at the time, and Kunga, pregnant with their first child, was too shy to speak more than a few words of English.

In the twenty-five years since we had met, Kunga had shrugged off her shyness, and with better English had come an understanding of our Western mores and values. Meanwhile, Karma had done well for himself. His family now lived in a substantial house, which they had built in stages. When money became available, they added another story. The last of the five stories was a rooftop level with a large balcony, and from there ladderlike steps led to a vertical pole at the apex of the building. Lengths of strong cord were strung from the pole's tip across to trees growing on the slope rising behind. Stitched to each cord were Buddhist prayer flags in five bright colors, each of symbolic significance in Tibetan Buddhism. The cords were like permanent clotheslines, but with the clothes replaced by timeless prayers. As the flags flutter in the wind, Tibetan Buddhists believe, prayers are dispersed across the land and into the cosmos. Most common among Ang Karma's flags was the prayer of the wind horse, in honor of which he had named his business.

The strike imposed by the Maoists had been for only one day, so Kathmandu life returned to normal, which meant busy roads and, in the old part of town, crowded, cobbled alleyways. Karma had work to do, so I

showed Barbara and the boys my favorite haunts and restaurants. Singapore was not a good place to buy clothes for winter in the Himalaya,
so we wandered from one trekking store to the next in search of the few
extra items of clothing that they would need to keep warm at 17,000 feet.

We were keen to get up into the mountains. The air in the deep valleys
of the Everest region is more turbulent in the afternoons, and so the flights
to Lukla are always timetabled for early in the day. Kathmandu's morning fog in winter often meant the cancellation of the Lukla flights, but on
the day that we flew, we were blessed with clear skies. Soon enough we
were sitting in the front of the eighteen-seater Twin Otter aircraft, with
the propellers roaring as we taxied down the runway. The flight to Lukla
is only fifty minutes, and the views of the rugged Himalayan foothills
are breathtaking. The middle hills of Nepal are too rugged for roads.
The steep terrain limits all agriculture either to narrow terraces covering
entire hillsides or to alluvial flats on the floors of deep valleys. Tiny vil-
lages nestle in the valleys or on ridge-tops. At the highest pass, between
forested mountains, the aircraft was only a few hundred feet above the
ground, and we saw children walking along a narrow dirt path toward a
distant school.

Lukla must be one of the most exciting commercial airstrips to land
at in the world. The aircraft appears to be flying directly into the side
of a mountain, and only in the last minutes does it become apparent
that there is a sloping shelf on the mountainside where the airstrip sits.
Rather than looking ahead between the two pilots at the narrow runway
rushing toward us, I watched the faces of Barbara and the boys. All three
of them were grinning wildly, but Barbara with less conviction. Only for
the final seconds before the wheels touched down did I look forward,
when it seemed inevitable that the Twin Otter would slam into the rock
cliff at the end of the runway. But as on every other time I had landed
here, the steep uphill slope allowed the plane to decelerate quickly, and
suddenly it was all over.

With us on the flight was Rudra Thapa, one of the Windhorse Trekking team. We drank cups of sweet milky tea in the courtyard of the
lodge next to the airport building while Rudra organized two porters
to carry our gear. A friend of Rudra's, Beeba Sherpa, would help him to
cook for and manage our small team.

Lukla is at an altitude of 9,000 feet, which is certainly high enough for people to experience mild forms of altitude sickness. Luckily, the first day's trek is all downhill, with the trail cutting across the mountainside to the banks of the Dudh Kosi River. It was an easy start to the trek, and we delighted in the fresh mountain air after the dust, noise, and crazy traffic of Kathmandu. That night we stayed in the village of Phakding, which we reached by crossing a long swing bridge that was decorated with prayer flags. For the next day and a half we hiked up the Dudh Kosi gorge until we reached another swing bridge high above a narrow canyon, which compressed the entire river. As the river smashed against the vertical cliffs, a heavy mist rose on the turbulent air to the level of the swing bridge, where we stood and marveled at the scene. Many of the rough planks on the bridge were broken or missing. The gaps were covered by flat rocks that had been dragged from the paths on either side. This kind of repair made Barbara wonder if any of the bridge was safe to walk upon. She found it to be sturdier than it appeared but still took comfort from the prayer flags.

Beyond the bridge we faced a continuous climb up to the Sherpa village of Namche Bazaar. Two-thirds of the way up the hill we caught our first glimpse of Everest. All but the tip of the mountain's summit was obscured by the walls of the gorge and the pine trees in front of us. Our boys were pleased to see the great peak but disappointed with how little of it was visible. They felt better when I told them that, over the decades, thousands of trekkers would have slogged up this hill, heads down watching their feet, without realizing they had missed their first chance to glimpse the world's highest mountain.

I paused to look at Everest and wondered whether I would ever return to its slopes. During the months since Michael Dillon's first call, I had thought about the possibility a great deal. My place on the expedition had been confirmed, provided we could raise the necessary financial backing. However, it did not look like funding was going to happen in the short term. With the expedition at least a year away, I was happy to be here among the mountains again, taking in a good dose of the Himalaya before we took up our lives again in Australia.

I looked up the trail and saw that Barbara was approaching a switchback that would take her out of sight. The boys had already rounded it, having rushed ahead, full of youthful energy. The main path consisted of continuous zigzags, angled gently to suit yaks carrying heavy loads, but I knew of a shortcut. From the lookout point where I stood there was a rough track up the steep spur formed by the forested hillside meeting the wall of the gorge. If I didn't waste time, I would emerge onto the main trail much higher than Dylan and Dorje. It was the kind of game a father likes to play with his sons.

IN NAMCHE BAZAAR we arrived at our lodge, which was owned by one of Ang Karma's relatives. When we sat on the porch to eat a late lunch, there was heat in the sunshine, but the air was much cooler. All of us were slowed down by the lower levels of oxygen, which was to be expected at 11,500 feet. It was Christmas Eve, so we declared Christmas Day an acclimatization day. Among our small presents to the boys in the morning were German Christmas sweets that Barbara had bought in Singapore, where the festival is celebrated with immense commercial zest. It was a very different scene in Buddhist Namche.

We gave the boys a wad of rupees to spend in one of the village's three Internet cafés. Dorje checked his e-mails and chatted on MSN to friends in Singapore and Australia. Dylan had been out of touch with his gaming clan for over a week. When he logged in, he learned that an American faction within his clan had accused him of funding a climb of Everest with money earned from the clan's tournament winnings. Dylan thought the accusation was hilarious in its naiveté about what a climb of Everest involved, but he appreciated the need to take the issue seriously. He typed furiously, arguing his case and turning the tide of opinion.

Our next day of trekking involved a spectacular and enjoyable hike. After lunching by the river at a tiny village with the endearing name of Punke Tenke, we climbed steeply through conifer forest. It was an unrelenting climb, drawing us closer to the mountains. The pine trees gave way to huge rhododendrons as the angle eased and we traversed the hillside. The climb ended abruptly with a short steep section that led to the crest of a ridge. Suddenly, there was a view of the famous Thyangboche Monastery, perched on the highest knoll of the ridge, surrounded by green pastures and a 360-degree panorama of glorious Himalayan peaks. Mount Everest was among them, although obscured by its sub-peaks Lhotse and Nuptse.

That night in our lodge our bedroom windows were frosted with ice, a silent welcome to winter in the Khumbu. Dorje had picked up a stomach bug at Punke Tenke, which affected his appetite that evening. Although still off-color the next morning, he wanted to keep trekking. However, by the time we reached the village of Pangboche, it was obvious that he needed to rest and recuperate. We soon found a comfortable lodge, and I spent a day hiking to fetch some medicine for him from the Khumjung Hospital above Namche. Dylan filled the day with a hike up to Ama Dablam Base Camp with Beeba. This proved to be the highlight of the trip for him, indicating that not all the best Himalayan experiences involve Everest.

Another afternoon Dylan and I took advantage of the perfect weather to head up the steep grassy slopes above the village. At first we climbed up a thousand feet to admire the view, but then I noticed silhouetted prayer flags on a rocky ridge another thousand feet higher, and this became our destination. The ridge continued up to Taweche Peak, its icy mass tempting us to go farther. The shadows were lengthening, but before heading down we sat among the prayer flags and looked up the valley to the Everest massif. I gave Dylan my camera, and while he busily snapped photos, I gazed at the mountains. Now that we were 2,000 feet above Pangboche, less of Mount Everest was obscured by the vast mountain wall formed by Lhotse and Nuptse. The most dramatic mountain in view was the closest one, Ama Dablam.

Although I had visited Everest Base Camp several times before 1981, I felt that my relationship with the world's highest mountain began in that year with my climb of Ama Dablam, which was 6,500 feet lower. The easiest route of ascent of this chisel-shaped peak was up a ridge that faced Dylan and me. In 1981 our expedition had tackled the steeper Northeast Ridge on the opposite side of the mountain, which meant the summit of Mount Everest was always in view, rising above the Lhotse–Nuptse wall. The higher we climbed, the more we saw of Mount Everest, but as we saw more of the mountain, we saw less of our teammates. So forbidding was the steepness and the difficulty of the route that all the climbers except Tim, Andy, and I packed up and went home.

Our base camp had been very close to the bottom of Ama Dablam's North Ridge. This proximity meant that from the lower reaches of the climb we were within shouting distance of camp. On the day we came down from the mountain, it was well after dark as we carefully rappelled the last of the ropes. We had drunk very little during our long descent from the summit, so Tim called out for drinks in the hope that our Nepalese base camp crew might hear his request. We gingerly descended the steep grass slope in the dark until we saw a small light bobbing up toward us. We did not know whether it was Mingma, Tenzing, or Narayan who was bringing us a thermos of tea, until we recognized Mingma's voice as he approached us.

Our 1981 expedition to Ama Dablam was one of my most enjoyable Himalayan adventures, partly because of the superb climbing offered by the North Ridge but also because of the great friendships that we developed with our Nepalese crew. Mingma and Narayan followed Tim and me on a climb of Trisul in India the next year, then Narayan and Tenzing played vital support roles during our climbs of Annapurna II in 1983 and Everest in 1984. The attitude to life held by these three men set me on the path of Buddhism, although it was a dozen more years before I embraced the Buddhist creed religiously.

The values held by Sherpas certainly work well in the mountains, where being aware of the fullness of the present moment minimizes the inattentive lapses that lead to fatal accidents. I also learned from them that this same attitude—of simply getting on with what has to be done—is the best way to deal with uncomfortable situations. I remember arriving one afternoon at a clearing on a forested mountain ridge during gentle but continuous rain. We had stumbled upon an unexpected camp site, grass-covered and level, the perfect escape from the weather, so I called it an early day. The members of my trekking group huddled under a tree, not complaining but looking miserable while they eagerly waited for the Sherpas to finish pitching the tents. I was out in the clearing with the Sherpas, who were working busily as if the rain was not there. Suddenly the drizzle became a torrential downpour. Water ran down into my sleeve as I held up a tent pole. I cursed while the Sherpas laughed and shouted at each other, stimulated by the force of nature and not annoyed by it. Half an hour later I was in my tent when the flap was unzipped by two kitchen boys, who offered me tea and biscuits. They were still soaking wet but still laughing, this time at the waterlogged biscuits on the tray.

Many people who visit Nepal are deeply inspired by the Nepalese attitude to life and vow to find pleasure in the simplest of things. However, after a week or two back in a modern city, with the cut and thrust of office politics and not enough time at home to do the many apparently important tasks, it is easy to overlook a promised subscription to the values and priorities of the people of Nepal. For me it was much easier, as I was working with deeply religious Buddhists and Hindus and at the same time climbing mountains—both powerfully centering influences.

I came to realize that the common ground of both climbing and spiritual practice is the state of being "in the here and now." Essentially, this is a focus of mind, which offers a simpler but somehow deeper and clearer appreciation of reality. During the most intense passages of climbing, the "here and now" keeps you alive. There is no analysis of what is happening, no judgments, and no plans of what to do next. You are kept alive by the awareness of ever-present danger, which focuses all your faculties on the decisions and actions directed entirely to your survival.

AFTER THREE DAYS of rest at Pangboche, Dorje was in good shape. It seemed that the medicine had worked for him. Not far above Pangboche, the valley opened out, typical of those above 13,000 feet. We spent one night at Dingboche, which on my first visit in 1979 had been a small yak-herders' village but now catered more to trekkers' needs than those of yaks. The next morning it was easy walking along the edge of an ancient lateral moraine as we headed westward below the huge Lhotse-Nuptse wall. The boys entertained themselves by skating in their trekking boots on patches of old snow which had melted and refrozen as ice. The sky was overcast and it looked as though a storm was on its way. Sure enough, not long after we had finished lunch at Dughla, the first few snowflakes fell. We followed yak trails across the slope until a side-valley forced us down to the main trail not far from Lobuche, a settlement of trekking lodges at 16,000 feet, which is big enough to be described as the last village before Everest Base Camp.

That night we discussed our options. Whichever day-walk we chose from Lobuche, we needed a dawn start. If the weather was good, I was keen to head up the steep grass slopes to the rocky knoll of Kala Patar, 1,300 feet above the Khumbu Glacier, because it offers a much better view of Everest than is available from Base Camp. However, bad conditions would not make too much difference to the Base Camp experience, because even on a good day the upper reaches of Everest are obscured by the mountain's massive West Shoulder. Base Camp is an iconic place that marks the absolute limit beyond which only climbers can go. It is, in effect, the finish line, whereas Kala Patar is the equivalent of the best seats in the grandstand.

The winter days were short, so we got up in the dark, had breakfast, and left our lodge at eight A.M. We made good time along the wide moraine trough that parallels the wide Khumbu Glacier. From the dry, sandy lake-bed of Gorak Shep, the slopes of Kala Patar disappeared into the cloud. With the entire sky heavily overcast, Base Camp was now our best option. We followed the crest of the moraine until the narrow ridge ended suddenly at a cliff. At the end of the ridge we ate our lunch, sheltering from the wind among the boulders.

From here the path dropped down the unstable moraine wall to the rough-and-tumble surface of the glacier. Barbara was concerned that she would not make it back to Lobuche before darkness fell, so she and Rudra began to retrace their steps, while Dorje, Dylan, and I continued with Beeba. I warned the boys that the moraine wall was constantly being undermined by the down-valley movement of the glacier and so the slope could be unstable. Once we had dropped down to the glacier, the track was well trodden, but it weaved up, around, and over various ice obstacles. All but the steepest ice surfaces were covered with shards of rock, splintered by glacial movement and the weathering power of ice, which made for good traction.

This was the boys' first encounter with a big Himalayan glacier. They were fascinated by the giant ice-mushrooms. They dropped rocks into the black depths of crevasses and skated on the frozen ponds. As we drew close to Base Camp and the upper reaches of the glacier, the ice flattened out and we navigated by moving from cairn to cairn. A highlight for the boys was a crashed helicopter, most of it in one badly damaged piece, its

victims long since removed and laid to rest. Few choppers are designed
to land at 17,500 feet, where the air is so thin. Dylan souvenired a small
piece of the machine, then we headed on to the camp itself. There was
no one in residence, but random rubbish—available in a dozen different
languages— distinguished the site from the rest of the glacier.

I pointed up to the Lho La, a gap in the high ridge between the West
Ridge of Everest and the peak of Khumbutse. From the Lho La a sheer
cliff dropped 2,000 feet to a steep right-angled bend in the glacier at
the base of the dangerously unstable Khumbu Icefall. I explained to the
boys that in 1984 we had traveled to the North Face of Everest via Hong
Kong, China, and Tibet, and that in the first weeks of our expedition we
had skied from our Camp One at 19,000 feet up to the Lho La. For me,
it had been an amazing experience to view from a dramatically different perspective the familiar territory of the Nepalese side of the mountain. I had been surprised by how insignificant Kala Patar appeared from
the Lho La—its small grassy ridge lost against the backdrop of steep icy
peaks.

Now I was looking in the reverse direction—from the Khumbu Glacier up to the Lho La. The pass appeared higher than I remembered, no
doubt because the minimizing effect of Everest was not in play. Everest was largely hidden by the clouds, but the boys felt no great disappointment. They were fascinated by the glacier and by the strangeness of
the frozen river of twisted ice and regarded every piece of rubbish as an
archaeological find.

I pointed out that the Khumbu Icefall, a vertical tumble of shattered glacier, could have been the work of a giant who dropped a thousand building-sized ice blocks from his land in the sky, creating a stack
of ice that reached up to the clouds. The dangers of climbing up the
treacherous icefall were as great as any faced by Jack as he scaled his
beanstalk. My teenage sons grimaced at the fairy-tale reference, so I
added the glaciological truth. The glacier begins at the head of the narrow five-mile-long valley known as the Western Cwm, which runs westward from the mountain face that joins Lhotse to Everest. Lhotse is the
south peak of the Everest massif and the fourth-highest mountain in the
world. The snowshed on the southern and eastern faces of these mountains accumulates in the Western Cwm and compacts to form a hanging

glacier, which—as it plunges down 2,000 feet to the broad, gently sloping Khumbu Glacier—creates the icefall.

Not surprisingly, the boys were more taken by the physical reality of
the glacier and by the adventure of exploring the place than they were by
an understanding of the mechanics of it. The afternoon was drawing on,
so Beeba headed off with Dylan and Dorje. I stayed back to enjoy some
quiet, contemplative time alone.

I pulled my camera out of its case and composed some moody photographs of the gigantic mess of the icefall. The light was bad, but I pressed
the shutter anyway. The scariest aspect of the Khumbu Icefall is that you
must pass through it to reach Everest's summit from Nepal. I considered
the shattered rocks around me, the tortured ice of the glacier, and the
dark storm clouds hanging over the scene. Revisiting these drove home to
me the immense forces that had shaped this landscape. Above the clouds
the sun would be shining brightly on the summit, creating extraordinary
beauty, but with no one there as witness. I knew how quickly the benign
beauty displayed by clouds high on a mountain could transform into a
deadly blizzard. Even soft, harmless mist engulfing the peak is enough
for climbers to lose their way, never to be seen again.

I wondered whether I wanted to play that dangerous game again.
Doubts had loomed large in Singapore, but now that I was here at the
foot of Everest—with the air already thin enough to be sensed only as
coldness being drawn into my nostrils—I knew that Base Camp was not
yet the finish line for my relationship with Everest.

Three

BEHIND THE EIGHT BALL

W HEN WE RETURNED to Australia, our feet barely touched the ground. Along with the chaos of unpacking from storage our furniture and household goods, we had to enroll Dylan and Dorje in school and generally reestablish our life in the Blue Mountains. I also had to find time to finish the book I was writing. *Fear No Boundary* was the life story of my mountaineering friend Sue Fear, and a large part of it dealt with her ascent of Everest. Although we had just returned from Base Camp, I did not have room in my mind to think about my own ambitions for the mountain.

On top of everything else that was happening, I became distracted by a phone call from Lucas Trihey, a longtime friend and onetime business partner. He had called to offer me my old Sydney-based job back as the editor of *Outdoor Australia* magazine. I had resigned only because the opportunity arose to live in Singapore, and I was now happy to return to my post. My acceptance meant that those initial months back in Australia were extraordinarily hectic, with a crazy combination of working on the book and the magazine simultaneously.

Once I had signed off on the book, there was time for Mike Dillon to introduce me to Christopher Harris, the teenager who wanted to climb Everest. Christopher had done all of his mountain climbing with his father, Richard. Both were tall and lean, and while Richard talked non-stop and with great enthusiasm, Christopher was happy to sit back and listen in the fashion typical of a teenager in the presence of an adult he had only just met. I remained caught up in the hustle and bustle of magazine life, but occasionally I managed to escape for a meeting about fundraising and other strategies with Mike and the Harrises.

The months slipped past almost unnoticed, accelerated by the constant busyness of work on the magazine. There was also much to do at home. Our small cottage was no bigger than our apartment in Singapore, but it had a spectacular view out over our thirty-seven acres to the rugged hills and cliff-lined plateaus of the Blue Mountains National Park. We had bought the property on the park's border only weeks before leaving for Singapore. We felt privileged to live in such a special place, but with collapsed fences to be pulled down, erosion, and all kinds of weeds to be exterminated, there was no shortage of chores.

Although I was perpetually busy, it was impossible not to think of rock climbing. Every time I came home and stepped through the gates, I faced the huge orange cliffs of Mount Solitary across the valley. Much closer were the six-hundred-foot-high sandstone cliffs that dropped away from our western boundary. My attitude to rock climbing had changed when I found myself with a wife, two kids, and a mortgage. Although I still found time to hit the cliffs, it was no longer with the obsessive regularity and intensity of my youth. During our Singapore years, my climbing was limited to holidays back in Australia and a few days on the granite domes of California's Tuolumne Meadows during a business trip. These days climbing provided time-out in the "here and now," usually with my closest friend, Greg Mortimer. Sometimes we would talk about our climbs in Antarctica, the Himalaya, or New Zealand, but usually we just climbed, Greg without a word, me constantly sending down comments, both of us focused on where we were and what we were doing in the different dimension of the vertical world.

On the morning of Friday, February 17, 2006, I arrived at my office just after eight o'clock. Climbing was on my mind because I hoped to spend one day of the weekend on the cliffs with Dylan. I made myself my usual plunger coffee, sat down at my computer, and switched it on. Rather than checking my e-mails, I got straight to work completing some notes for a presentation later that morning. After the meeting, and with the rest of *Outdoor* magazine's staff now at their desks, I opened my e-mail. Two messages in particular caught my eye—one from Mike Dillon, sent the preceding night, and the other from Richard Harris.

Mike's message was startling—the Everest expedition was under way, thanks to major sponsorship from Dick Smith Foods. There was enough money to fund Christopher, Richard, and Mike on a packaged expedition that left Kathmandu for Tibet on April 10, only seven weeks away. The implication was that more funds would have to be raised for me to join the team. Richard's celebratory e-mail was an invitation to a barbecue at his home the following day, which I happily accepted.

Not all of this was news to me. I was aware that Richard had been researching Everest expedition operators on the Internet and had decided that the best value was 7Summits, an Amsterdam-based operation run by Harry Kikstra. Richard was very keen for Christopher to tackle Everest in pre-monsoon 2006, as success would make him the youngest person to climb the world's highest mountain, and suddenly their dreams would be realized. However, I was completely unprepared for the breakthrough when it happened because there had been little progress on the sponsorship front during the preceding six months.

Those two e-mails on that Friday in February turned my life upside down. My first response was complete surprise, then sudden despair because it seemed impossible that I could join the trip. I felt that there was not enough time for me to ready myself, my family, and my employers for such a major undertaking. For the rest of the day I silently debated the issue while trying to do my work.

I called Mike to hear the news in person and to confirm my role if we hit our sponsorship target. I mentioned my dilemma to Sam Gibbs, the equipment editor for *Outdoor Australia*. Sam was one of the few people at Emap publishing who knew that an Everest expedition was in the offing. I told her about my misgivings, all the reasons why I had to say no, particularly those that related to the magazine. But she wouldn't have any of it. The publishers would have to let me go, she said, for the pragmatic reason that it would be good publicity for the country's leading adventure magazine.

That night I talked to Barbara. The decision had huge implications for her as well. She worked three days a week at a girls' school in Sydney, a significant distance from our Blue Mountains home. She had not changed her mind about supporting me, even though it would be a very hard two months for her. As well as her work and the commuting involved, Barbara would have to run the household, drive Dorje to his ice hockey matches and training, and keep Dylan on track with his studies in his final year of school. She offered me every encouragement, and I loved her even more.

When we turned up at the Harris family home the next afternoon, Richard was already busy at the barbecue, alternately chatting about Argentine wines and the Everest expedition. He was obviously delighted by the course of events. The hot tub was soon full of teenagers and children—among them were our two boys, Christopher and his brothers Nick and Ben, and his sister Katherine.

Two climbing friends invited by Richard had no doubt that I would be joining the team. I pointed out the difficulties created by the ridiculously short time-frame.

Neither of these two very experienced climbers would accept that argument.

"You're almost there," said Adam Darragh, a professional climbing guide who knew the challenges of getting Himalayan expeditions under way. Adam had guided the Harrises on New Zealand's Mount Cook, when Christopher became the youngest person to have climbed the formidable peak. "It will all come together by the time you have to go."

"Even if that's true," I said, "I need seven months to get fit for Everest, not seven weeks."

Harry Luxford chipped in with his take on the issue.

"I know your plan," he said. "You'll get fit hiking to the mountain, and by carrying loads up those glaciers."

"Doesn't work in Tibet," I answered. "At least, it doesn't with Everest. It's not like Nepal, where you trek in for a week. You drive to Base Camp on the Tibetan side of the mountain and spend all your days in a Landcruiser."

Harry just smiled. He had the "where there's a will there's a way" approach to life. I certainly couldn't play the age card with Harry—he was in his sixties and still climbing regularly.

These climbers whom I had known for years seemed to believe in me, which made me think that perhaps I should as well. It seemed that the reputation I had gained in the 1980s for making expeditions happen was still current. But this was a different kind of expedition—one that was already organized, with all permits, provisions, land transport, ropes, and tents taken care of. All that we needed was our personal gear—and an extra boost of sponsorship funds.

As we drove home after the party, excitement pulsed through my veins. Psychologically, the tide had turned for me. I had given up long ago the lifestyle of my twenties, where expeditions had been the theme of my life. These days there would never be an empty few months where I could just slot in an expedition. After the positive opinions expressed to me at the party, my mind no longer generated its usual excuses—the fullness of my life as it was now, the unfairness to my family.

Later that night Barbara and I talked through the issues at stake—the security of my job, the strain on our family, but also the opportunity for me to shrug off the burden of incompleteness that had been with me, to one degree or another, since I had turned back below Everest's summit two decades ago. For years I had told myself not to be lured by such a dangerous ambition, but now was a turning point, a moment to "speak now or forever hold my peace." If I failed to reach the summit, I would accept that it was beyond me. The burden of doubt would no longer weigh me down, and that in itself would be a kind of release.

MY MIND-SET CHANGED when there was a new sponsorship offer on the table. Mike hit the right chord with adventurer and author Bradley Trevor Greive, who had a strong interest in Everest and was aware of my climbing credentials. Courage is an integral part of any ascent of the mountain, and as Bradley had just delivered his latest book, *A Teaspoon of Courage,* to his publisher, the marketing tie-in was obvious. When BTG, as he is known to his friends, confirmed his sponsorship of the expedition, he was kind enough to organize a media launch at Sydney's Taronga Park Zoo, a straightforward procedure given his position as governor of the Taronga Foundation and sponsor of the Taronga Poetry Prize for young Australians.

When all the speeches had been made, Mike and I strolled up the broad path toward the café with Bradley. While we walked, he asked me a curious question.

"Do you wear special watches on these big mountains?"

I was more accustomed to questions about footwear and gloves, but the answer was simple.

"Yeah, they're marketed as 'wrist-top computers,'" I replied. "I have a Suunto that's got a compass, a barometer, three alarms, a stopwatch, and other features I've never bothered with. The altimeter's great because it can help you work out where you are in a white-out."

BTG nodded, then as we walked, he took his own watch off his wrist and handed it to me, asking, "Would this work up there?"

The watch and its band were of silver metal, heavier than my Suunto but not as bulky. I looked at its face: 10:15 A.M., March 14, Rolex.

I nodded. "Sure it would work."

"Would you wear it to the summit for me?"

"I don't know . . . maybe . . ."

He could see that I was flabbergasted by the suggestion.

"Why don't you wear it for a while and see what you think?" He slipped it on my wrist and showed me how to close the clasp.

That evening I could not work out how to take the thing off.

SUDDENLY SAND WAS POURING through the hourglass; I was scrambling in too many directions at once—work, home, family, fitness, logistics, and funding. The first step was to obtain two months' leave; otherwise there would be no expedition for me. I delegated tasks to my supportive coworkers, commissioned freelance writers with the major stories for the next two issues, then sought and obtained approval from David Kettle, the publisher at Emap responsible for *Outdoor Australia*. With so much to do, I knew there was a big possibility of arriving in Kathmandu burned-out and exhausted. Already underprepared for the gargantuan task of climbing the mountain, I could not afford to let myself slip any further behind the eight ball.

To have any chance of performing well on Everest with only six weeks' notice, I had to be disciplined with my training—which meant rigorous exercise at least five days a week. When at home, I extended my standard five-mile run to eight miles, sometimes with a bike ride at the opposite end of the day. At work, one lunchtime a week, I played football—very mindful of avoiding injury; on the other days, I jogged to the nearby pool for as many laps as I could manage.

Back home in the Blue Mountains, I was lucky enough to live ten minutes' jog away from the vertical cliffs of Wentworth Falls. Steps cut into the cliff linked with steep ladders allowed a six-hundred-foot descent to the bottom of the two-tiered falls. I began with a load of thirty pounds and was soon carrying fifty. A month later I was managing five circuits to the base of the falls and back—totaling 3,500 feet of up and down, with the whole routine taking four hours.

A week before we flew to Kathmandu, I took a day out of my ridiculous schedule to walk the Royal National Park Coastal Track from Bundeena, the southern outpost of Sydney. With me was my good friend Glen Joseph, whose company, Spinifex Interactive, had taken on management of the expedition website. Our walk was seventeen miles of spectacular cliff-tops and perfect beaches of pale yellow sand. Too many months had passed since Glen and I had had a proper conversation. In our enthusiasm to share stories we got lost twice. The track is generally regarded as a two-day walk, so there was no time to spare. When we found the trail again for the second time, we were careful not to take one more wrong step. The finish was a long steep hike up to the ridge above Otford with spectacular views from the top.

The adventure was not yet over—the ticket machine at Otford Railway Station was out of order, so when we boarded the train we were threatened with fines for not having tickets. Timing stayed tight until the end. Glen's car was parked at Bundeena, across the wide expanse of Port Hacking, and it was only because I ran ahead to the wharf that we caught the last ferry back from Cronulla. As the old wooden boat chugged across the bay, we congratulated each other on a great day out. The excitement of spending two months in the mountains was building up, and I could scarcely wait to be on my way.

ALWAYS IN MY MIND were the steps that I needed to take to help Barbara through the times ahead. Both Greg Mortimer and his partner, Margaret Werner, understood the implications of my decision to return to Everest, and when I spoke to them about looking after Barbara, they knew exactly what I meant. In 1988 Greg and I had sailed to Antarctica to climb Mount Minto, with Margaret in the galley as the expedition cook. Barbara, who was in the early months of her first pregnancy at the time, had looked after Margaret's three daughters. Upon our return, Margaret attended the home birth of Dylan, and Dorje a few years later. The bonds between our families remained very strong.

The highs and lows of parenthood had led to lasting friendships with Lois and David Horton-James and Tina Boys, the parents of Dylan's and Dorje's closest friends. All five boys attended the same schools, and we formed a natural support group for each other during some of the most interesting and challenging passages of life.

Before Dylan and Dorje reached school age Barbara and I had spent a lot of time at "Happy Daze," a magnificent secluded property where Richard Neville and Julie Clarke lived with their two young daughters. Julie had invited us to participate in a private play group at their spacious home. Among the other children were the son and daughter of Julie's brother Roley and his wife, Robbie. Barbara and Julie shared another parallel path—both were married to writers, so they needed that extra degree of tolerance while Richard and I were locked away with our manuscripts for months at a time.

As our children grew up and went to high school, they drew us down different paths, and then, of course, we went to Singapore. But in March 2006, Richard and Julie heard the call before we made it. Our friends invited us to dinner during those last weeks, but in the final days all that Barbara and I could manage was coffee and cake at Happy Daze on the Saturday morning before I left for Kathmandu. As can only be felt among friends, there was an unvoiced acceptance that we were in this together—a nebulous sense of a destiny yet to be realized. But on the surface it was all fun and witticisms as I battled Richard's eloquence with nonsensical interpretations of his words.

He photographed all of us constantly with his new digital camera.

"Don't delete any of those photos, Richard," I joked. "They could be the last ever to be taken of me in Australia."

Four

KATHMANDU

HIS HOLINESS THE DALAI LAMA told me once that Tibet has the purest air in the world. "As you have seen," he added, knowing that I had been there in 1981 and 1984.

I was not about to dispute it. Certainly in 1984 I had thought Tibet to be the wildest place I had encountered. The years I had spent traveling from one mountainous place to the next gave me some yardsticks to judge it by. We sat in the meeting room of the great man's residence at Dharamsala, perched on a forested ridge-top in the foothills of the Indian Himalaya. To the distant south was the haze of heat and dust that hovered above the vast plains of India.

Two decades had passed since that meeting, and during that time I became domesticated, like a wild dog which stumbles into a backyard, finds someone who loves him, discovers the joys of loving, and decides never to leave. But from time to time I did get restless, as does a dog under a full moon, and at those times my wife left the gate open.

When I flew to Kathmandu in 2006, the gate was opened wider than it had ever been. An expedition to Mount Everest is no ordinary leave of absence. One of my close friends, Narayan Shresta, had been taken by an avalanche on Everest eighteen years ago, and I had nearly died there myself a few years before that. I was older and wiser now—or at least more cautious—and committed to coming home from every mountain that called me away.

As cameraman, my role was to record our climb of Everest, a far safer motivation than an obsession with the summit. My own dream of summiting remained a shadow in the wings, but if Christopher Harris succeeded in his attempt to be the youngest person to climb to the peak, I hoped to be beside him, filming history.

On the day we were to leave Australia, and in case history was in the making, the media showed up at Sydney Airport to interview Christopher and film him with his family. This interlude gave me the opportunity to discuss with Barbara a problem that I had created. I had forgotten to wear my favorite Scarpa ZG10 walking boots to the airport, despite placing them squarely in the front doorway so that I had to step over them to get out of the house. I loved those boots almost as much as I loved Barbara. I would be in Kathmandu for a few days, so we talked about the possibility of using World Expeditions to deliver the boots to Kathmandu, as I had worked with the company for twenty years. However, it was a Saturday and their office was closed. My good friend Sue Fear had the home number of the general manager, but Sue had already left for Kathmandu with the goal of climbing Manaslu, the world's eighth-highest peak.

"If all else fails, I'll buy a second-hand pair from a trekking shop in Kathmandu." I pondered the option. "In fact, let's just do that."

But Barbara knew that because one of my feet had been shortened by frostbite, it was hard for me to find comfortable footwear.

"I'll find a way," she said. "Leave it to me."

Conversations such as these followed one after another and left no time for private moments of intimacy, especially with our families and friends forming one large amorphous group. My sister Julia's three young sons circulated actively, with my father and their father keeping watch. We had our customary coffee. Because it was the last possible opportunity before I left, I called Dick Smith and thanked him personally for believing in Christopher and making the expedition possible. It was a call I had been intending to make from the time my position on the team was confirmed.

Although everything I wanted to say to Barbara and the boys I had already said at home, I needed to say it again before I boarded the plane. But the opportunities were taken up by simple things, such as Dylan and

Dorje joking with their young cousins, too many camera flashes, and Mike on the job, filming us. Our last words were to the camera, not to our loved ones.

And while I was filled with an unexpected sense of dissatisfaction, I felt that Barbara was already prepared for it. She had told me that she did not want to know when I was on the summit—only when I was safely back down. For her there loomed the two-month void of my absence, which meant no dirty socks discarded on the floor, no whiskers in the sink, but also no watching the sunset together at the end of the day, no magic glances across the room, and only her in our bed.

AS WITH ALL EXPEDITIONS, there was a mental switch that took place when the plane left the ground. The all-important last-minute tasks no longer mattered because they were out of our hands. Mike and I had spent years of our lives in the Himalaya, but it was the first trip to Nepal for Christopher and Richard. However, there were new horizons for all of us because rather than the small private group that we had planned to be, we were about to enter the arena of large commercial expeditions.

When we landed in Kathmandu, the sky was thinly overcast, creating a drab and silent ambience. We were met by Harry Kikstra of 7Summits and two filmmakers, Kevin Augello and Milan Collin, who immediately began filming us. Harry quickly explained that he was also making a documentary, but of a German climber, Thomas Weber, who became visually impaired at high altitudes.

Harry had brought with him a sizable minibus, but its back door did not open, so our big bags and barrels had to be squeezed over the backseat. As we drove off, we introduced ourselves and chatted to one another. The streets were empty except for truckloads of soldiers. Harry told us that an all-day curfew had been declared by King Gyanendra in a desperate attempt to balance his authority against the growing power of the Maoist guerrillas. On some days the strikes were imposed by the Maoists and enforced with bomb threats—as we had learned from Ang Karma in 2004 when we came here for our Everest Base Camp trek. On other days the king called for curfews. Only tourist vehicles were allowed on the road. I fell silent, stunned and depressed by the troops at every corner and the roads barricaded by sandbags. All the shops had their shutters drawn and locked. We arrived at the Vaishali Hotel in the Thamel district of Kathmandu, where I had stayed seven years ago during the Australian-American Makalu Expedition. It had been a much cheerier place then.

I decided to call Ang Karma. While I waited for the receptionist, I glanced at the Nepali language newspaper on the counter with its stark photos of bloody rioting. Two of the staff hovered around the television at the end of the lobby, watching for updates. It was the worst day I had ever spent in Kathmandu.

Ang Karma was unavailable, but the receptionist kept trying. At last he picked up the phone.

"Karma Daai, it is Lincoln. I am in Kathmandu."

The news was a complete surprise because he had not received my e-mail. It was great to hear his voice, calm as always despite the horrible battles taking place in the streets.

"I will call you tomorrow after we know whether the king is to call another curfew. Probably the evening will be safe, and I can bring your friends to my house for dinner. So, Lincoln Daai, I will talk to you then."

THAT FIRST EVENING there were drinks at the lobby bar of the Vaishali Hotel, and the space was full of men, generally serious-looking, wearing 7Summits-Club.com T-shirts or similarly branded Windstopper jackets. I was at the edge of a conversation when someone mentioned that the expedition doctor was Russian. I had worked with Russian sailors on Greg Mortimer's Antarctic climbing cruises. The Russians were good fun when they let their hair down, but the rest of the time they seemed set upon establishing a national characteristic of being noncommunicative. And so when I heard the distinctive accent and idiom of Russian from the man beside me, I took the initiative.

I turned with a beer in my hand and said, "So you are the doctor?"

He smiled at me, a tall, balding man with glasses, the kind of person who looked like a doctor.

"No. I am the expedition leader."

Every e-mail, every discussion to this point, had implied that Harry Kikstra was the leader. He had debriefed us on the journey from the airport. He had answered our every question.

"But I have heard that the doctor is Russian."

"Yes. He also."

I could think of no other comment.

"I am Lincoln," I said, and I extended my hand.

He shook it with a strong, warm grasp.

"I am Alex." With a sweep of his arm, he gestured to the woman beside him, whom I had already noticed. "And this is my wife, Ludmila."

Ludmila smiled at me, tall and confident of herself and her appearance. I excused myself and made a beeline for Richard, who was standing by the bar.

"Yeah, mate," he said. "Harry and Alex have got some kind of arrangement. Harry is looking after us, though."

The next morning we learned that there would be a curfew enforced from eleven A.M., which gave us two hours of shopping time. The four of us set out with me leading the way, Richard and Christopher following, and Mike filming. We extracted Nepalese rupees from an ATM, bought snack food for the trip from a supermarket, picked up a few items from different trekking shops, and tracked down some medicines needed to supplement our medical kits. Suddenly all the shopkeepers started clanking down their roller-shutters, and soldiers appeared on the streets to make sure everyone was obeying the king's decree.

While we were shopping, there were riots elsewhere in Kathmandu. This became a pattern that repeated itself over the next few days, a mere frustration for us but a nightmare for the people of the city.

That evening at Ang Karma's house we enjoyed a dinner cooked by Kunga with "one dish by Karma." We sipped on Tibetan millet beer called *thongba*, except for Chris, who drank Coke. Karma's mountaineering business was going well. He had a Korean team on the north side of Everest—the climbers and Sherpas already in Tibet—and other teams on other peaks. Karma was optimistic about Nepal's future, believing that the current crisis would erupt in greater violence but that the ultimate result would be the return of democracy, with the Maoists a part of the government. As Karma drove us back to the Vaishali, we were stopped a half dozen times at checkpoints, with soldiers carefully shining flashlights on us before waving us on.

SEVERAL SURPRISES awaited me during the official expedition meeting, which began at seven o'clock on the evening of April 10. Alex was indeed the leader of the expedition. With him were other Russians—guides, camp managers, a doctor, and a communications expert. The biggest surprise was that thirty of us were waiting to be briefed—climbers from the USA, Ireland, England, Italy, Holland, Norway, Denmark, South Africa, Russia, and Australia—a huge mountaineering team by any standards. The climbing Sherpas, kitchen staff, and Tibetans, plus the Russian crew, more than doubled our number. Years ago I had decided that my ideal expedition size was four to six people, so what on earth was I doing here? The answer, of course, was that we had accepted the commercial expedition because it suited our purposes. If I admitted to any of these climbers that I had no idea I was joining such a huge team, I would be thought an idiot.

The mystery of the two leaders was also revealed. Harry and Alex were partners in a cooperative sense. Harry's business was 7Summits .com, while Alex's was 7Summits-Club.com. Harry's primary role was marketing, and for this expedition he had elected to be Thomas Weber's guide and the director of the film about his climb. In these circumstances, Alex had taken on the leadership role and management of the logistics for the expedition as a whole. He outlined the structure of the expedition, explaining that there would be an A-Team and a B-Team, and that each team would have twenty members. I was greatly relieved to hear that not all thirty were climbers—some were Russian guides, some were trekkers or filmmakers heading for either Advance Base Camp (known familiarly as ABC) or the North Col, and the remainder were summit climbers.

Alex outlined the trip. As soon as the curfews permitted, we would drive from Kathmandu to Zhangmu, the town on the Tibetan side of the Nepalese border. Because there were grave dangers in heading to high altitude too quickly, acclimatization stops were built into our itinerary. Acclimatization would continue after we arrived at Base Camp, the approach being to head up toward Everest, retreat to Base Camp to recover, then repeat the process, increasing the height and distance every time. In this way, we would ready ourselves for our summit attempts.

After the meeting, we walked a short distance down the street to the Rum Doodle Restaurant, which courts customers by offering free meals to climbers who have reached Everest's summit. All of us ate for free that night because it was the expedition's Welcome Dinner, courtesy of 7Summits-Club. I sat between two Americans, Slate Stern, an attorney from Santa Fe, and Vince Bousselaire, a preacher from Colorado who had mortgaged his house to fund his climb. I relaxed as I began to enjoy their company. Everyone seemed to be happy and excited, judging by the volume and volubility of the conversation.

When the food had been eaten and all the plates had been removed, and as coffee was served to those who wanted it, Alex stood up to make his welcome speech. His words were received well by all and forgotten moments later by many—such are the effects of alcohol. I was among those who were sober, and so his final remarks lodged in my brain.

"Tomorrow morning," Alex said, "we run to the Monkey Temple. This will be for seeing the fitness of you for climbing the Mount Everest. We want to see you have the fitness. We will run at seven o'clock before the breakfast."

I did not like the sound of this. Going for a run was okay, but I was worried by the concept of testing us and the military mind-set behind that. If Alex was going to operate a boot camp program, I wanted no part of it.

Nevertheless, at five minutes to seven the next morning, Mike and I went downstairs and waited outside. Christopher came down a few minutes later, but there was no one else in sight. In the dining room, set up at a table opposite each other, we found the two Americans I had sat between at dinner the night before, Slate and Vince.

"Slate's your man!" said Vince, when I mentioned the run. "I've still got a sore hip from running with him yesterday, so I'm going to take it easy."

"But I've already started breakfast," Slate protested, "and I wasn't planning to run today."

I looked at my watch. It was already seven fifteen.

"Alex said we should run to the Monkey Temple and back before breakfast. So where is Alex? Where are the rest of them?"

"Too much vodka," suggested Vince.

I looked through the window of the restaurant, but there was nobody waiting outside.

"I'm going anyway," I said.

Slate pushed his plate away and said, "Okay, I'll come. I ran there yesterday. It's a good route."

He washed down his coffee with some water, then we set off, with Slate leading the way out of the hotel compound and north along the narrow potholed street. Rather than an expedition jogging team of thirty, it was only Slate and I determined to reach the temple. We soon hit a major road and turned downhill toward the river. The road had a footpath, but there were too many pedestrians, even though it was only seven thirty in the morning, so we ran on the road. We crossed a bridge and ran along beside the river, which smelled and looked like a sewer. Slate started to draw ahead, so I increased my pace to catch up with him. Within minutes he had gained a two-hundred-yard lead. There was a bridge ahead, which meant a choice of paths, so I had to speed up if I was not to lose him. Luckily, he stopped at the bridge to adjust his iPod, and from there we ran together up a flight of steps to a Hindu temple. While Slate paused and looked around, I tried to get my breath back. Next was a road with high brick walls creating blind corners, which meant traffic was a danger. Finally, we ran along the tree-lined path that led into the grounds of the temple. The huge Buddhist stupa of Swayambhunath—our destination, the Monkey Temple—was on the top of the hill. Vince had mentioned that Slate had run up the stairs three times, so before Slate suggested the same discipline, I recommended that we walk.

It was many years since I had been to this place, as my favorite of Kathmandu's two big stupas was Boudhanath, which was more peaceful because it was not overrun by hungry monkeys. Both stupas were very similar—gigantic white masonry domes, each topped by a square gilded block. On each of those square gilded faces was painted a pair of all-seeing, all-knowing eyes. The blocks on each stupa were oriented so that every pair of eyes pointed to one of the four cardinal points. On top of each block was a thin conical tower, with shapes symbolic of the earth, the sun, and the moon at its zenith.

Because it was on the outskirts of town, one advantage the Monkey Temple did offer was a broad view across the city—but not now, at the end of Kathmandu's dry winter, when the dust was heavy in the valley and the precocious first rains of the monsoon had not yet fallen.

The morning was warming up, and I sweated heavily as we ran back to the hotel. As an adventure racer, Slate was very fit and he happily asked me questions as we ran. I tried to give short answers because long ones left me out of breath. At last I gasped, "Let's just run. We can talk when we get there."

Back at the Vaishali the waiters were still serving breakfast, for which I was grateful. I never asked Alex what had become of his glorious morning run, but I also never again worried about his military inclinations.

THE PROBLEM of my overlooked boots was resolved, thanks to Barbara. I phoned her from the roof of the hotel, using Richard's satellite phone, and learned they were on their way to Kathmandu. I also learned that Dorje had scored a triumphant goal against Blacktown, leaders of his ice hockey competition. The next day I rang the Radisson Hotel, where Sue Fear was staying. She had been delayed in Kathmandu by the curfews and promised to bring the errant footwear to me the following afternoon. True to her word, she arrived at the Vaishali, and we adjourned to the bar at the Rum Doodle Restaurant so that I could buy her a beer.

I was delighted to see Sue, quite apart from her role as the courier of my precious booty. I had called her in Sydney the day she left for Kathmandu to wish her good luck with her climb of Manaslu. Now I had the time to tell her that although I had never set foot on Manaslu, it was a special mountain for me. Its beautiful form loomed directly across the deep valley of the Marsyandi River during my prolonged and difficult first ascent of Annapurna II's South Face.

Sue blurted out her frustration at being stuck for a week in Kathmandu by the king's mindless curfews. On the climbing front, she was excited by the prospect of being on the same Manaslu expedition permit as Junko Tabei, who in 1975 had become the first woman to summit Mount Everest. Sue hoped to be climbing light and fast with Bishnu Gurung, a strong and experienced climber and a good friend.

She also gave me some advice. "Remember how I had stuff stolen on Everest? Well, I have heard some really bad stories recently."

It was not what I wanted to hear, but Sue loved to talk. She related some chilling examples of theft and deceit high on the mountain. I had suppressed my dread of the overcrowding on Everest and the resulting competition and opportunism, trying to pass off the confrontations as misunderstandings.

Both of us were leaving Kathmandu before dawn to avoid whatever travel restrictions might be imposed the next day, and so we stopped our reunion at one beer. Downstairs outside the Rum Doodle we hugged and promised to share stories afterward. With a quick kiss, she turned and strode down the narrow street, small in size, huge in confidence, not looking back. With my boots hugged to my chest—just where Sue had been—I watched her blend into the evening crowd. I never saw her again.

Five

HIMALAYA

THE VALLEY OF the Bhote Kosi gorge is one of the few breaches deep enough to allow a road to be cut across the backbone of the Himalayan chain. From above the border town of Zhangmu, the road is very narrow and exposed to rockfalls and avalanches. Much of the road skirts the lip of a vertical precipice. Although it's called a highway, it's high only in altitude. As the road heads deeper into the gorge it follows a series of ascending switchbacks, and it seems impossible that there can be a way through. Solace came with the thought that every slow hairpin bend that we rounded in low gear brought us closer to the Tibetan Plateau.

Because the roads were unsealed, the pure air mentioned to me years ago by the Dalai Lama was polluted by clouds of dust thrown up by our one-Landcruiser, two-minibus convoy. The badly tuned diesel fumes didn't help either. Our first acclimatization stop was at Nyalam, the first township above the Bhote Kosi gorge. Our itinerary scheduled two nights here, so that we could hike up to 13,000 feet each day, while sleeping more comfortably at 12,000 feet, the height of the town. This "climb high, sleep low" process is a proven method of triggering acclimatization responses.

Other expeditions had arrived ahead of us, and because ours was a large group, the only hotels or dormitories with sufficient bunks for us offered very basic facilities, and even then we were split between two locations. Unfortunately, basic facilities also meant minimal hygiene, and a number of our 7Summits-Club group fell ill with stomach upsets. During my years as a trekking guide, I had developed the habit of not rushing to secure the best room or tent site. In Nyalam, this habit meant that I slept with my head two feet from the squat toilet, which was directly beyond a plywood wall. I heard all sorts of ghastly noises as the local diarrhea bug notched up more victims.

The weather the next morning was excellent, so Christopher, Richard, Mike, and I set off to climb as high as we could—and still get back for lunch. Nyalam consists of one street—the road through town—so we hiked down it to cross the bridge over the river. We headed diagonally across the hillside to reach a rocky spur, which yielded steep scrambling that was easy but fun. We caught up to Noel Hanna, Lorenzo Gariano, and his brother, Giuseppe, who were deliberately climbing slowly. Henrik Olsen had a more aggressive approach. We were still heading up when he passed us, descending. He paused only long enough to comment on the ferocity of the wind above. Sure enough, when we reached the small rocky knoll that we had identified as our goal, we found prayer flags that had fluttered themselves into rags. The mass of the hillside had protected us from the worst of the wind, but here, at well above 13,000 feet, we were out in the open. I tried without success to welcome the coldness of the wind on my cheeks, because soon enough the cold would be part of everything we did.

Nyalam was in an undeniably beautiful setting, but the next morning everyone was happy to be on the road again. Before long the chain of Himalayan peaks that formed the border between Tibet and Nepal had disappeared behind us, and the valley ahead brought us onto the famous high plateau of Tibet.

The themes of the Tibetan landscape persisted day after dusty day—long flat-bottomed valleys between vast, rolling hills, which had either the softness of grass cover or the starkness of exposed rock. In the distance, there was always a mountain range or two on the horizon, but in no particular direction. Sometimes there was a white-capped peak. The journey to the Everest Base Camp was punctuated by high passes of 17,000 feet or more, where the vehicles stopped and we clambered out, battered by the freezing wind as we snapped photographs, then scrambled back into the minibus for a return to our iPods or our own private reveries.

As we drove, I was quite content to sit and stare out the window at the landscape passing by. Too many of my travels in recent years had been done in a hurry, and I was happy to take in the timelessness of the sparsely populated plateau. Of course, my thoughts did wander to the months ahead and to how I would cope with them. It had been seven years since I had worked as a cameraman on the world's fifth highest peak, but this did not concern me as there was little to forget. The challenges of the job are few but significant. Fingers numbed by extreme cold make it difficult to use some camera controls and impossible to use others. Above 24,000 feet it is very hard to hold a camera motionless while your lungs are gasping convulsively for air, yet a tripod is a burden too heavy to consider. In such a place there is no room for fancy camera angles and mood lighting, but that is okay because the mountain provides the moods. Perhaps I would find it easier when oxygen was being delivered from a tank on my back.

At least I could expect the Russians to have a good understanding of the oxygen system. The most popular system of oxygen equipment for high altitude is manufactured by Poisk in St. Petersburg. Russians and other Eastern European climbers have a reputation as being tough and fearless in the mountains. Polish mountaineer Wanda Rutkiewicz once said, "Each climber loses one finger or toe once in a while. This is a small but important reason for Polish climbers' success. Western climbers have not lost as many fingers or toes."

For me, successful climbing is not a Faustian pact with the devil of cold. The two toes trimmed for me by frostbite twenty-eight years ago were badge of honor enough for me, and I had no desire to buy success with more amputations.

Toughness was not yet apparent among the Russians, but they were proving to be pragmatic. Their approach to the language barrier was to ignore it. A week passed before I realized that one of our two Sergeys spoke good English (Sergey Kofanov had excellent English; Sergey Chistyakov had none), and that Maxim Onipchenko, our Base Camp manager, was also fluent. Igor Svergun was more forthcoming. I felt a bit foolish when I realized that not all the Russians were 7Summits-Club staff—five were mountaineers who were paying clients. Alex had introduced everyone to everyone back in Kathmandu, but with several dozen people in the one place it had been impossible to remember more than a few names.

For the entire trip from Kathmandu to Base Camp, Alex and Ludmila (also known as Luda) sat in the seat in front of me, which gave us the opportunity to get to know each other.

Early in the journey Alex turned to me and said, "I heard from Harry your experiences. You climbed to twenty-seven thousand feet the North Face?"

"Yes, in 1984, as part of an Australian team. We climbed a new route without oxygen."

"But you turned back . . ."

"I did. I wanted to stay alive. With only five hours to sunset, I was still above twenty-seven thousand feet. I calculated we would get to the summit at dark. That was just too risky for me, so I turned back."

"Because of frostbite?"

"It's so much colder without oxygen to warm you. I had frostbite before. My fingers recovered, my toes didn't. But it was too easy for me to get frostbite again. Frostbite could kill me up there, if my hands could no longer hold my ice axe."

"You think so?"

I nodded. Twenty-eight years ago during my first Himalayan climb, the frostbite to my hands had made me so clumsy that the 2,500-foot descent to camp in the dark had put me an extra four hours behind my partner.

"For sure," I replied. "Two of my friends reached the summit at sunset. Andy Henderson stopped one hundred and fifty feet short, already with frostbite. All three got to the tent at half past three in the morning. Andy's hands were like claws. We had no rope. We had to send him down alone with nothing in his pack so he wouldn't overbalance.

"If I was frostbitten as well, God knows what would have happened. Greg might have died because he had pushed himself too far. We were still above twenty-six and a half thousand feet, and I had to climb with him—right next to him—to keep him moving; otherwise he would have gone to sleep in the snow. I may not have been able to help him effectively if I'd had frostbite. It took the two of us an extra day to descend."

There was a pause as Alex constructed the scene in his mind. Then he summed up his thoughts and said, "It's an honor to have you with us."

I laughed. "I don't know about that. It was a long time ago."

· · ·

WHEN WE ARRIVED at Tingri, there was a mood of anticipation, as the small settlement was famous for its view of both Mount Everest and Cho Oyu, the world's sixth-highest peak. However, while Cho Oyu was obvious, Everest was forty miles to the southeast, with only its summit pyramid visible behind the foreground ranges. The sun was also against us, shining into our eyes and letting us see only Everest's silhouette.

Two days later, after acclimatizing near the small regional center of Shegar, everyone was expecting a much better view of the great peak from the crest of the Pang La pass. However, as our convoy headed south toward the ranges, the weather worsened. The final 3,000 feet of height was gained by almost an hour of slowly traversing back and forth across a huge rocky hillside, every turn a switchback.

As soon as we crested the pass, our two minibuses pulled into the widening of the road which served as a parking area. The only view was of the damp grayness of the clouds enveloping the ridge-top. A canvas tent provided accommodation for a family of Tibetans, who excitedly rushed toward the minibuses as we pulled in. They were selling local fossils and cheap trinkets that had come from Lhasa or Kathmandu. There was absolutely nothing here but rocks, yet the Tibetans had identified a business opportunity and members of our team set about assuaging their disappointment with some retail therapy. Meanwhile, I hiked up the track toward the best lookout point. Nothing could be seen, of course, except the mist.

In the silence away from the others, I considered the panorama hidden by the clouds. In the course of two treks and my 1984 climb I had stood at this spot five times. On two of those occasions, the peaks had been partly obscured by clouds. Three times the mountains had been etched so sharply against the impossibly blue sky that I could still view the scene in my mind. Beginning in the east with the pyramid of Makalu, I knew the skyline took in the profile of Kangchungtse, Chomolonzo, Lhotse, Everest, Nuptse, Changtse, Gyachung Kang, and Cho Oyu. I knew that beyond the clouds, nine peaks higher than 25,000 feet spanned the horizon, and that only Everest stood perfectly balanced, slightly left of center, the only one projecting three-dimensionality.

For a roadside mountain panorama, it could not be equaled any-where. Strangely, just knowing what magnificence lay across the valleys and beyond the clouds was enough for me to feel that we had arrived. In the vastness of Tibet, four hours more in the minibus was nothing at all.

THE FIRST SIGHTING of Rongbuk Monastery is always a surprise. On that final afternoon of driving, many miles of rough narrow road ran parallel to the river, much of it sixty to one hundred feet above a glacial torrent that is the product of snow-melt from Everest. Along that stretch of river there are no buildings at all, only the occasional ruined stone meditation hut high on a stark mountainside. Everyone who travels this route peers ahead in the hope of seeing Mount Everest, which is at its most majestic when approached from the north. But because the steep-sided valley is also narrow, even when the weather is good there are only a few glimpses of the mighty peak to be had before the final curve in the road, when the monastery buildings and the giant stupa leap into frame. Just as suddenly, the valley opens out to give the best view yet of Everest, and although center stage is taken by the world's highest monastery, the dramatic backdrop of the world's tallest mountain is overwhelming.

But on April 18, 2006, a less panoramic scene greeted us. Clouds hung heavy over the valley, so all that we could see of the mountains were the cliffs and talus slopes that form their foundations. On my most recent visit to the Rongbuk Valley I had trekked cross-country from Tin-gri, walking along the road at a pace that allowed me to remember the details of the route. And so, when the road curved away from the river and headed toward a small notch between ridges of moraine, I knew that we were almost there. As we crested the rise, the low, dark clouds swallowed the valley ahead. Snow blew diagonally forward in the direc-tion of the mountain we had come to climb. The mass of the monastery was starkly obvious, but its whitewashed walls made it ghostlike in the storm.

Ghosts certainly existed in this place. One million Tibetans had died at the hands of the Chinese since the People's Liberation Army began their invasion of Tibet in 1950. In the thirty years after the Dalai Lama fled in 1959, all of Tibet's great spiritual leaders either had been killed or had escaped into exile. With the living heart and soul of Tibetan Buddhism excised from the country, the Chinese were content to leave the shell of the religion in place as a tourist attraction and to present a front of tolerance. But the truth behind the façade was very different. Photos of the Dalai Lama were prohibited possessions, and only the simplest forms of Buddhist practice were allowed. Lamas who stepped beyond the prescribed guidelines were jailed—or worse.

In 1984 Rongbuk Monastery had consisted of one small room, resurrected from the ruins left by marauding Chinese troops during the Cultural Revolution. On my several visits I had witnessed the stages of its rebuilding. By 2003 there was a two-story meditation hall with wings on each side of a courtyard. Rooms for the monks along the wings reduced the courtyard's internal dimensions but provided good shelter. What was new in 2006 was a building on the downhill side of the road, directly opposite the monastery. It was obviously basic accommodation for the increased tourist traffic. The rooms appeared to be classically Tibetan in style, just like the small rooms in the monastery's courtyard, each with a single door and no window, each opening out to the sheltered area created by the U-shaped building. No doubt a larger room served as a kitchen and eating place. The driver of our minibus was not interested in stopping for photo opportunities or verification of my architectural theories. His reticence was understandable. It was snowing heavily, and he obviously wanted to get to Base Camp, unload his human cargo, and head back down the narrow road before it became impassable. The weather worsened as we drove past an alluvial flat, white with snow and punctuated by the shapes of fifty or more yaks. Most of the animals lay sphinxlike and motionless, their black coats not yet whitened by the snow. Before I could decide if this was a camp for the yak-herders or a fenceless holding yard for the yaks, the scene was behind us.

The higher we drove, the colder it became outside and the more the windows of the minibus fogged up. We were almost at Base Camp, yet no one would let me open a window. I laughed to myself at this attempt to postpone the realities of high-altitude mountaineering. In a month or two we would not be worrying about fresh air rushing in through a small window but about the possibility of the tents we huddled in high on the mountain being shredded by hurricane-force winds.

Six

TENT CITY

WITH THE SUMMIT of Mount Everest the most inhospitable place on earth, and with the base camps on both sides higher than any permanently inhabited place, people are understandably surprised when they learn that a road leads all the way to the Tibetan Base Camp.

When China invaded Tibet and added it to the Motherland, they also assumed ownership of the entire Everest massif. Chinese maps of the time portrayed Chinese territory extending as far south as Namche Bazaar. In the Everest region the true border between Nepal and Tibet runs from the summit of Makalu westward over the crests and summits of Lhotse, Everest, Pumori, Gyachung Kang, and Cho Oyu—very much the skyline as viewed from the Pang La. Of course, the optimistic Chinese border was not recognized by Nepal, India, or any other country. Nowhere else in the world could a border be less traversable than across the top of Mount Everest.

The Chinese came to their senses and corrected their maps. They salvaged some of their limitless national pride by mounting an expedition to Chomolungma (the Tibetan name for Everest). Their first task was the gargantuan one of constructing the Rongbuk Base Camp road that is in use today. With that achieved, they trucked in mountains of supplies and a climbing team of 214 Chinese and Tibetan men and women. Nothing could be further from the lonely experience of 1924—when a small British team including George Mallory and Andrew Irvine climbed close to the summit—than the Chinese siege ascent in 1960 under the leadership of Shih Chanchun. Completing the route pioneered by the British thirty-six years before, the Chinese planted the Red Flag on the summit on May 25, 1960.

THE ROAD TO BASE CAMP had improved since my visit in 2003. Well-engineered embankments and wider hairpin bends made it easier for longer vehicles to manage the steepness of the final moraine wall. Our minibuses chugged up with no difficulty. Ahead, the terrain opened out into a broad valley with a floor of gray glacial silt. I recognized a short ridge that rose twenty feet above the flats. On its crest was a two-room building that marked the outskirts of Base Camp. The concrete hut provided office space for the Tibetan Mountaineering Association (known as the TMA) and accommodation for its officials; it was inhabited only during the spring and autumn climbing seasons. Below it was a small grassy area that existed only because a spring-fed creek brought life to the dry ground. This beautiful spot was where we had set up our base camp in 1984, and we had had the place to ourselves. A large American team was the only other expedition on the Tibetan side of the mountain that year, but it did not arrive until after we had moved up the valley to our higher but more sheltered Advance Base Camp, much closer to the North Face.

The grassy area had survived the explosion of Everest expeditions over the preceding decade, but the spring water was no longer potable. The most obvious change was the growth of the shantytown of temporary tents where meals, alcohol, and the other services of a frontier land were sold. By 2006 the temporary settlement along the last stretch of road had doubled in size. Between two of the tents was Base Camp's newest permanent building, the small concrete cube that was the Rongbuk Post Office. The northern approach to Mount Everest had definitely become a tourist attraction.

The shantytown was politely known as the Chinese Base Camp. Beyond it was a vast alluvial flat. Most expeditions had set themselves up here. Our driver showed no mercy as he bounced and swayed the minibus across what was essentially a field of glacial silt, boulders, and dry watercourses filling with snow. With the visibility ahead limited to a few hundred feet, we drove past several encampments. Finally, rows and rows of yellow tents appeared to our left. The minibus jolted to a halt, and we clambered out into the storm. We had arrived.

There was no mistaking the conditions outside, but it was still a slap in the face to step out of the warm fug inside the vehicle into heavy snowfall and a strong wind. This was the reality we would be living for the next two months, so I took it on board immediately. None of us was fully dressed for a snowstorm, so there was some urgency about getting our gear into tents. I could see that our driver had dropped us at the base of a huge wall of moraine that was like a rock dam across the valley. I had never seen as many tents in the one spot—and that was without counting the base camps of other expeditions, now hidden in the storm. The tent city was laid out in rows, and as somebody who had decided not to live in a city back home, I wanted to avoid living in one here. My best option was to choose a tent at the end of a row, with only one row between my tent and the eastern edge of the encampment. Mike was in front of me and Slate to one side. A good set of neighbors, I thought to myself. Mike's neighbors were Christopher and then Richard, which was convenient for our small Australian team. I slung my daypack and cameras into the roomy yellow dome that would serve as my home for the next two months. I looked forward to making it into a comfortable refuge.

Soon there was a call for hot drinks and snacks in the mess tent. The tent itself was extraordinary. Bright yellow and semicircular in cross section, it was nine feet high, twelve feet across, and eighty feet long. From a distance it looked like a giant yellow caterpillar. The tent was divided into five compartments. Midlength was an entrance into the vestibule, which was about twelve feet square. The sides of the vestibule had door-flaps leading to dining areas about twenty feet long. There were small storage areas at the far ends. When I stepped in, Alex directed me to the right, as this was the zone for the B-Team. The climbers in the A-Team were directed to the left. Although climbers from one team could visit climbers of the other team, they were not allowed to dine with them. I felt like I was in school again.

Alex and his Russian crew certainly had their own way of doing things, and I was not sure that I was going to like it. If we were to be treated like schoolkids at Base Camp, how tightly would we be reined in when on the dangerous slopes of the mountain? Time would tell. For the moment I would just watch and learn.

Five collapsible metal card tables ran the length of the B-Team's section of the mess tent. Each table was set for four people. A mirror image of the layout had been set up across the vestibule for the A-Team. The Russian staff ate with us in the B-Team's mess tent, their tables at the end of the row. Their conversation, not surprisingly, was in Russian and they kept to themselves, with one exception. A man in his thirties with a young face but a hairline that was starting to recede took a spare seat at a table next to us and introduced himself.

"I am Andrey Selivanov," he said as he joined Noel, Lorenzo, and Giuseppe. "I am from Siberia. I am doctor, but now I am mountaineer. Welcome to Base Camp."

I assumed he was making himself approachable because he was the doctor and wanted everyone to feel comfortable in his presence. He was certainly friendly, but his English came to him slowly.

The Russians were squeezed between our table and that of four Norwegians. Petter Kragset, Johnny Brevik, Torbjørn Orkelbog, and Frode Høgset all spoke excellent English and shared a sense of humor that translated well. Climbing this mountain would demand a lot of fuel, so we set about sampling the hot drink options and the agreeably large range of biscuits. That first afternoon I concluded that we had landed on our feet. My years as a trekking guide had heightened my sensibility to what I called "the shithead factor." I judged that, this time around, we had escaped without someone whose unbearable ego might have prevented us from working properly as a team. I had experienced this too many times, not only when in the mountains but also when I took corporate groups into the wilds for a week of team building. On this expedition all of us shared a purpose that would allow us to take strength from one another, and yet no one could guess what events might push us together or pull us apart when we were high on the mountain.

Certainly the mess tent was a good place to get to know everyone, and there were plenty of good stories to share around. Three of the B-Team climbers had been on Everest the previous season. Petter Kragset had been a member of a Norwegian expedition, and while some of the team had summited, poor health had turned him around at the North Col. At an altitude of 23,200 feet, the col is high by every other standard but is just the real beginning of a climb of Everest.

Noel Hanna had also been forced to turn back at the North Col when his eyesight was compromised by a retinal hemorrhage. These are not uncommon at altitude, but usually vision is not affected. Noel had become aware of a large dark spot, which he knew was a danger sign. Doctors at Advance Base Camp had agreed that it would be unwise for him to go back up the mountain. Back in Ireland, Noel sought specialist opinions, and some key advice was to take Diamox, a drug used by glaucoma sufferers to reduce fluid buildup around the eye and so lower its internal pressure. Noel immediately realized this was a serendipitous recommendation. He knew that climbers had long been using Diamox to manage or inhibit the onset of altitude sickness, with some taking it preventatively for the duration of their expeditions. Although I had never used the drug myself, I had given it to trekkers in my care and had seen its positive effects. Noel arrived at Base Camp with a plentiful supply.

Oddly, the third returnee to the North Ridge of Everest had also retreated because of an eye problem, but on the highest reaches of the mountain. At 28,000 feet, in the deep cold of the night, Lorenzo Gariano had realized that the surface of one of his eyeballs was frozen. With several hours of climbing to the summit, he might have made it to the top, but he had not known how near his other eye was to freezing and so his only option was to descend.

Three climbers were facing a bigger challenge. Along with Petter, Henrik Olsen and Kirk Wheatley were close to completing the Seven Summits of all seven continents, their goal being the highest point on each. Everest was the last on their list, and I judged all of them as likely to succeed. Petter had already devoted months to climbing Everest, knew how to manage cold, and oozed determination. Henrik was a solid man in body and spirit, obviously fit, accustomed to the extreme cold of winters in Denmark, and a competent no-nonsense outdoorsman.

Of these three, I found Kirk the most intriguing. My first proper conversation with Kirk, who came from the UK, had taken place in the big dining hall of the grand hotel in Shegar. I learned that he was a professional diver, but not the kind who introduces bikini babes to the warm tropical waters of the Bahamas or the Great Barrier Reef. He operated at the other end of the spectrum, the murky depths of industrial diving, working on the maintenance and repair of marine and underwater structures. Kirk might spend three weeks in a pressurized capsule with two or three workmates without coming up to see the sky, let alone his wife and young family. At other times he repaired port facilities in darkness that came not from night but from the swirling silt at the bottom of the sea. Often he wore a mask with air pumped down from above because the work took much longer than any scuba system could accommodate. That kind of work required a particular type of person, someone who could work twelve hours straight while under several atmospheres of pressure and stay focused on the job. Kirk obviously had those abilities.

Because Kirk was someone who worked where the visibility was often less than the length of his arm, I wondered whether he compensated for the claustrophobic darkness of the depths by searching for the most majestic and all-encompassing views in the world. But in fact Kirk wanted to climb mountains because as a nonclimber he was excited by the challenge of climbing the Seven Summits.

"I'm not a mountaineer," he told me. "I'm a tourist in the mountains."

Kirk certainly had no pretensions, but I knew already that he had two of the attributes necessary for success at extreme altitudes—the ability to stay calm when there was very little environmental oxygen and the doggedness to persevere in dangerous situations. As for climbing skills and the intimidating cold, he would have worked out his strategies during his climbs of the other six peaks.

Kirk was talkative and cheerful in a sour, British kind of way and had initially attempted a unique sponsorship path. He had smoked a cigarette on the top of the six peaks he had summited and decided to approach tobacco companies about sponsoring his Everest ascent, which he would complete with a cigarette on the summit. He was knocked back, perhaps because companies such as Philip Morris, the Gallaher Group, and Austrian Tabac realized that tobacco was dangerous enough without linking it to the deadly risks of climbing the world's highest peak.

Also in the Seven Summits stakes was Christopher Harris. Before I left Australia, a number of people had questioned me about the wisdom of a fifteen-year-old climbing Mount Everest. I replied that it had already been climbed by someone only three months older than Christopher, so it was definitely possible. It was refreshing to find that among our expedition nobody questioned Christopher's goal of becoming the youngest fifteen-year-old to climb the mountain.

Everyone accepted that all of us were here for our own Everest experiences, which would surely vary enormously. Rather than Christopher's climb, the point of controversy was whether Irian Jaya's Carstensz Pyramid should replace Australia's highest peak, Mount Kosciuszko, as the Australasian summit. Alex voted for Carstensz because he said it was a climbers' mountain, unlike Kosciuszko, which was for walkers. Whether the quest should include Kosciuszko or Carstensz (which sits on the Australian tectonic plate) was never settled. Alex argued that Christopher should play it safe and climb both, but then his company, 7Summits-Club, had the vested interest of running expeditions to the chosen seven—and an ascent of Kosciuszko was not an expedition, it was a day-walk.

DURING THE TWENTY-TWO YEARS since I had turned back on Everest, much had happened on the mountain. In 1984 there were no operators of pre-organized mountaineering expeditions looking for clients, but today most climbers attempting the world's highest mountains join exactly that kind of trip. Professionally operated expeditions can be divided roughly into two categories. In the first are those who offer serviced expeditions, meaning that all services are provided—from permits, transport, and accommodation to food, tents, and oxygen. The climbers turn up with cash and their climbing partners and use their own expertise to climb the mountain as they see fit. In the second category are the commercial expeditions. These differ from serviced expeditions by their high ratio of guides to clients, their strict management of climbing protocols and processes, and their high standard of facilities, which generally include a doctor, a Base Camp manager, and modern communications. Also high are the prices.

If you asked any nonclimber how it is that people get to climb Mount Everest, a common answer would be along the lines of "they get fit and are escorted to the summit by a guide." Many would add the words "and pay $65,000." This perception of climbing Everest emerged from Jon Krakauer's enormously successful book *Into Thin Air*. Krakauer was commissioned by *Outside* magazine to write a story about the commercialization of Everest; because Jon was a climber, he figured the best way to approach the article was to be a participant.

He did not set out to write an overview of the different facets of modern-day Everest climbing but rather kept to the allocated topic of commercial expeditions. Fate intervened and gave him a tragic saga. Rob Hall and Scott Fischer were both charismatic mountain guides—they were friends but also rival expedition operators. The core of the action occurred on May 10, 1996, when thirty-three people were heading for the summit after leaving their high camp in the middle of the night. Most had turned back by early afternoon, but many were still close to the summit when a ferocious storm hit the peak. Climbers hurried down, but several remained near the summit. Rob Hall was one, staying beside an exhausted client. The storm worsened into a blizzard that raged through the night and into the next day. Both lead guides survived until late on May 11. Twelve people died on Everest that season, the deadliest on record. The death count would have been higher had not the members of other expeditions climbed up into the storm to rescue the survivors.

Around the world, people read Krakauer's account of these events, as much for the gripping nature of the story as for any insights into Everest. However, Rob Hall's and Scott Fischer's commercial expeditions became the prime examples of how Everest is climbed. The other ways of climbing Everest—private teams of world-class climbers tackling the steepest faces of the most rugged peaks, and small teams coming together on serviced expeditions to achieve their own private dreams—saw no limelight, leaving the myth that high-altitude mountaineering was all about being guided and being told what to do every step of the way.

Our 7Summits-Club expedition was somewhere in between these categories. Alex provided everything a serviced expedition includes, but he also managed the acclimatization and climbing program. Our twenty climbers would remain divided into the A-Team and the B-Team, with each team allocated one guide and one assistant guide as well as Sherpa support.

There was some discussion that first evening about the mind-blowing nature of our base camp. The facilities were those that I would have expected from a more expensive expedition operator. The consensus was that Alex had found the effective level of economy of scale, and while I appreciated the luxuries of our tents, the food, and the sauna/bath tent, I was stunned to discover the multimedia tent, where half a dozen laptops were laid out and a large television sat at each end of the room. I wondered what kind of economies might be enforced high on the mountain. Being famously tough mountaineers, the Russian climbing regimen might be very challenging. This possibility did not worry me because I was committed to attempting only what was safe and achievable regardless of what instructions I might be given. That was the only way to return home safely to my family.

Seven

EVEREST 2006

THAT FIRST NIGHT, snuggling into my sleeping bag after dinner, I had a mix of contradictory feelings. I was nervous about how Christopher would perform on the mountain. I remained nervous about how I would perform personally. The refrain "I have given myself only seven weeks to train for this Everest attempt" kept repeating itself in my head like the chorus of an overplayed popular song. Nevertheless, I was excited by the prospect of being among these mountains again because I knew I would thrive on the physical and mental challenges. The only time I perform at my limit is when circumstances demand it, and I was looking forward to finding out just how far I could go seven years after my last big expedition.

I slept well, waking with the slight headache that I expected after my first night at 17,000 feet. One of the most welcoming aspects of a Himalayan expedition is the wake-up call given by the Sherpas. That first morning, despite gloomy skies and fresh snow still settling on the ground, pairs of kitchen boys came by with thermoses of coffee and tea, welcoming everyone to our first morning here. This was a signal for us to get dressed and ready for the day. I stuck my head out, but there was no view of the landscape beyond the perimeter of the camp. Most of us stayed in bed until breakfast was announced half an hour later—the unmistakable clanging of a big spoon against an old oxygen cylinder which hung in the doorway of the kitchen tent.

As soon as I stepped out of my tent, I was surprised by the amount of snow that had fallen, more than double the quantity of the evening before. It was very unusual for spring and much more like a winter fall. On my way to the mess tent, I poked my head in the kitchen and greeted the crew in Nepali, and they beamed back at me. Such greetings were easy, and while I managed to converse in the language, I did it very poorly, with inappropriate verb forms and messy sentence structures. Sherpas and Tibetans have their own distinct languages, so they don't worry about others speaking bad Nepali.

Breakfast was a leisurely affair, largely because the weather did not favor any kind of outdoor activity. The cooks produced a huge variety of food and drink for breakfast, and I marveled at the range available on what was a relatively low-budget expedition. Alex had obviously discovered the economic benefits of buying in bulk. Everyone seemed to be in good spirits, with many of the climbers happy to sit there indefinitely, talking and joking.

My priority for the morning was to catch up with my diary. I knew that as soon as the weather lifted, life would get busy, not just with sorting gear and meetings about procedures and logistics but also with the mountain itself. I needed to finish writing about the last two weeks so that I could put the past behind me and give my full attention to being here at Base Camp.

When I had eaten enough, I returned to my tent and jotted down details, filling in some blank days from early in the trip. Then I set about organizing my tent properly by dividing it into zones. My sleeping zone ran down the middle, with my feet at the door. On my right side, next to where my head would be when I was lying on my back, were my books, notebooks, and cameras—my creative zone. Also on my right was a sports bag for clothes and a big nylon drawstring bag for bulky garments, like my fleece bib-and-brace and jackets. My weatherproof Gore-Tex gear was near the door, so that if it suddenly got cold while I was wandering around camp, I could just reach inside the tent and grab what I needed. To my left were my snacks, of which I had quite a lot. As a vegetarian, I was not sure how well I would fare in the mess tent. I had chocolate, sports bars and gels, plus suckable sweets to soothe my throat, which I knew would be made raw by the constant gasping of freezing oxygen-thin air. Barbara had helped me dry all kinds of fresh fruit. Next to the food were two plastic boxes containing my Pharmanex nutritional supplements, the best quality I could get. The rest of the left side housed my toiletries, a second empty bag ready for dirty clothes, my daypack, and finally, by the door, my footwear. I love the simplicity of having a tent to myself because I can really make myself comfortable.

When I emerged from my tent, I noticed that the huge dome that Harry had brought specifically for the two film teams was being set up, but nothing much seemed to be happening. At first I thought it was a case of too many cooks—there were three people in Harry's team, plus Richard, Christopher, Mike, and several Sherpas—but as I approached and became involved, I realized the problem was more fundamental. Whatever we tried to do, the tent fly appeared to be too small. Sherpas are always keen to get a job done, and a few poles were bent as we tried to bully the fly into place. Harry had wandered off but now reappeared with another tent fly. He told us that the tent fly that we had been struggling with was designed for suspension from inside the frame, so that the tent could be pitched as a single-skinned weatherproof tent. What Harry now brought was a larger fly that was meant to go over the top of the frame. The correct fly slipped into place easily. Our timing proved to be perfect. As lunchtime was announced by the clanging of the oxygen cylinder, snow began to fall more heavily.

The wind picked up strongly during the afternoon and not just at ground level. I was writing my diary when the yellow glow inside my tent—instantly followed by an increase in temperature—told me that the sun was now shining. At the same instant Mike called out to me.

"Lincoln, the clouds are gone, so we'll be able to see the mountain."

"I'll be right out," I replied, but I was caught up with the thoughts I was scribbling. It was half an hour before I stepped outside, cozily protected from the bitter wind by my down jacket.

The heavy clouds we had been under for days had now been swept from the sky. Our base camp was in a location that offered no view of Mount Everest. In one sense it was good that the mountain was invisible. It was as though we were assembled in a teacher-free classroom, where we did not have to worry about what punishment might be meted out to us. Some of our team had walked a few hundred feet beyond the limits of our extensive camp back toward the road-head to a point where they could see the great peak. I thought it more useful, in terms of fitness and acclimatization, to clamber up the steep moraine wall directly above our camp.

Climbers from other teams were tackling the slope as well, so I followed what was already a well-trodden trail in the snow. I quickly realized the trail had been established by Sherpas, as there were several cables, one of them thicker than my thumb, lying beside the track in the snow. I presumed these were for radio-phone communications.

When I reached what proved to be a false crest, there was still no view of Everest. However, I was startled to see a small but deep lake of perfectly clear water. I was even more surprised when I realized that what I had taken to be a thick cable running to Base Camp was, in fact, a hose that supplied it with water. I wondered what other creature comforts this huge Russian expedition might be holding in store.

Beyond the spot where the hose had been placed in the lake, I followed fresh tracks that led to the true crest of the moraine wall. As I approached, half a dozen figures were silhouetted against the majestic backdrop of Everest. After two days of gloomy skies, the colors and the clarity seemed surreal. I snapped a few photos, then plodded up to where everyone stood. Someone was hunched over a substantial tripod, and I realized immediately who it was.

"Fantastic view, Mike."

"Hi, Lincoln," Mike said as he turned and beamed up at me. "It's looking better all the time."

"Where are Richard and Christopher?" I asked.

"They came up as soon as the skies cleared," he said, "but they didn't put on much in the way of extra clothes, so they went down as soon as they'd taken some photos. I got some footage of them as well."

"There'll be plenty of other times to look at the mountain."

Mike nodded but said nothing.

I stood staring at the mountainscape. I had spent countless hours staring at Everest during our expedition in 1984—it is a sight that has no see-by date.

"Bloody cold," I muttered. "Makes you wonder why we even think about going up there, where it's going to be twice as cold."

I looked away from Everest and down at the many expedition camps that took what shelter they could from the low moraine humps that formed the perimeter of the glacial flat. From where I stood, the effect was of a snow-covered sports ground surrounded by different teams with color-coded encampments. The flat expanse of snow was now dotted with people looking up toward me and beyond to the mountain, some of them walking away, having had their fill of Everest. Others walked in pairs, their random tracks telling me they were going nowhere in particular but just enjoying a late-afternoon stroll.

My back was not only to the mountain but also to the wind. I felt warm and secure in my down jacket and thick fleece bib-and-brace. I was at peace among the mountains again, not looking out through fogged-up windows but standing shin-deep in snow with my hands thrust deep in my pockets. There was no sense of the hugeness of the task that faced us all—its discomforts, dangers, and uncertainties—though the fact that we were here implied all these things. Instead, as I slowly adopted the sharpening of focus and the concern with what really matters, I felt myself letting go of my questioning. The time had come for me to begin to listen to the environment and to renew my understanding of the parameters.

THE NEXT MORNING there was not a cloud in the sky. Everything was covered in snow, and although the air was cold, it melted quickly. Reflections from the intense white snow dazzled us and multiplied the melting power of the sun. Now that we were no longer crammed into our mess tents, we were no longer obliged to congregate only as the A- and B-Teams. Life became more social as we stood around chatting or sat in front of our tents, fiddling with gear.

Richard and Christopher spent a lot of time in the film tent. They were busy setting up the solar panels they had brought to power their computer, satellite phone, and weather station. They also used the tent as storage space. Mike was often with them, both to organize the camera equipment and to film Christopher as he attacked the Sherpas with his inflatable kangaroo and crocodile, or as he adjusted the weather station which he had set up just outside the big dome. I spent time there as well, just chatting or helping with the wording of the Web dispatches, which

Richard would then upload to Christopher's website. We had a very stable satellite phone, not only for uploads but for phone calls as well.

It was great to be able to talk to Barbara, Dylan, and Dorje, but it was also difficult. I wanted to hear how they were and what they were doing. I was happy to hear their voices, whatever they had to say. On the other hand, I knew that success on a big mountain depends on commitment and perseverance, and that there are times of great discomfort, danger, and emotional turmoil. Tough times could lead me to question what I was doing here—and it was only a small step from there to the desire for warmth and comfort and the need to be safely back at home with the family I loved. It was much harder to talk myself through such times of doubt when my loved ones were only a phone call away.

On my first eight major expeditions, spread across fifteen years, we had sketchy radio communications at best; at worst, we had mail-runners—or nothing. By 1999 things had changed. In March that year I was a cameraman on the Australian-American expedition to Makalu, where we filmed a documentary about Michael Groom, Australia's most accomplished high-altitude mountaineer at the time. After Michael and Dave Bridges had summited and were back at Base Camp, they were able to use the expedition's satellite phone to ring home with the news. The arrival of such portable technology had dragged me away from the intense isolation that had once been a major characteristic of expeditions. The new generation of climbers is blind to such complete remoteness, as almost every team now has a satellite phone and, often, a live website.

In October 1999 while I sat at my desk in Blackheath writing a newspaper column, I was stunned to receive an e-mail from a friend at Shisha-pangma Base Camp explaining that a few hours earlier Alex Lowe and my good friend Dave Bridges from our Makalu climb had disappeared beneath a huge avalanche, and that Conrad Anker, who had been with them, was definitely alive. The next day the deaths of Alex and Dave were confirmed on the American Ski Expedition website. It was bewildering to be sharing from the other side of the world the unfolding of the tragedy at the same time as those who were living it at Base Camp. The hope and horror of the avalanche hit me right there at my desk. This time around, on Everest, the members and organizers of our expedition had five different websites among them. I had been dragged into the seemingly innocent world of mountaineering websites.

WHEN VIEWED FROM the Tibetan Base Camp, the initial section of the climbing route is obscured, with only the upper reaches of the North Ridge visible above the foreground mass of Changtse's peak. The unmistakable asymmetrical triangle of Mount Everest towers behind, with its West Ridge cutting down to the right at an angle of forty-five degrees. The Northeast Ridge drops to the left at a much gentler angle. Access to this ridge is via the North Ridge, a broad snow spur that rises from the North Col. Climbers reach the crest of the Northeast Ridge at 27,900 feet, with only a little more than a thousand feet of height to gain before they can stand on the world's highest point. The catch is that the horizontal distance to the summit is more than a mile. There are no quick dashes to the top on this route, and this is what makes summit day so dangerous.

The low angle of the highest sections of the Northeast Ridge belies the difficulty of the climbing, as both sides of the ridge are steep. Only in a few places is it possible to walk along the crest. The rest of the time climbers traverse downward-sloping ledges on the North Face, often with loose rock underfoot. Each ledge finishes at a sheer drop or simply merges into the smooth slabs of the face. Climbers gain height by clambering from one sloping shelf up to the next. Usually this is a matter of straightforward rock-scrambling, but there are a few tricky sections where technical climbing skills are necessary. Those without the skills pull up on the fixed rope, which runs all the way to the summit of the mountain. However, this is a dangerous technique because the cord—which is only one-third of an inch in diameter—is sure to be seriously weakened in places. The damage is done by rockfalls or abrasion, or by a careless mountaineer puncturing a rope that is lying on the snow with the sharp point of an ice axe or crampon. The anchoring devices that attach the rope to the mountainside can loosen with time, which means they can pull out under a climber's body weight. Some ropes are old and have not been checked in years. Caution is required on all fixed ropes, and experienced climbers keep as much weight on their feet as they can in order to lessen the load on the rope.

The most intimidating obstacles of the entire climb are encountered on the upper section of the Northeast Ridge. They are three in number, each of them steep cliffs, which have the unpoetic names of the First, Second, and Third Steps. Prosaic names are not surprising, as there is not much scope for poetry at extreme heights. A more likely mental state is the hallucinatory one that comes when the mind rebels against exhaustion and lack of oxygen. At the roof of the world, the absurdities of an illusory state can be easier for the mind to accept than the logic of deadly reality.

The First and the Third Steps offer few challenges apart from sheer effort, but every climber who tackles the route approaches the Second Step with trepidation. Many climbers turn back here, and of those who continue onward to a summit which lies beyond their limits, the Second Step is often where they retreat to. For those who really have gone too far, this is where they can expect to die.

Above the Second Step, the ridge seems to broaden. In fact, it remains narrow but feels wider because there are fewer boulders, buttresses, and cornices cluttering the crest. Climbers heading for the summit along the ridge have the unbelievably precipitous Kangshung Face to their left and the steeply sloping North Face to their right. The lack of obstacles along the crest only makes the sheer drop on each side more obvious and the climbers more frightened. By this stage, climbers are either fired up to reach the summit or coming to terms with having bitten off more than they can chew. Two options remain for those who are struggling. Death is one. The other is retreat. The tragedy is that by this stage many climbers no longer have the capacity to make a choice.

I know these details because my life has been linked to Everest for over twenty years. My work as a trekking guide has taken me to the Nepalese Base Camp many times, and three times to the Tibetan side. I have climbed lesser peaks in the region which has Everest as an ever-present backdrop. Trekkers always ask me about Everest, about my 1984 climb and why we didn't use oxygen, and about how I felt about not reaching the summit. They ask my opinions on topics such as rubbish on the mountain, the deadly 1996 season, and how dangerous it really is. None has an easy explanation.

I am particularly knowledgeable about the North Ridge route because of the book I wrote in 2004 about my longtime friend Sue Fear. Sue was the second Australian woman to climb Mount Everest and the first to climb it from Tibet. Sue used to stop by Singapore for a few days or a week on her way to an expedition to the Karakoram or the Himalaya. During those few visits I taped thirty hours of interviews, which covered every aspect of Sue's Everest climb. I needed from her as clear a picture as I could get of the climbing route so that I could write about it as accurately and convincingly as possible. I kept asking questions until I could visualize each camp and each obstacle. It helped that I had hiked up the East Rongbuk Glacier approach to Everest a few months after Sue had reached the summit. Now I was about to discover how close my descriptions in our book had been to the truth.

Eight

EAST RONGBUK

O N THE MORNING that the A-Team were getting ready to head up to Intermediate Camp on an acclimatization hike, I entertained myself by watching Slate pack what he thought was necessary for a few days up the valley. The hike to Advance Base Camp and back would take three days, so with tents, sleeping bags, and the catering already set up at the camps, not much gear was needed.

Most intriguing among his gear was a black Darth Vader–like mask that Slate had constructed all by himself.

"So, you're intending to blast off into space from the summit, are you?"

"May the force be with me."

We got along very well. I never had to explain my bad jokes and I always nodded politely at his. He was very proud of his construction, so I did not criticize it any further.

"You know how I was really ill back at Nyalam with that cough?" he asked. "This will help me keep it under control."

"But how?"

"The beaklike thing is a heat-exchange breath-warmer."

"Like the Norwegians have?" I had been intrigued by the strange cigarette-packet-sized objects the Norwegians had been shoving into their mouths. "The ones they've got are white."

"Yep. Because they are Jedi."

"Right."

"Actually, they're pretty well the same, just a different brand of breath-warmer. Then I used this duct tape to keep out the wind and make a mask, and so I don't have to clench it between my teeth all day long."

"Petter swears by his and it hasn't even got cold yet," I said, "so maybe you're on to something. And if it doesn't work, you'll be able to mug people without them recognizing you."

"It's a win–win."

"And it keeps out the wind-wind."

Then I shut up so that Slate could concentrate. I did not want to be responsible for making him forget something vital. He was very well prepared and had obviously given careful consideration to how he was going to climb the mountain. And while I did not feel inadequate, I did wish that I'd had more time to organize my own personal gear. Six weeks from the day I got the green flag just wasn't enough to get myself fully prepared. As it was, I had done little more than pull out my favorite items of clothing and hardware and take a quick cruise through the Mountain Designs store in Sydney to replace worn-out gloves, socks, and a few other items. With ten expeditions behind me, and several dozen treks, I knew my basic needs. However, I would have liked some extra time to have checked out the latest technologies for keeping hands and feet warm and functional at extreme heights. And now that I knew about breath-warmers, I would have liked one of them as well.

When Slate had shouldered his pack and was ready to go, I offered him a high five, saying, "The American way."

We slapped palms as he mumbled something about watching too many basketball movies and that this form of hand greeting was not universal practice in his home country. Trust an attorney to be a stickler for accuracy. Then he headed off, pausing at the kitchen tent to stick his head in and say good-bye to the crew.

I decided I should start getting my own stuff sorted in preparation for my departure up the valley the next day. Christopher, Richard, Mike, and I would be hiking with other members of the B-Team—Harry Kikstra, Thomas Weber, Kevin Augello, and Milan Collin.

As it turned out, I was granted an extra day's rest. I developed a cough overnight and an upset stomach by morning. I was not badly sick, but I was aware that it would be a foolish move to sleep at a higher altitude until I felt better. Success at high altitude begins with preventing any illness or injury from getting worse. I limited myself to walking with my Australian companions as far as the turnoff which led up into the East Rongbuk Valley.

Back at Base Camp I relaxed in my tent and enjoyed a light lunch followed by a snooze. Apart from any other considerations, it was a great pleasure to be alone. I could be with my own thoughts and begin to recalibrate my brain to the immense challenge of climbing Everest. To this point, the journey had been excitement and anticipation, but now every action would have its purpose. On protracted expeditions it is easy to be knocked around by the inhospitable conditions. I had found that the best way to remain unfazed was to dress appropriately, keep my hands and feet warm, and not worry too much about anything else. The path to equilibrium is always easiest for me when I am by myself, and so I was happy to head up the glacier the next morning alone.

Most of our climbing gear had been lashed onto the wooden saddles of the yaks. When all the yaks were loaded, they formed a convoy, which was led the full distance to Advance Base Camp in one day. Because I was intending to sleep at Intermediate Camp, I carried everything I needed for a night on the ice, including my down jacket and other warm clothing. All these items remained in my pack as I trudged up the glacier. The weather was perfect and I felt strong, even though my pack was heavier than I had intended.

The first stage of the hike follows the long trough between the slow-moving mass of the Rongbuk Glacier and the unstable scree slope above it. The trough is the seam that separates the stationary mountainside and the movable ice. Such troughs are common access routes because they provide relatively level going, as was the case all the way to the junction of the East Rongbuk Valley with the Rongbuk Glacier.

I climbed steeply up a spur to get upstream of the gorge carved by East Rongbuk River. A mile up the valley, the river emerged from beneath the ice of the East Rongbuk Glacier, but as the flow was small, I was able to walk across a basin of glacial silt. Beyond the basin lay the worst kind of glacier travel, although it was nothing new to me. The lower reaches of every sizable glacier are a maze of ice pyramids, frozen ponds, ice slopes, and obvious but uninviting crevasses covered in loose shards of rock. The East Rongbuk is better than many, but it was still a chore to have to lose height, gain it, and lose it again, all the while knowing that the destination was much farther than it appeared because of the circuitous route.

Today the sun was shining strongly, so that despite a persistent wind my Gore-Tex wind-suit kept me more than warm enough. At last I came to the final deep valley, eroded into the glacier by a stream. The climb up out of that valley was the final leg to the 7Summits-Club Intermediate Camp.

The glacial landscape at the halfway point between Base Camp and Advance Base Camp was not the ideal spot for a major encampment. Consequently, the different expeditions were scattered across two separate ice ridges, which at least limited overcrowding. I recognized our long yellow-caterpillar tent immediately; it was identical to our mess tent at Base Camp but less than half the length. My delayed departure from Base Camp put me between the itineraries of both the A-Team and the B-Team, but a few members of the A-Team were still in residence. Dawa and Tendi, cooks in residence, served up plenty of food, which I ate with gusto. I was pleased to have a good appetite because a gain in altitude often suppresses hunger and causes nausea.

In 2002, I had hiked up to this point after leading a trekking group to the Lho La, but the weather had been so bad that I was unable to grasp the lay of the land. And so when I awoke the next morning, I was excited about the next seven miles. The terrain was more straightforward than the previous day, with the upper reaches of the glacier more open and less eroded.

For me it was a great day out in the mountains. Everest had been barely visible in the morning beyond the mass of Changtse. By midafternoon my perspective had changed. As the glacier rounded Changtse's long East Ridge, more of Everest revealed itself, and I could see that there was no need to venture onto the upper glacier, where there would be hidden crevasses. Instead, the moraine valley, with the glacier on one side and Changtse's ridge on the other, led directly to Advance Base Camp. Unfortunately, my heading westward coincided with the sun dropping behind the ridge, putting me in shade and exposing me to a dramatic drop in temperature. I pulled my down jacket on over my wind-suit and struggled onward. I was now at 20,600 feet. The shortage of oxygen forced me to take big gasps of the freezing air, which shocked my lungs and made me cough uncontrollably. This inevitable circumstance was the reason Slate had constructed his Darth Vader mask and why the three Norwegians made sure they were equally well equipped. Without such technology, I was bitterly cold, short of breath, and just wanted to be warm and at rest.

Not yet acclimatized to this height, I was not able to walk quickly toward the tents in the distance. As I crested a rock-covered hump of ice, I almost fell into the open doors of a small expedition's kitchen tent. It was a dramatic way to learn level space on the sloping glacier is utilized even when right by the trail. I plodded on, gradually realizing that Advance Base Camp stretched a half-mile up the moraine gully, gaining almost a thousand feet in the process. Because I was puffing hard and moving slowly, the 7Summits-Club encampment appeared impossibly far away.

At last I arrived at our tents, easily recognizable among the many dozens pitched along the moraine below Changste's Northeast Ridge. I whipped off my down jacket, unzipped my wind-suit, pulled on my cozy fleece bib-and-brace, and then I donned my down jacket again. Now insulated from the sunless afternoon cold at 21,000 feet, I staggered up to the signature yellow caterpillar tent for the refreshments I knew would be waiting for me. Every other time that I had been to this height I had been completely self-sufficient, carrying my own tent, stove, and food, or at least sharing these loads among my few friends. I was not complaining, but it felt decidedly odd to enter a tent where I was welcomed by smiling Sherpas offering a thermos of water, another of milk, six kinds of teabags, and three incarnations of hot chocolate. Despite the strangeness, the "village" setting made me feel less intimidated by the prospect of my first night in several years at 21,000 feet. When I woke at two A.M. with a headache, I was prepared—with a Panadol at the ready and a book to read until I fell asleep again. Years ago I had discovered that this was the best way for me to deal with high-altitude insomnia. The remedy became ineffective only when there was not enough oxygen for me to remember the preceding sentence, but at my present height I was a long way from that.

My first night at Advance Base Camp turned out to be more comfortable than expected, but the best way to acclimatize was to head back to Base Camp, where I would get the recuperative benefits of sleeping 4,000 feet lower. That morning, the sun beating down made the mess tent as hot as a greenhouse. I could not manage much breakfast, but I made sure I had plenty to drink, then I wandered back to my tent and repacked my belongings for the long downhill trek. The path out of the camp was easy to follow, with a good covering of shattered rocks obscuring the ice of the glacier beneath. Not far beyond the last tents, the path was interrupted by a steep-sided gully in the ice. Obstacles like this one were the reason I had brought with me a pair of trekking poles, which are best described as modified ski stocks. Their height is easily adjusted, which is a useful feature on steep terrain. The only time I use them is for balance and extra grip on glaciers where there are loose rocks and exposed ice—which is almost every glacier. With fourteen miles of moraine and glacier to be traversed multiple times, the poles saved me a great deal of effort.

The glacier curved to the north, and by that process the ice was contorted into ridges, like frozen waves. The terrain eased as the glacier straightened out, with shards of rock providing friction underfoot.

I made good time and caught up with a young man also heading down the valley. We chatted, and as we talked, I learned that he was the cinematographer for a two-person Norwegian ski team, although he himself was Swedish. His name was Fredrik Schenholm.

"They will ski the Norton Couloir," he said.

"I've been there," I replied immediately. "I can tell you about it."

He looked at me but said nothing; perhaps he was thinking that the couloir had been climbed only once, and that the chances of meeting someone from that expedition were highly improbable.

"I was part of the Australian team in 1984 that made the first ascent. I climbed to the top of the couloir, to where the snow ended. I could explain the lay of the land to your friends, if they're interested.'

"Okay," he said, which was about as noncommittal as he could get without being rude.

I wasn't trying to assert myself; I was merely excited to meet anyone interested in our route on the North Face, even if they were going to ski rather than climb it.

"I'm with 7Summits-Club and Alex Abramov. You'll know us from our giant yellow-caterpillar tent."

Then I was on my way. Maybe the Norwegian skiers would contact me; maybe they wouldn't. Just thinking about the North Face gave me a boost of energy. I continued to be amazed that no one else had climbed the Great Couloir (also known as the Norton Couloir) in the intervening twenty-two years. Very few had tried, despite it being such a major feature of the mountain and one of the most direct routes to the summit. On Mount Everest, tagging the summit sadly meant more than style and adventure.

THE TWO-DAY APPROACH to the heights of Advance Base Camp had been a workout for me and a great metabolic trigger for my body's acclimatization processes. The long one-day return to Base Camp was proving much easier. Once I had cleared the irregular contortions of the rock-covered ice pyramids that marked the end of the East Rongbuk Glacier, I moved with a rhythm and pace that felt just right for where I was and what I was doing. By midafternoon I was traveling at a good speed across a part of the route that consisted of small boulders.

I only stayed on track because the route was marked by cairns at regular intervals. Soon I caught up with three slow-moving figures ahead of me. They turned out to be Harry, Thomas, and Milan, taking it easy on a beautiful sunny afternoon. The sun was losing its warmth but not its power to heighten the warm colors of the orange and brown rocks. As I overtook my teammates, I made a few light remarks about the good weather and wondered to myself whether Thomas's vision was already impaired at these relatively low heights.

I was tired but content and wasted no mental energy on anything superfluous. I was doing what I needed to do at each particular moment, until I reached the point where there were no moments, only the continuum of my passage along the rubble-strewn trail. I made no attempts to put myself in this state; I just found myself there. It felt like the landscape was including me—as if the barrier between the living and the nonliving, between life and death, had dissolved. My enjoyment was no longer of the magnificent day or of the mountains but of an altered sense of reality, a disconnection from the flow of thoughts that normally had me planning, thinking, analyzing. I had stepped into a simpler state of being.

The change in my perceptions was confirmed for me when I became aware of the sounds of birds. Several types of bird live at these heights, but they are neither songbirds nor plentiful. At first I thought nothing of it—because I was not thinking, only moving through the landscape. I approached some boulders with the knowledge that there were Tibetan snow cocks behind them, and although I had seen nothing, I did not question the knowledge or how I came to have it. As I drew parallel with the boulders, four birds broke cover. Only able to fly downhill, they flew across the path in front of me, the loud *wap-wap-wap* of their wings warning other birds higher up the slope to take flight.

I had experienced this kind of connection to a world beyond oneself on the hardest of mountains, when danger had put all my senses on red alert. Afterward, as I descended from the last of the snow and steep rock, my senses remained tuned to the present moment. The sounds were more insistent, the colors were brighter, and my eyes seemed to take in everything around me without my mind asking them to look. It was an extraordinary feeling—it is one of the reasons that I climb. I had trudged up and down many tedious glaciers in magnificent settings, but never before had I experienced such rapture without the elixir of danger.

This state of heightened awareness stayed with me as I continued down the trail. The steep descent from the lip of the East Rongbuk Valley into the main Rongbuk Valley seemed much shorter than it had during the ascent, which was a measure of the extra effort I had needed to put in when plodding uphill, unacclimatized, at 17,000 feet two days earlier. The path through the boulders scattered along the moraine trough was obvious, thanks to the glacial silt underfoot which left a well-trodden trail.

There are dangers between Base Camp and Advance Base Camp, especially for heavily loaded yaks, and so the *yakpas* (yak drivers) had the habit of blessing the trail with prayer flags. With no trees or bridges from which to hang the lines of flags, they were placed individually on boulders at waist height or above and kept in place by a pebble in the center. The pebble or fragment of rock had to be heavy enough to hold down the prayer flag but not so large that it prevented the edges of the flag from fluttering in the wind.

I was no longer hearing birds, but I could hear distant wind-borne music. Ahead of me a dark blue prayer flag caught my eye, and I sensed that I needed to keep it in my sight. The flag was on a jagged boulder of gray granite at the level of my shoulder and was held down by a chunky rock the size of a bar of soap. Within a few feet of it, as I watched intently, the chunk of rock wobbled, the event confirmed by the soft *clack* as it moved. I was surprised less by the movement than by my attention being drawn to it before it happened.

During the last miles to Base Camp, my mind was open to everything. I saw a man leaning against a tall rock, wearing an Akubra hat and moleskin trousers and holding what looked like some kind of box. There are times when you see an object from a new perspective only to discover that it is something completely different. As I approached the man, the perspective changed, but he remained a man. A few steps farther his image had transformed into a stack of boulders. You can make mistakes when your mind is cluttered with thoughts but also when it is free of them.

Beyond the disappearing man, I saw the hindquarters of a small deer, similar to one that Mike had spotted silhouetted on the crest of a ridge. As I approached, I slowed down and trod softly, only to discover that the deer, too, was no more than a shape among the rocks. These were obviously hallucinations caused by tiredness and hypoxia, but I believed I would not have seen the shapes at all had I not been in a heightened state of awareness.

If nothing else, the experience gave me an insight into the origins of Tibetan animism, where spirits are believed to exist among the rocks and mountains are courted by *pujas* at Base Camp and ceremonies in monasteries. I was not seeing any spirits, but I managed to maintain the feeling of belonging to the landscape until I stepped into the mess tent at Base Camp. Back at our mountain home, instantly there were practical matters which required my attention.

. . .

ON A SUNNY but windy afternoon a week later, when hiking up the glacier with Christopher, Richard, and Mike, I pulled into Intermediate Camp and was amazed to find the mess tent full. This only happened because the B-Team caught up with a few members of the A-Team, who had decided they needed an extra night there before pushing on to Advance Base Camp. This was perfectly acceptable because there is often personal variation in the rate of acclimatization, and there were enough tents, plenty of food, and two eager cooks. What I didn't realize immediately was that there were two extra people, Vitor Negrete and Rodrigo Raineri.

The two Brazilian mountaineers had attempted Everest by this same route the year before. Vitor had summited, but Rodrigo had been forced to retreat 150 feet below. The fact that he turned back at that point indicates both the enormous physical effort required for that final section and the debilitating effects of extreme altitude, even for those using oxygen. As chance would have it, Harry and Vitor had stood on the summit of Everest at the same hour on the same day in 2005 but until now had not had the opportunity to compare their triumphs.

The Brazilians knew only Harry and Alex, so that night I chatted with Vitor, wanting him and Rodrigo to feel welcome among a tent full of strangers. Vitor explained that he and Rodrigo had been climbing partners and best friends for fifteen years, and that they had returned to Everest to put themselves back on an equal footing—both would be Everest summiteers.

"But this time it will be a little different," he said. "I will climb without oxygen."

"I've always climbed without oxygen," I chipped in, "and on Everest, at twenty-seven thousand feet without it. The problem is that there's not enough oxygen to keep you warm or to let you think properly. If you want to think, you have to stop moving."

Vitor smiled, and I felt I had said enough. I did not want to be telling someone who had already stood on the top of Everest how to climb the mountain.

"It will only be me without oxygen," he continued. "Rodrigo will use it."

I wished them luck.

IN LATE APRIL it was time for all of us, both the A-Team and the B-Team, to leave the glacier behind and move up onto the slopes of Everest itself. Members of the A-Team had hiked up to Advance Base Camp the day before, so they were fresh and rested when the B-Team arrived from Intermediate Camp late in the afternoon.

"Tonight," announced Alex at the dinner table, "everyone will meet with the Sherpas. Those climbers who have asked for a personal Sherpa will meet him. Other climbers will meet with team Sherpas. This will be after dinner."

Alex was never one to give advance warning of his meetings, probably because he did not see the point, and he wished to avoid questions ahead of time. Everything would be explained when necessary, so why worry? After dinner the Sherpas and climbers squeezed into the yellow tent. It was a tight fit, with many of us standing. Alex said a few words about the importance of the Sherpas' various roles, then introduced Mingma Gelu Sherpa, who was the expedition *sirdar* and in charge of the Sherpa crew. There were twenty Sherpas in total, all of whom had been busy establishing our three camps on the mountain—Camp One at the North Col, Camp Two at 25,000 feet, and our High Camp (or Camp Three) at 27,300 feet. Alex had proudly announced that the 7Summits-Club camp at the North Col had the only mess tent and toilet tent on the mountain. If nothing else, the extra loads meant that there had been no shortage of work for the Sherpas.

Mingma explained that all the Sherpas were from his village or district and were his brothers, cousins, or uncles. All of them had climbed Everest at least once, and several had climbed other 8,000ers as well (peaks above 8,000 meters, or 26,250 feet). All were well trained in the ways of the mountain and in the safest ways to use the fixed rope.

To me, it was a strange scene. Because of my very basic grasp of Nepali, I had come to know a couple of Sherpas who had traveled with us from Kathmandu; apart from that, I knew nothing about any of the crew assembled before us. However, those of us who had booked a Sherpa to climb with now had to choose or be chosen, and everyone's decisions had to be made in a matter of minutes. This was a decidedly odd way to select someone with whom you would be sharing life-or-death situations. But it was also classically Russian to get a result by setting the cats among the pigeons. We had no choice but to take Mingma at his word that all of his Sherpas were up to the job required.

The A-Team was heading up to Camp One at the North Col in the morning, so the priority was to get them sorted. Harry had already selected the two Sherpas, Pemba and Passang, to accompany him and Thomas. When the dust settled, there were not too many choices left. The ambience was similar to a school dance, when the last girls and boys finally stepped out onto the dance floor.

As the climbers who had linked up with their Sherpas went outside, the tent emptied. I saw four men sitting together, and among them I recognized Lakcha, one of the Sherpas who had helped us erect the giant dome tent in the snowstorm during our first morning at Base Camp. I remembered us joking together, his gold front tooth obvious every time he smiled. His English was at about the same level as my Nepali, which meant we could communicate readily. He was strong, solidly built, and outgoing—all of these attributes were obvious at first glance.

Lakcha indicated to me almost immediately that he would be able to hold the team of four Sherpas together. It was not a strategy on his part; he merely stepped up and introduced the other three—Pasang, Dawa Tenzing, and Dorje. Ironically, the others had better English than Lakcha. Dawa Tenzing was shy but prepared to say what he thought; Pasang was more forthright and definitely wanted to be treated as an equal; while Dorje, who could not have been long out of his teens, was initially reserved but very much aware of what was going on. He smiled broadly when I told him my younger son shared his name.

I had been talking to the four men in Nepali, saying that I wanted us to climb as friends and that I hoped we would enjoy our time together on Sagarmatha, the Nepali name for Mount Everest. Then I turned to

Richard, Christopher, and Mike, and we went through the introductions in English.

It had been a long day and now it was definitely time for bed. We agreed to meet in the morning, then said our good-nights. I slept well, secure in the feeling that we had a good crew to help us.

Nine

EVEREST THE HIGHWAY

THE 7SUMMITS-CLUB Mount Everest Expedition officially began with a *puja* at Advance Base Camp. For both Buddhists and Hindus, *puja* is a word from the ancient Indian language of Pali meaning a ceremony of honor and devotion. No Sherpa will set foot on Mount Everest unless a *puja* has been performed. The 7Summits-Club Sherpas, who were already setting up camps and carrying supplies up the mountain, had attended an earlier *puja* of their own.

At Advance Base Camp, our ceremony began with the building of a *chorten*, which can be an elaborate structure but at 21,000 feet was a basic square stone tower 5 feet high. A vertical pole emerged from the *chorten*, with its tip being the point of attachment for radiating strings of prayer flags, which were fastened to an irregular circle of rocks on the ground.

With the place of worship established, the Sherpas laid a plastic tablecloth on the rubble at the base of the *chorten*. Food offerings were placed on it, and a Sherpa who was also a Tibetan Buddhist lama sat on a sleeping mat in front of the offerings. He began to chant prayers that were appropriate for Chomolungma, a Tibetan and Sherpa term that translates as "Mother Goddess of the World." Several goddesses are believed to inhabit the upper reaches of Everest, but only Chomolungma is invoked as the mountain's name.

It was a beautiful day, perfect for a *puja*. The lama chanted constantly as he blessed the food. Sprigs of juniper were burned as incense on both sides of the *chorten*. The Sherpas placed their climbing tools—ice axes, boots, and crampons—on the *chorten*, and we climbers were invited to do the same. Mine were among the first. The wafting smoke from the burning juniper bestowed blessings on the climbing equipment, and the eating of the blessed food and drink did the same for everyone who chose to partake.

The expedition members, both Sherpas and climbers, sat on sleeping mats behind the lama. The ceremony lasted an hour, finishing with a crescendo of cymbals and the ringing of a handbell as we all threw handfuls of rice into the air and the flames. The lama handed to each of us a red thread of string "blessed by the Dalai Lama." Climbers and Sherpas alike tied them into loops around their necks.

The festivities were over, but there was plenty of food still to be eaten. It was the day that the A-Team and their Russian guides and Sherpas were to head up to the North Col, so none of them sat around for long. Instead, they shouldered their packs and trudged up the path toward the mountain.

BEFORE WE HEADED UP to the North Col for the first time, we followed the main track one afternoon through Advance Base Camp to the uphill limit of the tent village. The highest camp, and hence the closest to the mountain, belonged to a Chinese expedition at 21,300 feet. That put them a half-mile away and 300 vertical feet above our 7Summits-Club camp. It doesn't sound like much of a hike, but after a big lunch in the stuffy mess tent, we did not have spare energy for walking. Nevertheless, we slowly set off, ever conscious of the need to acclimatize.

After a few minutes we reached an expedition where there was some camera work going on. Suddenly I recognized Bob Killip, an Australian climber I have known since the 1970s. I had heard he was on the mountain somewhere but hadn't seen him until now. Bob was a member of the Himalayan Experience (known as Himex) expedition, which led me to recognize the man at whom all the cameras were directed. It was New Zealander Russell Brice, the most experienced expedition operator on the north side of Everest.

At the same moment, Bob saw me, hurried over, and whispered, "G'day, mate." The first thing I asked was why we were whispering.

He smiled and said softly, "Russell's got six Sherpas just about to get to the summit. He's watching them through his telescope and talking to them on the radio. The three guys with the big cameras are making a doco for the Discovery Channel, so we have to keep it quiet."

I nodded, then whispered, "Maybe we should catch up later, when we're on our way down."

Bob gave me a thumbs-up and turned back to watch the action. We had arrived at the Himex Camp at a crucial moment in the 2006 season. The Sherpas had climbed to the summit ahead of all foreign climbers in order to fix a continuous line of rope from the bottom of the mountain to its very peak. On the world's tallest mountain, hundreds of lengths of rope totaling many thousands of feet were put in place every pre-monsoon season by the Himex team. Other expeditions contributed by supplying rope, Sherpa labor, or money to help cover the cost of both. The expeditions that did not contribute still used the ropes put in place by Russell's team, invariably leaving him out of pocket for the service he provided.

The morality of rope use was certainly not an issue I had had to deal with. On the big mountains I had climbed, the only fixed ropes I used were those placed by me and my climbing mates. We set up ropes only on difficult sections where it was impractical or dangerous to carry the heavy loads needed to establish and stock the high camps. Between the roped sections we used our ice axes to gain purchase on the snow or ice. When the shaft was shoved deep into a snow slope, it provided a solid handhold; when the pick of the ice axe was chopped into ice or hard snow, again it provided a secure grip. When we encountered rock, we climbed it as we would at sea level—pulling upon ledges and edges with our hands, then holding ourselves in balance while we stepped up with our feet. There was joy in the acrobatic maneuvers as well as in finding a route through the obstacles. We had a different attitude to fixed ropes—ascending a fixed rope with a big pack full of supplies was necessary drudgery, just another part of the hard work of climbing a big mountain. Pleasure could be experienced on fixed ropes, but it came from the scenery and the physical workout, not from the ascent. The climbing of fixed rope is a repetitive process of sliding a special ascender up the rope, with the one-way clamp securely attached by a short line to your waist. With this system, there is little need for handholds or ice axe placements.

OUR FOURSOME plodded slowly up the trail away from the Himalayan Experience Camp. Because the walk was not something we were compelled to do, I felt less energetic about the task. There was no campsite we had to reach, as our tents were below us. It was the perfect example of being motivated by a goal or, rather, of being unmotivated because we had set no real goal for the afternoon. We were here only to explore and acclimatize.

We sat at our high point and took in the view down the broad gully. With more than a hundred tents, Advance Base Camp looked like a jamboree where the organizers had got their map coordinates wrong. The scene was extraordinary, given the altitude. Also surprising was that Russell's Sherpas were summiting on April 30, very early in the season, thanks to impeccable weather up high. The heavy snowfalls at Base Camp were a low-level aberration during what had been a perfect few weeks.

Richard turned back, and Christopher followed shortly afterward, but Mike and I sat there taking in the view. I told Mike the story of how I first met Russell.

"It was February 1978," I began, "and Tim and I were training hard for our first Himalayan climb. We slogged up to Plateau Hut, an amazing place on the edge of a huge ice shelf halfway up Mount Cook. In the hut we met two guys who were on a quest to climb all of New Zealand's ten-thousand-foot peaks in one alpine summer. Turned out they were Russell and his Irish mate, Paddy Freaney. They had climbed Cook and Tasman, the highest peaks in the country, and were waiting for a chance to tackle Mount Dampier, a rocky bump on a ridge between Cook and Tasman. They had been holed up in the hut for seventeen days straight, waiting for a good day. They were tough characters and did not believe in niceties for the sake of it. After seventeen days, they didn't believe in niceties at all. Eventually they ran out of food and left. But they came back later in the season, climbed Dampier, and knocked off the remaining ten-thousanders as well. You have to remember that the lowest glaciers are at an altitude of around three thousand feet, so we're talking about significant climbs here."

We began to walk down the slope, and Mike related his first dealings with Russell.

"I first met him at Thyangboche," he began. "It must have been 1980 or '81, after he had just climbed Ama Dablam."

"Must've been 1980," I said. "It was the North Ridge. We climbed the same route in '81 but with a variant start."

"I was shooting a film with Ed Hillary at that time," continued Mike. "And ten years later Russell was on the 'ballooning over Everest' doco that I was shooting. He was looking after the logistics and the Sherpas. But this is the first time I've seen him since then."

Although I had not crossed paths with Russell again, I had heard of his exploits. His 1981 attempt to climb Mount Everest with only his old mate Paddy came to a close when the pair was turned back at 25,000 feet by strong winds. The fact that they had made such an audacious attempt with no Sherpa support was a good indication of their willingness to take on big challenges.

Fifteen Everest expeditions later, Russell was just as prepared to face those challenges. When I had interviewed Sue Fear for her book, I had learned more about him. Sue joined his 2003 Himalayan Experience Everest expedition not only because of his reputation as the best operator on the north side of the mountain but also because they had made a good impression on each other some years earlier on Cho Oyu. In all his years as an Everest expedition operator, Russell had faced only two deaths. The first had been Marco Siffredi, who in 2002 willingly attempted to snowboard down the North Face but did not survive. The second had occurred this season, only three weeks before we ran into him, when Tuk Bahadur Thapa Masar, who had been working on the fixed ropes with other members of the Himalayan Experience team, succumbed to complications from high-altitude pulmonary edema after being evacuated from the North Col to Base Camp. It was a freak death, as it is unusual for edema to kill at the relatively low height of the North Col. Russell was devastated.

. . .

ON THE WAY DOWN, Mike and I stopped by the Himalayan Experience Camp so I could keep my promise to Bob Killip, and so Mike could
catch up with his friend Jen Peedom, a camera operator for the Discovery
team. As we reached the mess tent, and before we could find Bob and
Jen, Russell stepped out.

"Hello, Russell," I said, before he wondered who was walking into
his camp. "It's Lincoln."

"Welcome," he said, and shook my extended hand.

"And this is Mike Dillon . . ."

"Yes," said Mike, in a rare interruption. "We met on the ballooning
expedition."

"Of course," said Russell. "Come and have some tea."

So Mike and I sat down in the kitchen tent and the cook handed
around cups of tea. I mentioned that I was a good friend of Sue's and that
we had talked in great detail about her Everest climb for the book we had
written together.

"And you're in the book," I said. "Have you read it?"

"No, actually. I live in Chamonix. I doubt it's available in France."

With Mike, he talked about the two ballooning expeditions they had
been part of, the second of which was the first balloon flight over Everest.
Then Russell and I talked a little about mutual climbing friends, which is
an easy topic of conversation when you don't know a fellow mountaineer
very well. Then I commented about the weather, which at Advance Base
Camp is far from a subject of idle banter but a vital part of everyone's
plans.

"Best weather I can remember," said Russell.

He told us that not only had his Sherpas gone to the summit, but they
had run the ropes 150 feet down the Southeast Ridge as a sort of joke
against the Sherpas coming up from the Nepalese side of Everest—a way
of saying "we got here first."

We thanked Russell for the tea, and then he told us where we could
find Bob and Jen—not that it was difficult in the compact campsite. The
four of us had barely reintroduced ourselves when we were joined by a
fifth figure, a short man rugged up against the cold.

"Hi, I'm Mark Inglis," he whispered. "My voice is shot, but I thought I'd introduce myself."

Suddenly I realized why he was short. Twenty-four years earlier, Mark's legs had been amputated below the knee. He and his partner, Phil Doole, had survived two weeks' sheltering from a storm and extreme winds in a crevasse on the top of the Middle Peak of Mount Cook, but by the time a helicopter was able to airlift them to safety, they had suffered frostbite so severe that they both became double-amputees.

I thrust out my hand. "Hi, Mark, I'm Lincoln. Remember, I interviewed you about this climb of yours? Before I knew I'd be coming as well."

"Sure, mate," he croaked. "And you wanted to get your hands on some PeakFuel, too."

"Yeah, but I ran out of time."

He shrugged understandingly, saying nothing, to give his voice a break.

"So your voice will be okay?"

"Hope so."

"Sorry. I've got to stop asking you questions."

He smiled, and to show I was holding back my questions, I said nothing at all. Bob and Jen started talking to Mike. My interview with Mark for *Outdoor* magazine had been about his goal to become the first double-amputee to climb Mount Everest, having tested his prosthetic legs by climbing Cho Oyu with Russell.

I had phoned Mark again when I knew I was going to Everest because I wanted to get my hands on the energy gels that he manufactured. For twenty years Mark had been a winemaker, with his focus on the flavors. It was his skill with flavors that had given his PeakFuel energy gels a good reputation. Gels had been developed as instant nutrition for cyclists, marathon runners, and adventurer racers, but they were also ideal for extreme altitudes where mountaineers frequently did not have the energy to dig into their packs for food but could easily suck the gel out of a foil sachet. The difference with Mark's line of gels was that they tasted good.

Mark knew that he shouldn't talk, but when he found that withholding his voice was too hard a chore, he excused himself and returned to his tent. The four of us shared an Australian perspective on what was happening in this extraordinary place, until the temperature dropped sufficiently to send Mike and me back to our camp.

The next morning I was sitting outside my tent, packing and getting ready to head up to the North Col for the first time, when I became aware of somebody nearby.

"Hey, dude," said a voice. "Is that you, Lincoln?"

I looked up to see the smiling face of Ken Sauls, his beard a bit more rugged than the last time we'd met.

"Sure is," I said. "What the hell are you doing here?" I stood up and gave him a hug, squeezing him as hard as I could to make him think I was as strong as he was.

We'd first met in Bangkok in 1999, me coming from Sydney, Ken coming from Los Angeles, both of us en route to Kathmandu to join the Australian-American Makalu Expedition. He had introduced himself as the cameraman, which meant that we shared the same role—only he looked like a hardcore rock climber with muscles on his muscles. Turned out that's what he was.

"Long way from Silverton, Colorado," I said.

"Yeah."

"Small world, eh?"

"Nah," said Ken. "Just running out of places to hide. You know how it is . . . IRS . . . Jealous husbands with big fists . . ."

"Hear you climbed Everest a few years back with Sue Fear?"

"Yeah, that was filming with Russ. This year I'm working for Discovery, but still with Russ. That's how I heard you were here."

"You only just got me. We're about to head up to the North Col for the first time."

"Yeah, we'll have to catch up at BC. Sink a few beers."

He slapped me on the back and sauntered back up the hill. It was great to see him. We'd clicked on Makalu, but afterward the trickle of e-mails had slowly dried up, both of us too laid back to keep the cycle going.

BY MIDDAY the B-Team was trudging across the uppermost reaches of the East Rongbuk Glacier, a huge snow bowl contained on three sides by the Northeast Ridge of Changtse and the North and Northeast ridges of Everest. The low point in Everest's North Ridge was the North Col, and that was our destination. There was little breeze, and the sun reflecting from the mountain walls had us baking in the bowl. There was a well-trodden path across the snow, with a line of dots up the snow face below the North Col, marking the line of fixed rope, and with each dot a climber.

Our small Australian party was now four teams of two, as each of us was traveling with a Sherpa. I had directed Lakcha to Mike because I judged him to be the most useful and experienced person when it came to Mike's filmmaking needs. Pasang and Dawa were with Richard and Christopher. I had suggested that Dorje accompany me because he was young and keen, and I felt that, for our short time together, I could be his mentor. The ratio of four Sherpas to four Westerners was the safest option for us, given the special factors of Christopher's young age and our filming of his climb.

We flopped into the snow at the base of the fixed ropes and had a quick drink and a snack before starting up the ropes. The slope was at an angle of only forty degrees and the snow was a good consistency for the sharp crampon points clipped to our boots, so the process of climbing was straightforward. The difficulty came from the altitude. I knew that on any expedition, the first climb up to 23,000 feet is very hard work. I also knew that it would get easier with every subsequent ascent.

There were dozens of climbers on the ropes and a dozen behind us. No doubt there were many more who had already reached the col. I told myself not to be bothered by the crowds and to enjoy the considerable pleasure of being on the mountain again. After all, there is only one Everest.

A climber overtook us, carrying a multicolored Berghaus pack. I noticed it because I had taken one exactly like it to Carstensz Pyramid in 1993. It had given me good service over the years, and I still used it for hiking in Australia. Our pace on the fixed rope was dictated by the speed of those above us, which was not fast. The man with the Berghaus pack was in more of a hurry. Rather than being delayed by the fixed rope full of climbers, he climbed ten feet to the left of the rope. It was not a hugely dangerous thing to be doing, as the snow was good and the slope not too steep. His approach could be compared to cycling in traffic, which is safe enough if you have the right skills and know what you are doing. I became a little frustrated when the climbing train on the rope above slowed down. I looked ahead to see if there was an obvious reason for the go-slow, and I saw Mr. Berghaus climbing confidently and drawing farther away. It was only later, when it had been mentioned in the media, that I realized that this thirteen-year-old Berghaus pack had belonged to David Sharp.

Clouds came in during the afternoon and we climbed up into them. I had dressed for a nonstop push through to the col, planning to have only short stops for filming. However, a serious "rope-block" developed above us, forcing us to stand still minutes at a time and then only moving up a few feet before waiting again. With only thermals and a light fleece jacket underneath my Gore-Tex wind-suit, and with no concerted exercise to generate heat, I became uncomfortably cold. A steep section near the lip of the North Col was slowing everyone down, some climbers much more than others. I unclipped from the rope to step past a few slow-moving people, then clipped back on before tackling the steeper part. I warmed up during the climb and was relieved to reach the first tents. My relief that the up was over evaporated when I realized that the main North Col camp was beyond a huge crevasse spanned by three aluminum ladders strapped together, which rose upward at an angle of forty-five degrees. I climbed the ladders, filming my feet stepping from rung to rung, which meant I had only one hand to keep my balance on the rope. Luckily, Christopher and I wore the same La Sportiva boots, so the feet that I had filmed could be passed off as Christopher's when Mike got the film to editing stage. At the same time, Mike filmed Christopher from below on the ladder. It had started to snow, and I was getting colder by the minute, so I was pleased to put the camera away.

Soon enough we were at the main camp. I had expected a crowded campsite, but there were more tents than I thought possible pitched in a long hollow beneath a sheltering ice cliff. We were a hundred yards away from the lowest part of the col, which was not protected from the wind by the ice cliff.

The 7Summits-Club mess tent contributed to the crowding. It was much smaller than those at Base Camp and Advance Base Camp but still the biggest tent at the North Col. I certainly found it welcoming, with the stoves chugging away producing heat and hot tea poured into my mug by Dawa the cook. Already in residence were Harry, Thomas, and their Sherpas, Pemba and Passang. When I heard Richard and Christopher arrive, I grabbed the camera and recorded their snow-covered entry into the tent.

There was plenty of good food for dinner that night, but none of us ate very much—the altitude was now 23,182 feet. Richard and Christopher headed for their sleeping bags early, as did Thomas, but Harry and I were in no hurry to retire to our tents. I expected a long cold night, with sleep interrupted by waking and gasping for more air to breathe, and that proved to be the outcome.

The difficulty of high-altitude sleeping is the inevitable fall in breath rate as you doze off to sleep. At normal altitudes your body needs less oxygen while you are sleeping, and sleep triggers a slower rate of breathing. The problem at high altitude is that the slow rate is still triggered when you finally manage to sleep, but soon the emergency "not-enough-oxygen" light turns on in your brain, and you wake up gasping for breath. I made my first night at the North Col endurable by reading a book for an hour or two in the middle of the night. During that time I did not let my breathing operate in auto mode. I breathed deeply but not forcefully, making sure my lungs were full with every breath. This got more oxygen into my system and allowed me to sleep more deeply for the rest of the night.

Clear skies greeted us the next morning. The sun shone brightly on the North Ridge of Everest, but the shadow of the ice cliff above us kept our camp bitterly cold. Irregular gusts blew whirlwinds of yesterday's fresh snow around the camp. I figured we were being buffeted by the edges of turbulence caused by a strong wind blowing over the lowest and most exposed part of the North Col.

I clambered onto the cornice above the tents so I could peer down over the névé of the East Rongbuk Glacier. From three o'clock the previous afternoon we had continually climbed up through clouds. Now, under clear skies, the view from the cornice was a revelation. Suddenly I remembered how high it is at 23,000 feet and how spectacular the views are from this elevation.

Advance Base Camp no longer looked like the world's highest village. The colorful collection of tents had been swallowed by the moraine trough below Changtse's Northeast Ridge. Looming above me was Changste's East Face, edged by its South Ridge. Its sheer size and mass made it impossible for me to forget that we had not reached even the halfway height of the lowest of Everest's subpeaks.

To the north, Everest's main summit was tucked behind the farthest point of its long Northeast Ridge. The snowy pyramid, which hid the true peak, looked so impossibly far away that I could not begin to conceive what had to be endured to reach the final summit. Suddenly, whirling snow blasted the camp and distracted me—a perversely welcome disruption. Spindrift stung my face and my exposed hands, and the camera I held was too cold for the snowflakes to melt upon its black surface. Cold, tired, and unacclimatized—now was not the time to think about what kind of miracle would be needed for me to climb the inconceivable.

Ten

SKY BURIAL

IN MID-MAY THE CLIMATE on Everest changed. The first month of the 2006 season had delivered weather that was better than it had been for many years. The wind blew as often as usual but rarely as strongly as in other pre-monsoon climbing periods. The afternoon storms were both less regular and less ferocious. In that sense, there were more good days than bad. But the weather had no influence on the ominous change in circumstances. It was the human interface with the mountain that altered in the middle of May. The change of climate was one of atmosphere, and the new atmosphere was death. Even on a good day on Everest there are many ways for people to die.

At the beginning of the 2006 Everest season, there had been four fatalities. The first to die had been Himalayan Experience's Tuk Bahadur in April. Two weeks later, on the opposite side of the mountain, ten Sherpas from several different expeditions were carrying supplies up the Khumbu Icefall. The climb of the standard ascent route on the Nepalese side of Everest begins with the notoriously unstable icefall. Unfortunately, there is no other way to gain access to the high valley of the Western Cwm. As the Sherpas followed the ropes upward, a huge ice tower (or serac) toppled onto a neighboring one, shattering both. Large chunks of ice, some of them the size of cars, tumbled onto the route followed by the Sherpas. There was no time to run—and nowhere to go. Six of the Sherpas were hit by the debris. Three were injured, but Dawa Temba, Lhakpa

Tsheri, and Ang Phinjo were buried beneath the ice. Unlike a snow avalanche, where buried climbers can sometimes be dug out, the jumble of
broken glacier ice was like being buried under truckloads of boulders. It
was fifty-year-old Ang Phinjo's forty-ninth expedition to an 8,000-meter
peak, as any mountain over 26,250 feet is known.

The deaths were a sobering start to the season and, for me, a reminder
of why I was climbing the north side of the mountain. There was nothing
as inherently dangerous on the Northeast Ridge route, but the difficulties
concentrated on the long and exposed summit ridge made the final climb
more challenging.

APART FROM THE SHADOW of those deaths, there was nothing but
good news until the middle of May. The fine weather was holding, and
long-range forecasts suggested it would continue to do so. Although the
Himalayan Experience Sherpas finished setting the fixed ropes on April
30, the first Western climbers did not reach the world's highest point
until May 11.

On May 14, ten members of the Indo-Tibetan Border Police Expedition reached the summit with four Sherpas. Rumors travel fast at Advance
Base Camp, where many different expeditions are clustered close together
in limited space. We heard that one of the successful Indian climbers had
descended to the Second Step, and then tore the oxygen mask from his
face before jumping off the cliff. It was such a crazy story that we dismissed it as a wild rumor, but two days later—after a second team from
the Indian Army Expedition summited and the organizers put out a press
release—the basic fact was announced that a Constable Srikrishna had
died during the descent from the summit.

Any further speculation about Srikrishna's demise was suddenly
replaced by talk of a climber who had spent a night out on the Northeast
Ridge. It seemed that no one knew who he was or which expedition he
was with, but his passage up the mountain—and partway down—was
noted by others high on the ridge at the time. Then the dreadful news
surfaced that climbers from two expeditions had passed by the terminally weakened climber during the night. In total darkness it is difficult
to judge the state of an unmoving body. Most of those climbers had

thought he was either dead or resting—the two usual states of anyone slumped beside the fixed rope above 27,800 feet. A few of the climbers who passed him that night thought he was alive but assessed him as being impossibly close to death.

However, by the time the two expeditions, Himalayan Experience and the Turkish Everest Expedition, were wearily plodding down the ridge in groups of two or three after their summit attempts, it was broad daylight. It was then that more climbers from both expeditions realized that the man was alive, thirty-six hours after he had set out for the summit.

At Advance Base Camp, Russell Brice had taken it upon himself to identify the unknown man, and one possibility seemed more likely than any other. The head Sherpa of the Himalayan Experience team, Phurba Tashi, was able to identify David Sharp from his passport photo, which they found in the man's luggage.

This basic information about the tragedy was instantly broadcast on websites. It was exactly the kind of dramatic, controversial story that the mainstream media picks up in a flash. Dispatches full of assumptions and misinformation, padded with a few facts, were broadcast around the world.

When I heard what was going on, I did not know what to think. I certainly did not jump to any conclusions. Base Camp seemed close to the dreadful events that had unfolded, but in fact I knew too few of the details to invest emotional energy in an opinion. It was not that I did not care about David Sharp, just that I did not yet know the truth of his circumstances. In the past, newspapers in Australia had written that I was missing, assumed dead, when the fact was that our small expedition had no radio communications on the mountain, only a mail-runner at Base Camp. After my first Himalayan climb, a journalist had written that my minor frostbite was so bad that I would never walk again, but I was to have more than thirty years of climbing and trekking ahead of me. I was keen to hear the facts about David Sharp, but I would not be seduced by the rumors or the outraged opinions of people who knew less than I did.

The topic was not foremost in our minds when Mike and I hiked across the glacial flats to the Himalayan Experience Base Camp. We needed the exercise, and I wanted to congratulate both Ken Sauls and Bob Killip on having reached the summit.

When we arrived at the Himex Camp, we were pointed to their large rectangular mess tent, set up to cope with the wind. As soon as Bob saw us, he leaped to his feet to share his triumph but grimaced as he put weight on his frostbitten toes.

"Congratulations, Bob!" I said, before I thought to ask about his injuries. "Well done!"

"Thanks, mate. It was hard, man. So cold."

"I'll bet. And you remember Mike from ABC?"

"Sure. Welcome." Then he said to us both, "I'm the oldest Australian to summit. Fifty-three. Should get a photo of me and young Christopher. Youngest and oldest Australians."

For the moment at least, Bob's exuberance at reaching the summit overshadowed the issue of his frostbite.

"That would be a great outcome for the season," I said, "Christopher topping out as well."

"It would be," agreed Mike. "Christopher's watching a DVD at the moment."

We sat and listened to Bob's account of his climb. He had arrived at Base Camp less than an hour earlier, so his story was fresh, and it began with the fact that he and his rope-mate, Mark Inglis, who also summited, had been unlucky enough to pick the coldest night of the season for their summit push.

"A lot of guys got frostbite up there. Much worse than this." He gestured at his toe. "Much worse."

His words reminded me of the latest tragedy.

"What's the story with David Sharp?"

Bob paused and grimaced. "He was history from the first time we saw him. It just felt like I was walking past a dead body—that's how far gone he was."

It was a very unfortunate affair, and the media kept feeding on it, but eventually the full story of David Sharp would come out. I could imagine he would have wanted the truth to be known.

WE DID NOT SEE Bob Killip again, as he would be preparing to leave for Kathmandu while the four of us spent the next day readying ourselves for our own summit push. Late in the day news came through that one of the Norwegians had died skiing the Great Couloir. There was no more information until the morning, when we learned that it was Tomas Olsson. The name meant nothing to me. I knew only of Fredrik Schenholm, the photographer whose details I had jotted down when we had crossed paths. Tomas had been attempting to rappel into the very top of the couloir, where the snow was ski-able and the real descent could begin for both him and his partner, Tormod Granheim. The anchor he'd used for his rope had held long enough for him to rappel one hundred feet—then it gave way and he fell the last forty feet to the top of the couloir and beyond. I remembered the spot well—it was my high point in 1984—and I knew it was too steep for him to be able to stop.

Tomas fell over 6,000 feet to his death. In a state of shock, Tormod had to climb down the rock-face to the top of the couloir. He must be a very skillful mountaineer, I thought, to have been able to complete the short descent without a rope. From that point, the obvious escape route was to do what he had come to do—ski the wide gully of the couloir. He managed it safely, but on that day there would have been no satisfaction in becoming the first person to achieve the feat. High-altitude extreme skiing is exceptionally dangerous—both men would have known the risks, but that did not make Tomas's accident any more palatable.

Richard, Christopher, and Mike set off after breakfast the next day, but I was in no particular hurry. Richard was not in good shape, so he would be traveling slowly with Christopher. Base Camp was deserted because the A-Team had moved up to Intermediate Camp the day before. When I was finally ready to go, I was treated to the arrival of the garbage truck. The piles of bagged-up rubbish were in a dry watercourse less than thirty yards from my tent, so I witnessed the full show. The truck pulled up, a team of cheerful Tibetans leaped off the load, and then heaved the bags of rubbish up into the truck in a competitive manner, as if there was a prize for speed and accuracy. I snapped a few photos of the scene. This was the first expedition I had been on where there was a garbage-removal service. On other climbs we had carried rubbish down to below the snowline and burned our combustibles there because the Sherpas did not want to offend the mountain gods with unclean smoke.

Noncombustibles we buried. I suspected that the Tibetans were excited about the work because it was one of the rare ways to earn money in this part of the world. Expeditions arrived with their own staff, not leaving much room for local employment. When the truck was loaded, the Tibetans hauled themselves up onto the top of the rubbish and disappeared in a cloud of dust.

It was time for me to disappear as well. Casting my eyes around the empty camp, I thought briefly about the members of the A-Team, who would be arriving at Advance Base Camp today. The chances were that we would not see them until they returned from the summit, with or without success. Several climbers had already gone home without setting foot on the mountain. Bill Tyler had hurt his back and headed home with his wife, Barbie. Vince Bousselaire, who the previous year had attempted Everest from the Nepalese side, was now forced to retreat from Tibet as well. It was altitude problems that sent him packing from ABC—his goal of placing a Bible on each of the Seven Summits put on hold. Torbjørn Orkelbog learned that his wife was pregnant and took the first Jeep out of Base Camp, choosing new life over possible death.

Three hours later I was well into the walk. I plodded slowly up a steep part of the trail where the ice was thinly covered by rocks. A figure was coming toward me, but I thought nothing of it. He approached quickly, and I expected he would slow down so that we could pass each other easily. Instead, he maintained his speed and overtook me on the uphill side, leaving me no room to step off the track. As he brushed past me, the lilt of his body caused a ski to swing and whack me on the shoulder. The unexpected blow almost knocked me off balance.

"Hey!" I shouted after him. "Watch what you're doing!" He turned and looked at me as I rubbed my shoulder, as if he did not understand.

"You hit me with your ski and almost bumped me off the path."

"I am sorry," he said, his hand raised in a conciliatory gesture. "I was not aware."

"It's okay," I said, raising my hand as well.

He nodded and continued down the path.

A few steps up the path, I realized that the man must have been Tormod Granheim, the surviving skier, still stunned by the death of his friend. I looked back, but he was already gone.

. . .

AFTER I RECOVERED from my thoughtless confrontation, I increased my speed until I caught up with Mike and the others not far from Intermediate Camp. When we had arrived here during our first hike to Advance Base Camp three weeks ago, snow had covered the rocks and ice of the glacier. Now the ground was bare rocks and patches of hard ice, and the intensity of the high-altitude sun hitting soggy yak dung released an aroma that made the place smell like a stable. By late afternoon the temperature had dropped dramatically, and with the warmth went the stench of the yak dung.

The next day was Thursday, May 18, and we awoke to find not a cloud in the sky. Mike, Christopher, and I felt strong, but Richard was finding it tough. If worst came to worst, he would monitor Christopher's climb from the North Col. The three of them began to plod up the slope to the main trail above. My pack was full, ready to go, but rather than following my friends, I snapped some photos around camp to compare with those of three weeks ago when there had been much more snow.

As I put my camera gear away, Tendi stepped out of the kitchen tent and called out to me.

"The Brazilian man—he is dead. They tell me on the radio."

"*Hajur?*" I said. The word for "yes" meant "please repeat."

Tendi stood there saying nothing, perhaps so I could absorb what he had just said. I scrambled the few yards up to him, and he told me again. A Brazilian climber had died the previous afternoon. He had reached the summit without oxygen but could not come down. He had chosen to climb completely unassisted. In the end he called for help, and a Sherpa had been able to bring him down to the High Camp at 27,000 feet. It was there that he died.

I was stunned by the announcement, almost directly after the news of Tomas Olsson. Vitor had told me that he would climb without oxygen and that his friend Rodrigo would not. It had to be Vitor Negrete, Harry's summit-mate of 2005.

I thanked Tendi and Dawa for looking after me, and for the news, sad as it was. Then I shouldered my load and trudged up the short slope to the easy trail that led along the crest of the glacier. I walked slowly because I wanted to be alone with my thoughts.

By midafternoon I had caught up with Richard, Christopher, and Mike, just as a team was hurrying down the mountain. Toward the end of the line was a Sherpa carrying someone on his back, all wrapped up, hands and feet buried under bandages, someone not yet dead but as unresponsive as a sack of potatoes.

"Japanese," muttered Richard, as we let the team past. "I asked the Sherpa. That poor guy spent the night out at twenty-eight thousand feet. Lucky to be alive."

What was it that this mountain did to people? I thought. Then I realized that was the wrong question. Blame could not be apportioned to the mountain. The question was: Why did we expose ourselves to it?

It was a very sobering sight. I wondered how they had rescued him from such an inaccessible place. We were not far from Advance Base Camp—there would have to be someone there who would know. Eventually, I discovered from Billi Bierling that the man being carried was not Japanese but a Sherpa member of a Japanese expedition. His name was Ang Temba, the *sirdar* of the Tochigi Mount Everest Expedition. The team of four Japanese and three Sherpas had reached the summit around midday on May 17. They'd celebrated with hugs and photographs and then set off down the mountain. Ang Temba had been last to leave the summit and had felt very weary as he descended. He'd rappeled the Second Step and continued down, still behind the rest of his team. His weariness overwhelmed him, and he'd sat in the snow to rest. When he awoke, many hours had passed, night had fallen, and he had run out of oxygen. He had realized he would have to stay put until daylight.

At dawn, three Tibetans climbing up the mountain had told Ang Temba they would help him on their return from the summit. He'd known he could not wait that long and had begun to stagger downward.

Ang Temba had been intercepted by Phil Crampton, of the Summit-Climb Expedition, who'd already had his hands full. Very early that morning he had aborted his ascent at the Second Step so that he could bring down teammate Juan Pablo, who had been stricken with cerebral edema—even staying put with that serious form of high-altitude sickness would have been fatal. Survival had depended on descent.

Meanwhile, veteran guide Dan Mazur had continued upward with the remaining SummitClimb climbers, two of whom had reached the summit. Expedition *sirdar* Jangbu Sherpa was helping Phil with Juan Pablo when they encountered Ang Temba tangled in the ropes. They'd checked on Temba's condition and found him lacking coordination—also a symptom of cerebral edema. But he had seemed strong enough and sufficiently connected to reality to be able to continue down. Jangbu had looked after him while Phil headed down with his charge. Both the sick men survived, but when Temba was safely down the mountain, he had fallen apart. His legs had become paralyzed, which was the state he was in when we encountered him on the trail. He had also lost his memory, a problem which rectified itself over the coming weeks.

As the climbers from the 7Summits-Club A-Team headed up the mountain, they'd also passed Ang Temba as he was being helped down. When the A-Team arrived at Camp Two at 25,000 feet, guide Sergey Kofanov and the Sherpas frantically pitched spare tents to replace several that had been destroyed by the strongest winds yet experienced this season. The mountain was revealing its potential. Luckily, the winds had since died down, but not everyone was able to cope with the altitude and the dry cold air.

Despite his high hopes, Petter Kragset's breath-warmer had proved ineffective against his uncontrollable coughing. For the second time in two years Petter was forced to descend from Everest, the final peak of his Seven Summits quest uncompleted. Johnny Brevik chose to retreat with his friend, while David Lien decided that he was content with reaching Camp Two. The effort had been enormous and would not lessen as he climbed higher. Nor could he expect any mercy from the elements or the decreasing amount of oxygen in the air. He decided to quit while he was ahead. Frode Høgset waited for his friends at the North Col, which had always been the cutoff point for his own personal exploration of Everest.

AT ADVANCE BASE CAMP on the morning of May 21, I was up early to monitor the progress of our A-Team in their final hours to the summit. The sun shone on the summit, but the entire Advance Base Camp area was in shade, keeping it bitterly cold. I had expected Alex to be up early, like me, reporting on progress with his eyeball frozen to his big telescope. Instead, he was smart enough to stay in his sleeping bag, attempting contact via radio. I shrugged off my impatience and returned to my tent.

By breakfast time an hour later, much had changed. Not only had the sun reached the camp and warmed the air and the insides of our tents, but also, through the telescope, figures could be seen on the final snow pyramid. We took turns watching them, dots moving almost imperceptibly, a mile and a half above us in the sky. It was an extraordinary sight. The climbers were hidden for the final half-hour to the summit, with Alex keeping track only by radio.

Sixteen members of our team summited that morning. Guides Igor Svergun and Sergey Kofanov helped clients Arkadiy Ryzhenko, Henrik Olsen, Kirk Wheatley, Noel Hanna, Lorenzo Gariano, and Slate Stern to achieve their dreams. The Sherpas who orchestrated this extraordinary success—Furba Kushang, Passang Gyalgen, Mingma, Renjin, Pasang, Jangbu, and Nima—were led by Mingma Gelu.

Although Igor Plyushkin, Ilya Rozhkov, and Ronnie Muhl climbed to the Second Step at 28,400 feet, all three had to turn back short of the summit. Remaining at Advance Base Camp and hoping to reach the top were Harry, Thomas, Pemba, Passang, Christopher, Richard, Mike, and me, along with our other Sherpas, Lakcha, Dorje, Dawa Tenzing, and Pasang.

During the past six days we had heard of four deaths on Everest and two narrow escapes. But with so many of the 7Summits-Club team summiting on this glorious morning, perhaps the tide of death had turned away from the mountain. I certainly hoped so because on this beautiful day it was our turn to head for the North Col to begin our summit push. If everything went according to plan, we would reach the highest point on the planet on May 24—Dylan's eighteenth birthday. In two hemispheres there would be cause for celebration, but I would not have the breath to blow out any candles.

Eleven

RUSSIAN ROULETTE

B Y LATE AFTERNOON on May 21, my optimism had vanished. Alex and Doctor Andrey had spent most of the afternoon on the radio, attempting to sort out some problems with Igor Plyushkin, who was at 25,500 feet in a tent just above Camp Three. Everything was being said in Russian, so I had no idea of the nature of the discussion. I was waiting to speak with Alex because I wanted to confirm arrangements for my summit push the next day.

The situation with our Australian team had changed dramatically that morning. After breakfast the four of us had set off for the North Col with our four Sherpas. Richard was feeling weak so he went ahead early with a light pack. That left Mike, Christopher, and me, and the four Sherpas, loosely walking together. Uncharacteristically, Christopher was plodding along slowly at the back with the Sherpas, so half an hour out of Advance Base Camp, Mike and I stopped and waited for the others. When Christopher arrived, he crumpled onto a rock and gasped that he could not breathe. I leaped to my feet, stretched out Christopher's legs, and got him to sit back against me. This freed up his chest and diaphragm so that when I instructed him to take deep breaths he found that he could do it. Once he was breathing properly, I ran ahead to fetch Richard, over-taking Harry, Pemba, Thomas, and Passang on the way. Although I was acclimatized to being above 21,000 feet, running was very hard work. Another half an hour later all of us were back at Advance Base Camp.

Andrey took over, stabilizing Chris with an hour of breathing oxygen and meanwhile determining that he had suffered a "collapse," a severe drop in blood pressure.

By chance, Italian mountaineering legend Simone Moro had just appeared on the scene, after climbing up the Nepalese side of the mountain and down the Tibetan side. It was his third ascent of Everest. Simone knew Alex and had dropped by for a chat. Simone had a keen interest in high-altitude physiology and shared his thoughts with Andrey, because he had suffered from the same set of symptoms, but only once, with nothing like it ever troubling him again. However, I suspected that the expedition would be over for Christopher.

And so it was that I sat with Luda on the rocks outside the communications tent, waiting for Alex to be free. At last Alex joined his wife and me, but before I could start talking about logistics, another woman appeared from inside the tent. She was weather-beaten, with sunbleached hair, and wore a huge red down jacket. Immediately, she began to talk—with a strong French accent—about her husband.

"They are saying that he is dead, but the Sherpa said he was alive when he left him. So maybe he is alive."

Obviously this was a conversation being continued.

"From yesterday he is dead," said Alex. "Maybe before. From the radio we have heard this. It must be he is dead now." Alex shrugged, his gesture emphasizing what he considered to be the obvious. The Russians tended to have a black-or-white view of things, with no interest in exploring shades of gray.

"If that is so, I must have Sherpas bring him down."

"I meet him," said Alex. "He is big man, maybe two hundred twenty pounds. Not possible to bring from there. I think twenty-eight thousand five hundred feet."

The radio crackled inside the tent, so Alex disappeared to take the call.

The woman turned to me and began to talk. Her name was Caroline. She had climbed up to the High Camp with her husband, Jacques-Hugues Letrange, and his friends and climbing partners, Roland De Bare de Comogne and Freddy Journet. At the High Camp, Caroline's Sherpa had said she must go down, that to go on would be too dangerous. She had stayed until the Sherpa told her she was too weak to remain at 27,000 feet.

"And so I come down, but I hear at the North Col he is dead."

I could understand the confusion of her conversation with Alex. I explained that at high altitude time and memory can be clouded by lack of oxygen—as she must know, having been there herself. I reminded her that many of the Sherpas do not have good English and that they often confused past and present tenses.

Caroline accepted each of my points but continued to find pockets of hope in the events that had unfolded since Jacques-Hugues had been regarded as dead on the evening of May 17. She told Luda and me that her husband had fallen against a rock and had bruised his side. Perhaps the injury slowed him down, she said. Perhaps it was an internal injury and that he was not suffering from cerebral edema, which was what the Sherpa who had climbed up to help him had initially surmized.

I understood why she was putting forward an alternative to cerebral edema—the only outcome of prolonged exposure to it at extreme altitude is death. I had witnessed the condition from a rescuer's perspective. During an expedition to Mount Trisul in the Indian Himalaya, a member of the team we were guiding was incapacitated by cerebral edema. John Coulton had become separated from the team in a snowstorm at the relatively low altitude of 19,000 feet. He was adequately equipped to survive a night out, but when we found him the next morning and brought him back to camp, we discovered he had developed cerebral, and possibly pulmonary, edema.

The only cure for high-altitude-induced edema is rapid descent, so while Tim Macartney-Snape and Geof Bartram led the rest of the team down the mountain, Michael Groom and I attempted to bring John down as fast as we could. I had asked Michael to help me because, after three days trapped in a storm, he was the strongest man left standing. John quickly became less coherent and insisted on sitting in the snow. I attempted to carry him, but the extra weight forced me to sink knee-deep into the snow, which made it impossible for me to move. Instead, Michael and I put John's arms around our shoulders and staggered for ten or fifteen yards until he refused to support any of his weight. We had to let him sit in the snow again, muttering incoherently, until we were able to get him to stand upright again. Using this stop-start process, we reached a steeper slope, which made it easier for us to lose height more quickly. John was able to walk with less support but plenty of rests, and he had recovered almost completely by the time we reached our base camp. Had we not managed to bring him down that day, he might well have died.

I refrained from saying to Caroline that an internal injury was not good news for her husband, whose location alone put his life on the wrong side of borderline. I was shocked when she mentioned that he had been left on the mountain four days earlier. To my mind, he was obviously dead and she must find a way to accept this. She was grave but not tearful, and I sensed her constant talking was a way for her to deal with the emptiness she could not yet fathom.

The sun had long since left us, and with it went its warmth. Now I was shivering, but I tried to hide it because Caroline needed to be heard. I learned that Jacques-Hugues Letrange had been collecting samples of snow and ice from different places on the mountain for research into the history of Everest's climate. From the data, French scientists hoped to learn more about global warming. I was unclear about how much Jacques-Hugues's two friends, Roland and Freddy, would have been able to do for him at those impossible heights. They had conveyed to Caroline much about his situation but not enough to provide any sense of closure. Any questions on the subject, I was sure, would only open her wound even further.

She said, "I have not found anybody who has seen that he is dead."

"It is four days now."

"But I must talk with someone who has seen him dead." She held her breath. "Otherwise I cannot be sure. If you meet any Sherpa or climber who can tell me they have seen him dead, please find me and tell me."

"I will," I said softly. It was the only tone I could trust my voice to manage. "I will do that for you."

Then she described the location of her camp.

BECAUSE OF THE COLD, I went straight to my tent. The small vestibule was filled with my pack, still bulging and ready for my summit bid. In it was the Australian flag handmade by Margaret Werner and taken to the summits of K2, Chongtar, and Manaslu. I pulled on my down jacket and lay on my sleeping bag, thinking about the events of the day. The possibilities of the next few days were also beginning to tie a knot in my stomach. There was no denying the seriousness of this game we had chosen to play.

A hot drink was sure to warm me, so I walked across the loose rocks to the mess tent. To my surprise, A-Team climber David Lien was there. It was good to see him, but I was not ready to talk to anyone. However, I made the effort to ask about his climb because, although he had turned back at Camp Two, it had been an amazing experience for him. Even now, twenty-two years since I had been to that height on the North Face, I could still conjure up the magnificent view. It was a personal altitude record for him, and as I listened to his tired enthusiasm, I began to loosen up and remember why I had come here. I had a lot of respect for people who trusted their intuition and turned back before being forced to by dire circumstances. Not enough people on Everest listen to that inner voice.

I had not expected to see David, but I was astonished when a commotion outside the mess tent was followed by Slate stepping through the door.

"How on earth did you get here?" I asked, standing up in surprise.

He must have descended from the summit to Advance Base Camp in one grueling, unbroken epic. Consequently, he looked exactly as I expected—he had been "processed" by the mountain. He had lost weight (not that he had any to spare to begin with), his sunburned face had been freeze-dried by the wind and the cold, his hair set a new record for bad-hair days, but most telling was the look in his eyes. It was a sight I had seen before in the faces of my companions when we had managed to descend alive from some unspeakable ordeal. Words said nothing; there was no spare breath to speak with, the whole experience conveyed only in the eyes.

"I don't know," he said. "Doesn't matter. Good to see you, man."

"Good to see you, too."

He had collapsed onto a chair. I went to grab his hand, but before I could shake it, he had to peel off his gloves.

This was not a simple process because he had come to regard them as a second skin, so I slapped him on the shoulder instead.

"Congratulations! I watched you on the summit triangle through a telescope. At least, I think it was you. Everyone looks the same when they're the size of an ant."

He managed a smile.

Chandra, one of the cooks, came into the tent with a hot lemon drink for Slate, who thanked him. Chandra nodded and congratulated him as well.

"It's such a long way," said Slate. "I was the only one to make it to the North Col camp. The weather got bad up high for the others, so they stayed above me at Camp Two."

"I can't believe you've come all the way from the summit to here in one day. And that's after having started climbing at Camp Three."

"Yeah, I might have overdone it. But Alex and Andrey insisted I come all the way down."

"You'll be all right. A good week's sleep and you'll be just like new."

He attempted a laugh, knowing it would take much more than that. Then his laugh became a cough. Now that he was warming up, he undid some zippers and said that he would take his boots off—cumbersome, heavily insulated mountain boots—but he neglected to do so. We sat there drinking tea and eating biscuits while he talked about the hardship and the sheer size of the mountain.

There was a mixture of moods in the mess tent that evening. David and Slate felt weary but relieved, so everything was fine by them. The numbing sadness I had felt after talking with Caroline had lessened with Slate's return, but I was anxious about my own path because so little separated the experiences of the distraught French woman and my exhausted American friend. The Russians were invariably in good spirits at dinnertime but not today. Whatever the issue was with Igor, it had not yet been resolved.

When we had eaten, I told Christopher that despite his apparent recovery, I felt it would be very dangerous for him to go high on the mountain. My advice was for him to abandon the climb for this season. He said nothing because he was holding back his tears. Not long after that conversation, he left the tent. I had to admire Christopher for staying committed to the climb, despite all the hardships, despite being ten or twenty years younger than all his teammates, despite being on the other side of the world from the haven of his family. The illness of his father and the spate of deaths must also have been playing on his mind.

I felt more tired than I should have, given that I had been away from camp for only two hours during the day. It was the emotional load that was weighing me down, and I was happy to wriggle into my sleeping bag.

I WAS UP EARLY on the morning of May 22, and so was Richard, who wanted to talk with me. I suspected that he was going to ask me not to go up the mountain because it might disappoint Christopher too much; he had already mentioned the possibility of this to me. But, in fact, he wanted to talk to me about Christopher taking another shot himself. He and Christopher had been inspired by Simone Moro's optimism. Andrey was noncommittal, saying that it was not his decision. It was not my decision either, but with Christopher having come so far, and with Richard out of action from a sprained ankle, I reluctantly agreed to be involved. But on this morning, another perfect day, we had not even left the outskirts of Advance Base Camp when Christopher felt his breathing beginning to fail again. He intercepted the event before there was a crisis. The game was over.

After a rest and more oxygen back at the 7Summits-Club Camp, Christopher quickly returned to normal. Richard made arrangements with Alex for their gear to be taken down to Base Camp the next day. There was a mood of acceptance, and I sensed some relief at the dangers being past.

Richard turned to me and said, "Lincoln, the mountain's still there, mate. You might as well go for it. We've got plenty of oxygen up at High Camp, so you might as well use it. And I'll give you the Iridium phone so you can call Barbara from the top."

I smiled and thanked him and felt another half-hitch add itself to the knot in my stomach. There was the option of returning down the glacier with them, which I considered only long enough to reject it. This was the opportunity of my lifetime, the one that I had dreamed about.

My pack was ready. All I needed was to square the climb with Alex. I went to the radio tent, where Andrey was manning the radio. I waited for the chance to talk with Alex, who had gone up to the North Col. I needed to sort out the logistics of my ascent, but Andrey, in his curt but not insensitive fashion, reminded me that Igor Plyushkin's rescue was still under way and that we needed to keep the airways clear because he was standing by to give medical advice as it was needed.

Lunch was served, so I returned to the mess tent. There was constant noise in the radio tent, with the crackling of messages between Igor Svergun, the guide at Camp Two, and Alex at the North Col. In between were what I assumed to be Andrey's advice, given quietly but insistently. I did not want to interrupt, but I did want to be ready for any chance that I might get to speak with Alex, so I returned to the radio tent and squatted next to Andrey. I was in that position when there was a rare silence in the radio traffic.

Without looking my way, Andrey spoke to me. "It is no longer a rescue."

Igor Plyushkin was dead, the tenth fatality of the season.

The radio burst into frantic Russian, so I did not even reply to Andrey. I simply stood up and walked out of the tent.

I found Richard, Christopher, and Mike sitting on chairs in the sun. I sat on a low rock and broke the news. Mike groaned softly; Richard shook his head. Christopher said nothing, but I imagined that now he was relieved not to be going back up that dangerous mountain. We sat there in the sun.

"Still going up?" asked Richard.

I paused, then said, "Yeah, but I'll go up tomorrow. Alex and the guys don't want to worry about what I'm up to. I'll just stay in the background."

The four of us continued to sit there, not saying much. Slate and David had left that morning. The only other Westerner at Advance Base Camp, apart from the Russian crew, was Kevin Augello, Harry's filmmaker. Kevin had had a very difficult time acclimatizing and had arrived at the camp for the first time only two days ago. He had made several previous attempts but had always been forced to turn back. He was obviously delighted to have made it. Acclimatization is a different process for everyone. Better late than never. Occasionally, one of us would make a remark about nothing in particular, but mostly we were with our own thoughts. I could hear the stoves being fired up in the kitchen tent behind me.

Andrey called out to me from the radio tent.

"Lincoln. It is Harry. He wants you."

PART TWO

DEATH'S OWN COUNTRY

MT. EVEREST
29,035 feet

3RD STEP

2ND STEP

MUSHROOM ROCK
1ST STEP

CAMP THREE
27,200 feet

Richard Harris, Christopher Harris, me and Michael Dillon at the launch of Christopher's Climb, Taronga Park Zoo, 14 March 2006. *Photo by Matt King/Getty Images*

Barbara and me, the week before I left for Kathmandu and Everest. *Photo by Margaret Werner*

In the afternoon of our first full day at Base Camp, the clouds cleared to give us a spectacular view of Everest, although Changtse obscures much of the mountain. *Photo by Lincoln Hall*

The many tents that comprised the 7Summits-Club Base Camp included rows of yellow accommodation tents (plus a few grey ones), our long yellow mess tent, and the long blue tent that was our radio shack, DVD theatre and web café! *Photo by Lincoln Hall*

We acclimatised gradually by making several hikes to higher altitudes and back. Here, I am at Advance Base Camp, ready to leave for our first climb to the North Col. *Photo by Michael Dillon*

At Advance Base Camp at 6400 metres, climbers and Sherpas joined in a *puja*, a Buddhist ceremony to honour the mountain. *Photo by Lincoln Hall*

Mike negotiates the aluminium ladders that span a crevasse immediately below the North Col. *Photo by Lincoln Hall*

From the North Col, we climbed part-way up Everest's North Ridge to acclimatise. The large white gully in the centre of the North Face is the Great Couloir, which our Australian team had climbed in 1984. *Photo by Lincoln Hall*

As we climbed the North Ridge towards the summit ridge, our camp at the North Col shrank behind us. Beyond it is the mass of Changtse. *Photo by Lincoln Hall*

I arrive at our High Camp, at an altitude of 8300 metres. That night I left for the summit. *Photo by Harry Kikstra/www.7summits.com*

The most difficult obstacle on the climb to the summit is the Second Step, which requires great care when both ascending and descending. Most summit climbers set out from High Camp in the middle of the night, so the Second Step is usually climbed in darkness. *Photo by Harry Kikstra/www.7summits.com*

From left, Dawa, Dorje and Lakcha on the summit, shortly after 9 am on 25 May 2006. *Photo by Lincoln Hall*

The majestic view from the summit of Mount Everest. Looking along the North Ridge, the view is dominated by Changtse, around which lie the Rongbuk (*left*) and East Rongbuk glaciers. *Photo by Lincoln Hall*

My summit photo, taken at 9.30 am on 25 May 2006 just below the peak of Everest, immediately before the rocky descent that leads to the snow triangle where things began to go wrong. *Photo by Dawa Tenzing Sherpa*

As dawn approached on 26 May, Dan Mazur, Jangbu Sherpa, Andrew Brash and Myles Osborne found me, confused but alive, sitting near Mushroom Rock, high on the North-east Ridge. *Photo by Andrew Brash*

Dan and his team had to prevent me from clambering over the lip of the North-east Ridge. The Kangshung Face, which begins at this lip, falls extremely steeply for several thousand metres. *Photo by Andrew Brash*

Having only just survived the descent back to the North Col, and then further down the mountain the following day, I welcomed the lower altitude (still 6400 metres!) but I was utterly exhausted. *Photo by Harry Kikstra/www.7summits.com*

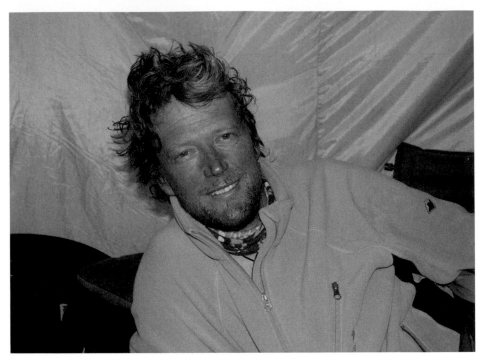

Fatigued and frostbitten, but glad to be alive and at Advance Base Camp. *Photo by Jamie McGuinness, Project Himalaya*

Alex (*left*) and Andrey keep me company while preparations are made for my descent to Base Camp. *Photo by Jamie McGuinness, Project Himalaya*

Preparing to descend from Advance Base Camp, 28 May. *Photo by Jamie McGuinness, Project Himalaya*

Six hours after leaving Advance Base Camp, I arrive at Base Camp, grateful to be one day nearer to home. *Photo by Harry Kikstra/www.7summits.com*

At Base Camp I offered my thanks to Chandra, our chief cook, and his two Tibetan helpers. *Photo by Harry Kikstra/www.7summits.com*

I was very glad to have the opportunity to thank Pemba, in particular, for his part in my rescue. *Photo by Harry Kikstra/ www.7summits.com*

Barbara met me in Kathmandu, as did a large press contingent. Here, we are leaving the Nepal International Clinic after I received a check-up. *Photo by Devendra M. Singh/AFP/ Getty Images*

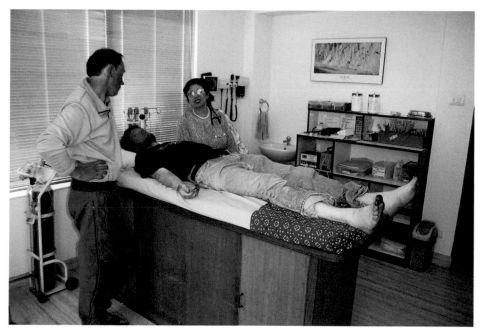

Dr Andrey Selivanov hands over his patient at the CIWEC Clinic in Kathmandu, and discusses my frostbitten fingers and toes with Dr Pandey. *Photo by Michael Dillon*

In Kathmandu I was delighted to meet with Andrew Brash (*left*) and Dan Mazur (*right*). Also with us is Andrew's wife, Jen. *Photo Hall Collection*

At my request, Alex organised a reunion with all the 7Summits-Club Sherpas. In the red vest is Dawa Tenzing, and Pemba is on the far right. *Photo by Michael Dillon*

Another large press team awaited us at Sydney Airport, but they were very respectful of my weakened condition and my inability to speak properly. *Photo by Bill Hearne/Newspix*

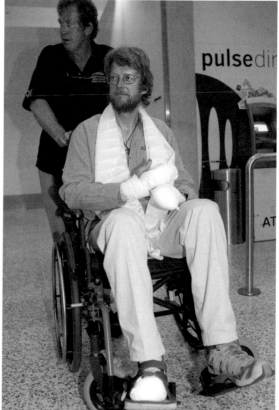

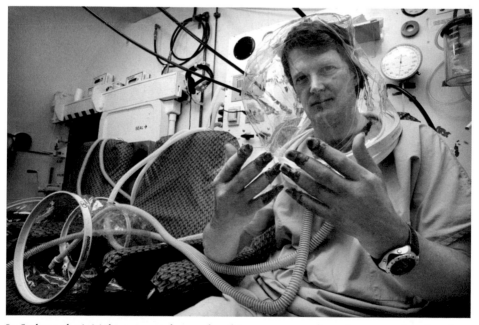

In Sydney, the initial treatment for my frostbite was to spend two hours per day, five days a week for a month in the hyperbaric chamber at the Prince of Wales Hospital. *Photo by Brett Faulkner/Newspix*

Back in the Blue Mountains, Barbara and I asked a visiting Buddhist lama, Ngakpa Karma Lhundup Rinpoche, to lead a *puja* ceremony. It was also a wonderful chance to thank our family and friends for their support. To my left are Dorje, Barbara, and Margaret and Max Hamilton. *Photo by Michael Dillon*

Nine months after my night out on Everest, life is back to normal – more or less – for all of us. From left: Dylan, me, Norbu, Barbara, Dorje and Tosca. *Photo by Lucas Trihey*

Twelve

BIG STEPS

I T WAS A SIMPLE ANNOUNCEMENT with huge implications. Harry had radioed to let me know that his team of four was heading from the North Col to Camp Two the next morning, en route to the summit, and I was welcome to join them. My immediate thought was that I had to leave straightaway or I would be climbing in the dark. Harry had explained how they had spent the day at the North Col, not wanting to get in the way of the rescue but wanting to be available if they were needed. Milan would stay at the North Col to do some long-shot filming, but Harry, Thomas, Pemba, and Passang would leave after breakfast. I told him I was on my way.

Despite the delicacy of the situation, I had to speak with Alex. Because of the rescue-turned-burial, many Sherpas had climbed up to Camp Two. When I finally managed to talk to Alex, he insisted that I climb with the Sherpas allocated to the Australian team—a total of four—even though Richard and now Christopher and Mike had dropped out. This number of Sherpas, he said, would be much safer, not only for me but for Harry and Thomas as well. However, the only Sherpa from our team that I had been able to find was Dorje, and we needed to leave immediately.

Ten minutes later, both of us shouldered our packs, still ready from the day before. I said my good-byes, then we set off together, hiking as fast as we could. Soon we began to meet 7Summit-Club climbers descending to Advance Base Camp. Arkadiy Ryzhenko, who had summited, and

Ilya Rozhkov, who had turned around at 28,700 feet, took up only a minute of our time because both spoke little English and we no Russian. All we did was shake their hands and step aside to let them pass. At five- or ten-minute intervals we stopped to congratulate Henrik, Kirk, Ronnie, Lorenzo, and Noel. Meeting us allowed each of them to take a rest. As I welcomed them, I was silently thankful that they were alive. I expected that our familiar faces, clean and not yet trashed by the mountain, reminded them of the haven of Advance Base Camp, which would soon replace the hell they had been through.

Their feedback about conditions on the mountain was welcome, but I was keen to keep moving. Seeing the last of the A-Team disappearing down the ice gully toward Advance Base Camp was proof that summiting and surviving were not mutually exclusive.

Dorje and I turned and followed the ice gully uphill to a level area, where we put on our crampons. Although we did not need the spiked frames on our boots for crossing the flat glacier, we would need them on the snow face leading to the North Col. It was simpler and safer to wear them from this point.

By the time we had attached our crampons, the sun had left us for the day, so we walked the breadth of the glacier in the shade. Dorje and I were less than halfway up the fixed ropes when the temperature dropped dramatically. My down suit was stashed at the North Col because I had not wanted to carry warm clothes up and down between Advance Base Camp and Camp One for the rare occasions that we needed our warmest gear. But today, with our very late start, I knew we would feel the cold. I had packed a down vest, which I now put on, so that my core at least was warm. Dorje wore his down suit from Advance Base Camp, so the late start was no particular inconvenience for him.

Harry was pleased to see us at the North Col. Thomas was an intriguing character with a sharp intellect and many amusing stories, which he told in perfect English. But he did have a Germanic seriousness which could be off-putting. Thomas was a man with a career who had found mountaineering, whereas Harry and I were committed climbers who had been forced to find careers. It gave us a similar outlook, and with a shared sense of humor, too, we found that we got along very well. At the North Col, however, Thomas was subdued. The nature of his visual impairment was such that his eyesight became less effective the higher he climbed. Here, at 23,200 feet, his vision was already significantly compromised. He told me that all he could see were shapes. Nevertheless, we were in good spirits in the mess tent. We had not forgotten Igor's death; that evening it seemed to make us value life even more.

One problem of sleeping on snow is that it compacts, not just from body weight but also from body heat. The disfiguration of the snow under the thin nylon floor was made worse by the amount of sitting that took place in the tent—a lot of time was spent putting on and taking off boots or shuffling through gear looking for gloves or goggles. The 7Summits-Club sleeping tents were shared—the A-Team would occupy them for a few days, followed by the B-Team. By May 22, after several weeks of regular occupation, the floor of my three-person tent—which would only ever accommodate two at the most because of the inevitable discomfort factor—was shaped like a crater made by some minor missile. Sleeping in the curvature of the snow bowl was like lying in a frozen hammock. Given the circumstances, I slept reasonably well, thanks to the ritual of my midnight read with my lightweight headlamp.

The next morning I woke early, partly due to the bomb crater. Harry, Thomas, Pemba, and Passang had set off on the long climb to Camp Two not long after breakfast, breathing oxygen from the moment they left camp. I was in no hurry because I needed to wait for Lakcha and Dawa Tenzing to arrive from Advance Base Camp, as Alex had requested. When they joined us, our group would be nine, with a ratio of two Sherpas to each Westerner. After Igor Plyushkin's death, Alex was limiting the risks as much as he could.

Lakcha and Dawa Tenzing arrived at the North Col at 10:30 A.M. but stopped for a late breakfast before tackling the second leg to Camp Two.

Dorje and I left them to their recuperation. Now that I was not filming, I could dispense with the stop-start approach of a cameraman and adopt a slower pace that I could maintain for hours at a time. I elected to do without oxygen for as long as I could. The first 1,500 feet of height gain was a simple matter of plodding up a broad snow ridge. I had climbed the first six hundred without oxygen with Mike and Christopher ten days earlier as an acclimatization exercise and saw no reason to begin using it now.

Had the weather been fine and relatively calm, I would have been happy with the uninteresting but strenuous task of hiking up the easy-angled snow ridge. The amazing panorama would have compensated for the repetitive nature of the climbing, the view improving with every step. But today the constant winds prevented any such improvement. My hood was pulled tight around my face and gave me tunnel vision, so the climb became boring and uninviting. The sky was clear, but the winds blasted us with snow, obscuring the outline of the mountain and making nearby rocks appear as black shapes. The higher we climbed, the stronger the wind blew. At around 24,300 feet I was feeling totally uninspired, and decided the cure was to ask Dorje to reach into my pack to turn my oxygen on. The climbing became easier immediately, which was pleasing, but the oxygen mask made it hard for me to see my feet—not exactly a safety feature.

Two hundred feet higher, at the junction of the snowy ridge and the rock-face above, was a campsite where the last of the tents were being packed up by Sherpas because all the climbers from that team were already off the mountain. Soon it would be the end of May—the close of the climbing season—and the number of climbers had decreased markedly. This suited me fine, as I had never before had to deal with crowds on a big Himalayan mountain and did not want to start now.

Our Camp Two was approximately 500 vertical feet above the abandoned camp. On average, the rock-face was no steeper than the ridge had been, and the bright blue fixed rope that had been laid in place for the 2006 season showed us the easiest way up to our camp.

The camp itself would not have met safety standards anywhere. The slope was a mass of loose rocks, which meant that tents could only be pitched if they were propped up on slabs of rock that had been piled together to form rough platforms. Each tent had its own platform, in every case too small, so a part of every tent overhung nothingness. It was not a place that induced a good night's sleep.

The tent that Dorje and I chose had a particularly lumpy floor. We worked out that the only place level enough for the stove was in the doorway. While Dorje melted snow for drinks and dinner, I carefully squeezed outside to take in the view. The wind had dropped to almost nothing, which encouraged me to take photos.

It had become a magnificent afternoon, with views in every direction. Behind and above us was the unbelievable mass of Mount Everest, which had only seemed bigger with every upward step. Stretching to the east, beyond the cascade of lower peaks in the middle foreground, were the rocky brown hills of Tibet. On the skyline were distant snow-capped peaks, with names known only by nomadic yak-herders.

Camp Two was an obvious turnaround point—after negotiating a couple of snow-filled rock gullies, it was a simple snow ridge all the way down to the North Col. I had not come up here to contemplate retreat, but I found that my feelings were taking me in that direction. I understood how David Lien had been happy to call it quits at this camp, where the A-Team had found their tents destroyed by wind. It was beyond this point that climbers drove themselves to their deaths, either because unbending ambition overpowered common sense or because the determination to overcome the cold, the discomfort, and the danger was as unwavering as a GPS-programmed missile locked on to its target. Most climbers survived, of course—some of them because they had turned back here.

A maiden expedition to Mount Everest is the biggest first date you'll ever have. You need to know when to say no, when to back off, and when to open the throttle. I knew what I was up against. Did I want to face that nightmare of choices and judgments in a place where the latest bodies had barely frozen solid? Was this place where I stood now not high enough? Was it not beautiful enough? I did feel some fear within me—it is always present when I am on a mountain—but it was not fear that was steering me away.

There had been so much death this season—a ludicrous amount, given the good weather. I had wanted no part of it, and yet already I had been drawn in. I gave advice to a man who was to climb without oxygen, and he died because he followed that path. I witnessed an ocean of grief in a woman who had lost her husband. I heard wild tales of a man trapped between life and death but with no option to choose either. I heard rumors of another whose reality had become so distorted by the oxygenless air that he had leaped to his death. Everest had taken four lives from the hundreds of locals employed by the guiding industry. One of our teammates had expired while I had waited by the radio, ready to be the next man to step up in line.

I did not want to be that next man.

I returned to the tent, and Dorje grinned as he protected the stove while I moved past. I asked him what was involved in the climb to 27,000 feet the next day.

"A big climb," he said. "Not much place to rest. You have to keep moving. Otherwise can be problem."

I wondered if he was hinting that I might not be able to match the pace necessary to get to the camp. I pulled out my diary and drew a line down the middle of a blank page. On one side of the page I wrote the reasons why I should go up, and on the other side the reasons why I should not. Then I read through what I had written. There were good reasons on both sides of the page, so I put the diary away and deferred my decision to the morning.

Dorje insisted on cooking a freeze-dried meal, but all I wanted was fluid. I had some snacks and energy gels that would satisfy me. I tried to tell him in Nepali that I hated freeze-dried meals, but I had never learned the word for *hate*, and he cooked it anyway. It proved to be as repulsive to me as always. I knew the fault was not Dorje's, and not entirely the fault of the freeze-dried. At this height, I had no appetite for food and could not stomach the amount of fluid I needed to drink. In the cold, both were slow to prepare on our lightweight, low-powered stoves.

Dorje attempted to eat enthusiastically, but I could tell it was a struggle. He kept insisting that I take more, but as a vegetarian I was expert at politely refusing food that I did not want to eat.

When we wriggled into our sleeping bags, I expected to have a sleepless night. I put my oxygen mask on and set my regulator to less than half the daytime flow. Soon I slipped into a dozy kind of sleep. Without sensing the transitions in and out, I must have drifted into a proper sleep at some point, as the night passed much more quickly than I expected. It was the best sleep I had ever had on any expedition at such altitude, and I attributed it entirely to sleeping with a low flow of oxygen.

THAT SAME NIGHT, the C-Team members of the SummitClimb Everest Expedition were settling down to sleep at the North Col. They called themselves the C-Team because they were the also-rans from the expedition's summit attempts in the middle of May. While Phil Crampton and Jangbu Sherpa had been helping Ang Temba and their cerebral edema–stricken client down from the Second Step on May 17, two other members of the A-Team had reached the summit. Two days behind them, SummitClimb B-Team members Andrew Brash and Myles Osborne had been forced to retreat in the face of bad weather. With expedition leader Dan Mazur, these four plus Phil Crampton formed the C-Team and were ready to make a final shot at the summit at the end of the season.

THE NEXT MORNING Lakcha stuck his head in the tent and chatted in rapid Nepali to Dorje.

"Good morning, Lakcha Daai," I called, wanting some advice drawn from his considerable experience.

"Good morning," he said.

"I don't know whether I've got the strength to do this. You've seen me climb. What do you think?"

He laughed. "Only you can know!"

He was saying that reaching the summit depended on how much I wanted to push myself and how much I was prepared to risk. His laughter said he could tell me neither of those things.

Lakcha said a few more words to Dorje about the oxygen they would carry, then he disappeared out the door.

I picked up my diary and opened it.

On the left-hand side of the page I reread what I had written the previous evening.

SHOULD NOT GO UP BECAUSE:
1. *I would have a better chance of surviving and returning in one piece if I went down now.*
2. *Don't want to leave Barbara in the position of Caroline Letrange.*
3. *Don't want Dylan and Dorje to have no father.*

These three were the same reason—namely, variations on not wanting to die.

4. Don't want to spoil the run of great experiences I have had on my previous expeditions.

Essentially, I did not want to cope with a climate of death that I felt came from a generational shift in values on Everest.

5. Don't want more frostbite.

In a way, this seemed a wimpish, relatively trivial reason, but then I thought that there were very few sports where the participants expect to lose extremities or worse.

6. Don't want to have to give superhuman effort and endure the intense discomfort of high altitude.

This was also nothing more than an excuse, given the discomfort I had already put myself through when acclimatizing.

7. Don't really need the summit.

So why was I here? It was the kind of excuse a school student would use for not doing their homework.

On the right-hand side of the page I had written the pros.

SHOULD GO UP BECAUSE:
1. Owe it to Barbara.

Barbara had encouraged me to make this climb, sacrificing many things during the two months I would be away. She wanted me to succeed for my own sake. I owed it to her not to squander the opportunity I now had.

2. Owe it to myself.

Friends who understood the radical nature of our climb in 1984 would introduce me with the words "Lincoln has climbed Mount Everest." I would then be asked, "And did you get to the top?" "No," I would say, and inevitably they would emit a deflated "Oh," as if I had embarrassed them with the answer. The fact that I had made the expedition happen and was largely responsible for getting everyone down alive counted for nothing. Twenty-two years of that was enough. I also wanted to find out whether or not I could get to the top.

3. Owe it to the boys.

I knew that Dylan and Dorje experienced a different kind of put-down. "So your Dad's climbed Everest?" their schoolmates would ask. "Did he get to the top?" When my sons answered "No," the kids were dismissive, understanding even less about the reality of climbing Everest.

When I had woken myself up at 3:30 A.M. on the walkout from the Makalu Expedition in 1999 so that I could call Dylan on his eleventh birthday, he had asked me if I had reached the summit. When I'd replied "No," I had received that same deflated "Oh."

The answer was obvious. I would climb Everest for Barbara, I would climb it for the boys, and I would climb it for me. And while I was at it, I would climb it because it was there.

Today was May 24, Dylan's birthday. When we reached the High Camp at 27,000 feet, I would ring him on Richard's phone with my best wishes. I would tell him that while I was not yet on the summit, I was on my way.

IN PACKING THAT MORNING, there was not much thinking involved, as everything I had carried up was coming with me, except my diary and SLR camera. The most time-consuming part of getting ready was putting on my harness and boots in the tent. It wasn't until I emerged from the tent that I realized it was another perfect day. Of course, I knew that our tent was precariously pitched on a slope, but I was unprepared to deal with the huge drop. It was like stepping out onto the wing of an airplane. But once I had clipped my crampons to my boots, pulled my oxygen mask onto my face, and attached my ascender clamp to the rope, I felt at ease again, despite the visual restrictions of the mask. As I began to move up the fixed rope, I was immediately reminded of the difficulties imposed by the altitude; even when breathing oxygen, I understood why Dorje had warned me about the day's climb. It was obviously more involved than yesterday's snow slope.

As we moved away from the camp, we encountered low rock walls, only two or three feet high, that we wended our way between. There were some big step-ups, which were simple enough, but they did take extra effort. I took a few too many of these at once and had to stop and breathe hard. We had climbed only 150 feet above the camp when we came to a broad shelf across the slope, with plenty of room for a tent. It seemed that one had recently been packed up, as the ground across the entire flat area was well trodden. There was a long pile of rocks on the downhill edge of the shelf, while on the uphill side lay an amazing flat block of rock, almost the ideal dimensions for a park bench. Dorje and I were a little ahead of Lakcha and Dawa Tenzing, so we immediately sat on the rock. It was a great campsite—much better than ours—but an inconvenient distance from the other tents.

My eyes were first taken by the view—out across Changtse and westward to the peaks on the Nepalese border. But then my eyes dropped to the long pile of rocks in front of us, which had been stacked in a curiously regular fashion. At the same instant Dorje and I realized what we were looking at.

"Igor," said Dorje.

It was Igor Plyushkin, buried beneath a pile of stones, his boots and trousers visible between the rocks. Suddenly it made sense that the whole area had been heavily trodden. This was one of the jobs the Sherpas had been doing only two afternoons before. I had known of Igor's death from the moment it had happened, but now it was macabre—the magnificent panorama, a perfect campsite with its God-given perfect park-bench rock, forever haunted by the centerpiece of a semi-open tomb.

When Kirk Wheatley had passed Dorje and me on our way to the North Col, he had told us about finding Igor slumped on the slope, but with a tent not far below him. Kirk had sat with him for twenty minutes and had finally been able to urge Igor into the tent. It seemed that Igor had pushed himself too far and too hard. He survived the night but the next day fell sick only fifteen yards into the descent, complaining he could not breathe properly. Extra oxygen, medicines for altitude sickness, and injections of adrenaline did not save him. He was an accomplished climber, who had won the coveted Snow Leopard Award for climbing all five of the former USSR's 23,000-foot peaks in less than forty-two days.

Before we left, I began to say a Buddhist prayer for Igor, one that I had memorized in Tibetan eleven years ago, but after a few dozen syllables, the remainder of it disappeared from my mind. Perhaps the prayer had been taken for Igor; perhaps I had just lost the lot.

That morning when I had decided to go for the summit, I had accepted that there was an atmosphere of death and that I would have to take it in my stride. Now was my test. There was no insensitivity in my decision to continue—just an extra resolve to play everything very safely.

Soon I began to enjoy the climbing, as we were in an incredibly spectacular place with enough challenging sections to keep me engaged and enough horizontal sections to ease the effort. There were another eight or so climbers not far from us, and we slowly gained on them. We had a brief stop for a snack and a drink and then continued climbing. Because bluffs rose above us, our view of the mountain was restricted, so every buttress we rounded revealed a different scene. Although I enjoyed the variety of the climbing, it seemed to go on forever. I was amazed at how long it took to reach our highest camp. The last 500 feet was a long slog up a wide slope with good views across to the summit pyramid. Disconcertingly far above us, near the top of the snow slope, was the cluster of our tents—Camp Three, or High Camp. I set myself a rhythm, which matched the pace of the man above me, Scott Woolums, the leader of the Project Himalaya team we had been climbing among all day.

As we approached the tents, Scott veered off to the right while I continued upward. The first two tents were occupied, and Harry shouted a greeting to me as I passed.

"Welcome to High Camp!"

I merely waved, deeply tired and wanting to find a tent. Again we faced the propped-on-rocks syndrome. Every tent seemed as insecure as the next, so I chose the nearest empty one. Dorje was not far behind me, and as soon as we were settled inside, I took my ice axe with me to visit Harry, who was only ten yards away. The axe would provide the means for me to stop myself if I slipped.

I squatted outside in my big mountain boots, which are not designed for squatting.

"Sit in the doorway," said Harry. "It's more secure."

Then he laughed. Security needed to be redefined before being applied to this highest settlement on earth. Admittedly, the tents not taken down would all have blown away within a few weeks of our departure, but for the time being, it was a settlement for nearly two dozen people.

I flopped into Harry's tent and accepted a drink. I did not take much because all our water bottles were almost empty, and in each tent it would take a couple of hours in the cold oxygen-thin air to melt enough snow for a couple of decent drinks each. Simple pleasures were not easily won up here.

Although I had some basic knowledge and had used my oxygen set effectively enough over the past two days, I asked Harry to run through the system again. Tomorrow would be the climax of the climb, and I wanted to be sure I knew everything I needed to know. The system was not complex, but at high altitude routine tasks can prove challenging. I also wanted to confirm the location of our spare bottles.

"Don't worry about that," Harry said. "The Sherpas have got it under control, and you'll be together."

I had not been using my oxygen set around camp because it was cumbersome when unpacking and taking photos, but now I was beginning to feel lightheaded. Harry passed his mask across to me, and I pulled it over my mouth, inhaled, then passed it back to him. We continued this as we talked. It was like being in an anti-opium den where we partook of oxygen to prevent hallucinations.

Because Harry had summited Everest the previous year, I asked him about the final climb. It was only a matter of hours away, and there was nothing like a recent update from the horse's mouth.

With our summit strategy agreed upon and my other questions answered, I carefully climbed back uphill. I stopped by Lakcha and Dawa's tent to tell them I had spoken with Harry and that our departure for the summit would be at 11:30 P.M., which was much as they expected. It was still a beautiful afternoon. All we needed was for the weather to hold for another twenty-four hours. I squeezed into the tent, which was at an even more ridiculous angle than the one at Camp Two.

We were now at 27,300 feet—I couldn't blame the Sherpas for not going to the same lengths to make things comfortable.

Once inside, I called Dylan on the Iridium phone and wished him happy eighteenth birthday. Barbara had not returned from work. When I rang back again later, I spoke to no one, only Barbara's message on the voicemail that finished with the words "We'll get back to you as soon as we can."

I thought how nice it would be for all of us to be together, but the thought lasted only a minute.

I left them with a message, the short, sharp sentences of extreme altitude. "I'm feeling strong. The weather's fantastic. We'll be leaving at midnight. I love you all."

From that moment on, my whole being was focused on climbing as far as I was able to climb, and then returning safely.

DESPITE HARRY'S WISH that we start up the fixed rope at eleven thirty, only he and Pemba were ready at that time. It was midnight when I clipped on to the rope, with Lakcha in front and Dorje and Dawa Tenzing behind. I felt clumsy and awkward in my big boots and oxygen mask, and with the hood of my down suit pulled around my face. The doziness, which had been my best attempt at sleep during the few hours I lay in the tent, had not worn off. The first fifty yards were tough, but soon I had warmed up and found my rhythm. By the time we had reached the first sections of steeper rock, I found myself really enjoying the challenge of climbing, with the best part of those first hours being the Exit Rocks, a steep cliff that led us to the Northeast Ridge.

By now we had mingled with members of the Project Himalaya expedition who had left camp before us. We had overtaken a few climbers as they rested at different spots. When they consolidated as a team on the narrow but flat crest of the ridge, Lakcha, Dawa Tenzing, Dorje, and I moved to the front. I thought Harry and his team were still somewhere ahead, but I had no idea if anyone else was up there with them.

The batteries in my headlamp were fading quickly, so I asked Lakcha to unzip the top pocket of my pack and take out the spare. I stopped next to a large boulder on the crest of the ridge, figuring this was something solid

against which I could lean while Lakcha found my headlamp. I turned off
the fading light and became aware of the beauty of the night. I felt much
closer to the stars, although in the scale of the universe they were no closer
at all. The darkness was intense, seeming to exaggerate the updraft of cold
air from the Kangshung Face.

Unfortunately, at that moment other climbers caught up to us,
and I realized that Lakcha was almost blocking the trail, as he looked
for my headlamp. We squeezed against the boulder to let the climbers
past.

One of them said, "Whatever it is you're doing, would you do it somewhere else?"

There was nowhere else to stop on this narrow ridge, but I thought it
an eloquent sentence in the circumstances. I later learned that Harry had
been directly behind me, that these words had come into his mind as a
favorite phrase of his. But he had not voiced this or any other phrase, had
not removed his oxygen mask. I was discovering that life in the Death
Zone was so far removed from the everyday world that telepathy had
become an aberrant part of reality.

At last Lakcha handed me my headlamp and we were on our way, just
ahead of a few more Project Himalaya climbers. My big worry on this
final day to the summit had been that I would get trapped behind a line
of many climbers waiting for someone to overcome an obstacle. This was
a frequent problem at the Second Step, the hardest part of the climb. And
yet here I was, already causing a traffic jam myself. But I had wasted only
a few minutes, whereas sometimes climbers lined up for hours at the Second Step. The lines were nothing like Saturday morning at the supermarket. Here, on the roof of the world, four people spending half an hour
at the Second Step was enough to ruin the summit chances of the people
behind them, so tight are the safety margins on Everest. The maths was
easy, even at this altitude.

I was now in the middle of the Project Himalaya team, which was
no inconvenience to anyone, provided I kept moving. The height gain
along this first section of the ridge was gradual, and when we reached
a significant rise, we did not have to slow down because the fixed rope
traversed the slope. A trail had been well trodden into the fragmented
rock, following the natural strata. We made good speed—if speed can

ever be the appropriate word close to 28,000 feet. My new headlamp was bright, but it still illuminated only a six-foot circle around me. I was moving well when suddenly I saw a body beside the trail. I immediately thought of "Green Boots" and David Sharp. Before the death of Igor Plyushkin, Alex had warned us that these would be the first bodies we would encounter.

Green Boots was the name given to a now-anonymous Indian climber who had died on the mountain in 1996. He had died with the top end of his body under a low rocky overhang and only his legs and lower body protruding. I was so startled by the body that I did not even take in David Sharp as a separate entity, until the wave of emotion had subsided and I realized that his body must have been there, too. Seeing Igor's grave the day before was the first time I had encountered a body on a mountain. All my other dangerous climbs had been on untrodden ground or challenging routes. In New Zealand I had climbed routes where people had died, but the bodies had always been removed.

It was strange to be marching past dead people in the dark, strange enough to make me believe in ghosts. Soon we reached the base of the First Step, junior cousin to the infamous Second Step and the first of the three cliffs that form steps in the ridge, visible from afar on the Northeast Ridge skyline. Several climbers were resting at the base of the First Step, partly because at this point there was enough space to do so but presumably also because this was the first of the acknowledged difficulties of the final climb to the summit.

Lakcha and I kept moving. I could feel a growing tension at the prospect of tackling the First Step, but it proved to be a simple rock-scramble, just on a larger scale than the other obstacles we had surmounted. At the top of the Step, I caught up with three figures, one of whom was Harry. I knew it was him because he flashed his light on me and waved me to sit down. We sat beside each other for a few minutes, saying nothing because of our oxygen masks. Lakcha sat with us. After doing nothing for a few minutes, I began to feel the cold. I felt encouraged by the fact that I did not need to rest.

"What's happening?" I asked Harry.

"Nothing," he replied, lifting the edge of his mask. "We're just waiting for Thomas and Pemba."

So, if Thomas and Pemba were not here, who were these other two people? It didn't really matter. We were all here for the same purpose.

"You might as well push on," added Harry. "You're going faster than us."

"Great. We'll do that."

Lakcha and I set off immediately, with Dorje and Dawa Tenzing behind us at a slightly slower pace. The ridge had leveled off, but as we reached steeper ground, the trail again followed the rock-strata across the slope. We passed three more climbers sitting on a ledge, and I wondered how many were still ahead of us.

After a few steps I realized why they had stopped. The fault line that exposed the outward-sloping ledge suddenly disappeared. I was not overly concerned because the fixed rope continued across the rock-face. The familiar blue rope was anchored at the blank section, so that when I clipped my carabiner past it, I was in a safer position to clamber across to where the narrow ledge continued. The step across proved to be much easier than it appeared in the darkness. Lakcha had climbed up a few feet to another ledge system, which we followed around to a shallow amphitheater. I immediately noticed someone sitting up against the cliff off to the side, but with all of us wearing oxygen masks, there was no conversation. I shone my headlamp up the rock buttress beyond the amphitheater. Suddenly I realized from ropes hanging vertically down the cliff that we had reached the Second Step, and that no one was climbing it.

Lakcha wasted no time in moving across to the ropes. It was a slight step up into an alcove, which narrowed as it rose upward. This kind of feature is not welcomed by climbers because the holds invariably face downward, rendering them useless. Several ropes were in place, as different climbing parties sought the best option for scaling the obstacle. I stepped back while Lakcha quickly climbed up and disappeared from view. Then it was my turn, but I did not manage it well. I am a flexible climber, so I decided to bridge the gap with my legs, but I neglected to factor in the limiting effects of my down suit, the tight leg loops of my harness, and the weight of my cumbersome mountaineering boots. When I swung my right foot across, it only scraped the far wall and, for the first time on the climb, I fell. My weight was caught by my ascender-clamp locking on to the fixed rope. I was ten feet above the ledge, with my heart thumping.

Thankfully, the darkness hid the enormous drop beneath me. I was able to haul myself up to a level where my feet were on a narrow flat ledge, and while I was able to balance there, the handholds were very insecure. By moving up, I had shifted my weight to my feet. I reached down to waist level to slide my ascender up above me so that the rope could again take my weight. Unfortunately, the ascender was jammed—when I had fallen and swung to the right, one of the spare ropes had been caught by the clamp. I could no longer move the ascender in either direction. Had I been in a less precarious situation, I would have abandoned the ascender and climbed onward without the rope, but that was much too dangerous to contemplate. Otherwise, I could disconnect myself from the ascender, which was shaped for right-hand use and replace it with my left-hand unit. However, my left-hand ascender was at Base Camp. I slid my wind-protective goggles to my forehead in order to assess the problem—my main concern was that the rope which bore my weight might be damaged.

Time was ticking away, and Lakcha would be wondering what had happened to me. Thinking about Lakcha brought Dorje and Dawa Tenzing to mind, so I removed my mask and called out to them before realizing that they were just below me and ready to come up the ropes. I turned back to the jammed ascender and, in the light from my headlamp, concluded that the rope was perfectly safe. I grabbed the errant rope and jerked it strongly. With the first jerk, it came free and the problem was solved. Still, I was aware that mental processes could be suspect at 28,500 feet, so I reassessed the damage and came to the same conclusion. Only then, with Dawa Tenzing almost at the level of my feet, did I continue up the rope.

I was still panting heavily from the adrenaline surge, so it was an effort to drag myself over the lip of the cliff and onto a steep snowy ledge. It was now an easy matter to climb up the soft snow to a pair of ladders lashed to the cliff. It seemed incongruous to have a ladder as the key to climbing Mount Everest, but no one even questioned it. The shorter of the two had been placed at the upper section of the Second Step in 1975 when a Chinese expedition made the second ascent of the mountain from the north. The first ascent of this twenty-foot-high obstacle by a Chinese climber, in 1960, had taken three hours at the cost of severe frostbite. In 1975 the Chinese had also fastened a tripod to the summit, but it was blasted away by the jet-stream winds within a year. The second and longer ladder had been donated by a client of Russell Brice so that climbing the upper step would become less time-consuming and, therefore, safer. I was thankful for its presence, as I had heard many stories about the Chinese ladder being just that much too short for an easy exit to the ledge above.

The ledge proved to be small, but once I had my ascender attached to the upper rope, I could see the difficulties were over. I looked down to check the positions of Dorje and Dawa Tenzing. Dorje was almost at the top of the ladder, with Dawa Tenzing waiting at its base. A final steep but straightforward snow slope led to the crest of the ridge, where Lakcha was anxiously waiting.

Paradoxically, the crest of the ridge felt much more exposed and, hence, more dangerous because there was no longer a cliff-face in front of me. Nothingness dropped away on both sides. The edge of the darkness was softening, but there was not yet a hint of light. The way was open, the deadly specter of the Second Step replaced by Chomolungma, Mother Goddess of the Earth.

Thirteen

THE ROOF OF THE WORLD

BEYOND THE SECOND STEP I had the feeling of walking in the sky. A sudden breeze confirmed we had reached the crest of the main ridge. I could sense the space around me and wondered what could be seen when there was light. I stopped and put a gloved hand over the beam of my headlamp. In the darkness the ring of mountains surrounding Everest was only an amorphous presence below a sky still full of stars. I wanted to see those invisible mountains, just as I had wanted a visual register of the landmarks we had passed. The Exit Cracks, the First Step, Mushroom Rock, and the Second Step were names familiar to me, but my images of them had just been distorted views captured briefly in the narrow beam of my headlamp. A mountaineering instinct deep within linked my safety to my knowing the mountain intimately—the backbone of its ridges, the cold flesh of its snows, the surrounding landscape. I was impatient for dawn and the sights that would come with it.

I dropped my hand from the headlamp and the beam lit my way. Lak-cha had drawn ahead, but after my short rest, it did not take long for me to catch up to him. Dorje and Dawa Tenzing were following but at a slower pace because they were breathing a lower flow-rate of oxygen from their tanks. Both had summited Everest in previous years and knew what they were doing. The gradient became gentle again and we seemed to be making good time.

I began to sense that the heavens were losing their blackness. Since leaving Camp Three, everything I had seen of the way ahead had been limited to whatever had been contained within my headlamp's moving circle of light. When I tilted my head too far to the left or right, the beam vanished into the sky; it did the same when I tilted the beam upward to where I knew the summit must be. But now there was some texture in the darkness surrounding the cast of my headlamp. Within minutes, vague shapes were appearing ahead of me. Most obvious was a dramatic increase of steepness where the Northeast Ridge melded into the heart of the mountain. It was impossible to judge the distance in the fading darkness, but I guessed that the summit pyramid, formed by the convergence of the Northeast Ridge, the West Ridge, and the Southeast Ridge, was only a few hundred feet away.

The line of fixed rope had been running ten feet below the ridge but now began to slant upward. Thirty feet ahead of me, Lakcha was approaching the crest. Against the gunmetal-gray sky to the north, I could distinguish Changtse and the indistinct mass of Gyachung Kang and Cho Oyu. These sights were familiar to me from 1984, as well as from the last two days. Now I was eager to reach the ridge and see the view to the south, across the Kangshung Face and east to the Makalu massif—country I had never seen from the west. I hurried, although of course the view was not going to disappear. When I reached the crest, I could tell that dawn was not long away. I was impatient to look down on Makalu, where seven years earlier storms had shrugged me off its slopes, but the granite pyramid was part of the darkness. A colorless sky silhouetted Kanchenjunga, over fifty miles away on the eastern horizon. The light was coming quickly now, and I could see that gray cottonwool clouds filled all the glaciers and valleys, lifting the giant peaks free from the earth. The Makalu massif took shape, but the main peak was as yet indistinguishable.

As Lakcha and I approached the Third Step, the sky continued to lighten. Sue Fear had told me that the step was straightforward, that the snow slope above was long and tiring but only because of the altitude. She had added that the summit itself lay back beyond the snow slope and was reached by an awkward, circuitous traverse across the top of the North Face. All I could see beyond the step as we drew close to it was the line of blue fixed rope disappearing up the snow slope.

The ridge became very narrow, which put us at the lip of the Kang-shung Face. There were a couple of rocks to be stepped around, which required focused attention. While Lakcha dealt with the obstacle, I looked down and across to Makalu, its majestic shape now apparent. To me, 28,765-foot-high Makalu is the most beautiful mountain in the world, a feeling that dates from when, as a young mountaineer, I first saw its dramatic profile in the pink light of sunset. Its magic has never faded for me.

As I looked down on Makalu from Everest, I felt a different kind of joy. Being above the world's fifth-highest peak gave me no sense of conquest. Rather, there was a sense of fulfillment now that I could see for myself the classic Everest-climbers' view of Makalu, an image already sharp in my mind from photos taken by others during the last stages of Everest's Southeast Ridge route. Although I was high on the North Ridge, the view of Makalu was very much the same. The message that came to me from this glorious sight was that I would climb Mount Everest.

The summit was less than 500 feet above me, and I knew in my heart that nothing would stop me reaching it. Another two or three hours of lung-busting climbing and I would be there. I was already a thousand feet higher than I had been on the North Face in 1984, and my determination to succeed, should the chance ever come my way, had strengthened with each of the twenty-two years that had passed. I was in good shape, with adequate oxygen, perfect weather, and the company and support of three great Sherpas whom I had come to know and trust.

As I took in the view and its implications, my thoughts delayed me. Lakcha continued toward the Third Step. I glanced down the ridge and saw that Dorje was only thirty feet below me. Dawa Tenzing was another hundred feet behind. I raised my hand, my thumb up in encouragement—the only kind of communication possible when wearing an oxygen mask. Then I turned and stepped over the rocks blocking the ridge.

It was only a few minutes to the low cliff of shattered rock that formed the Third Step. With less snow, it may have been more difficult, but today it looked straightforward. Lakcha sat down as I approached and pulled a thermos from an outside pocket on his pack. Suddenly, it seemed like a very good idea to take the weight off my feet. Without removing my pack, I sat on a rock and leaned back in the snow. I unzipped the front of my down suit and pulled my water bottle from one of the large inside pockets. I was pleased that my Black Diamond high-altitude gloves had kept my hands warm enough through the night. The weather was definitely on our side. There was scarcely a breeze, but I was beginning to feel cold, even though I had been inactive for only a few minutes. I wondered if I was cold because I had taken off my oxygen mask to take a few sips of water. Dorje arrived and flopped down into the snow, and a few minutes later Dawa Tenzing did the same. I zipped up my down jacket and tightened its hood around my face. Whether it was inactivity or the few minutes without oxygen, I was ready to get going. As soon as Lakcha stood up, I was behind him, and we turned to face our next obstacle.

The difficulties of the Third Step were limited to a few steep chunks of rock at the very beginning. Snow had accumulated over the rocks above the initial steep section, giving us the straightforward option of climbing the snow. Where the angle eased a little, there was a body slumped in the snow. Harry had warned me that we might encounter the body of Marko Lihteneker, who had been with Alex's 7Summits-Club expedition the year before.

It was only the extreme effort required at altitude that made the snow slope a difficult climb. The snow was in perfect condition, soft enough for a foothold to be kicked into the surface but firm enough for it not to collapse. The height gain of around 150 feet demanded much more than 150-feet's worth of work. There was some respite when the line of footsteps turned right and we began to traverse the slope so that we could edge around a large rock buttress onto the uppermost section of the North Face. The snow thinned until we were climbing completely on rock, still traversing at first, then heading straight up the cliff. Mercifully, the cliff lay back from the vertical, making it the most enjoyable rock climbing I had encountered on Everest so far—and there was not much left on the mountain to surpass it. The climbing was not particularly difficult but was continuous, and no doubt some of the enjoyment came from the fact that this cliff would take us to the summit. It would have been even more pleasurable had we been in the sun.

In this positive state of mind, I was stunned to find myself climbing across a rock-face and suddenly noticing two bodies lying side by side. They were head-to-toe, but with boots on, in the ruins of a tent that had been destroyed by storms. No one had mentioned this couple, who were less than one hundred feet below the summit. Surely that proximity would have generated some comment. For some reason I thought one of them was a woman, possibly because of the intimacy of their bodies lying so close together, but I had no other evidence to support this feeling. Their heads had been scalped by particles of wind-borne ice, and their brightly colored nylon clothing was in rags. The worst thing was the anonymity. They had obviously been here for at least a year—no storms this season could have wreaked such dreadful damage—and yet I had heard nothing. I knew the names of other bodies I had seen on the mountain: Igor Plyushkin, David Sharp, Marko Lihteneker. And I must have passed, unaware in the dark, Vitor Negrete and Jacques-Hugues Letrange. Even Green Boots, the Indian man who had been lying half in a cave by the track for years, had some kind of identity. But I knew nothing about this pair. It seemed so tragic that they had no names, no way for me to wish their souls well, no way to speak of them. I turned my back on them because that was the only way I could show some respect.

I continued up the cliff. The climbing was still good but with a few larger ledges covered with snow that led me to guess that we were close to the final summit ridge. I remembered Sue Fear's warning that the rock climb did not lead directly to the summit, and the photos she had shown me matched what we saw as we reached the ridge. The summit was obvious, perhaps only fifty feet above us, but we were separated from it by the corniced ridge, which ran for perhaps another hundred yards. The cornices overhung the Kangshung Face. It was too dangerous to go anywhere near those fragile, unpredictable lips of ice, so the fixed rope traced a route across the very top of the North Face as it curved over to meet the top of the Kangshung.

Enough people had been up here, during a season that had seen the best weather in years, to have trodden the snow into a definite track to the summit. I walked carefully along the icy path, making sure my crampons bit into the surface. The blue line of fixed rope led all the way to the summit. At first the height gain was slight, with the path weaving in and out of gullies while maintaining a gradual but constant rise. A slip while crossing one of the gullies would have very serious consequences, as there were long distances between anchor points and a huge amount of sag in the rope. If I slipped, I would tumble at least thirty feet down a slope that increased in steepness as it continued. The virtually horizontal rope would sag under my weight, making it impossible for me to use my ascender. Climbing back up the hard ice at that altitude would be very difficult. Such a fall would probably not result in serious injury; the danger was that I might lack the strength to get back onto safer terrain. I dispelled all such thoughts and focused on placing my boots exactly where I wanted them to be.

At last the ridge joined the steeper slope of the summit dome, although it was more of a half-dome, as the Kangshung Face still dropped almost vertically from the summit. I could see prayer flags stretched out along the summit, and the top of an oxygen bottle, which at first I mistook for the head of someone sitting just over the crest on the Nepalese side of the mountain. Another string of prayer flags led down from the crest toward the huge drop of the Kangshung Face; others dangled down the face itself. Some flags were frozen into the slope, and so they no longer had the winds capturing their prayers and dispersing them to the heavens.

I felt incredibly privileged when I realized that the summit of Mount Everest was deserted. Perhaps there were climbers approaching from the south side—I would soon find out. The crest of the summit itself rose like a small breaking wave, creating a final one-foot-high step. I paused for an extra breath, then stepped up onto the highest point on the planet. Twenty-nine thousand and thirty-five feet. I was alone on the roof of the world.

I pulled up the sleeve of my down suit and looked at the time. It was 9:00 A.M. exactly, according to BTG's Rolex. It had come a very long way from Taronga Zoo on the harborside in Sydney. I was halfway to returning the watch to him, but with the difficult and dangerous half of the journey ahead of me.

Lakcha arrived two minutes later, having graciously let me lead the way so that I could arrive first. I could see Dorje was approaching the summit dome, but as yet there was no sign of Dawa Tenzing.

I took in the panorama around me. Makalu, of course, and the jagged ridge-tops of Lhotse and its subpeaks. Lhotse is the fourth-highest mountain in the world. All the mountains around and beyond it are giants as well, and yet now they seemed too low to be of consequence. Even

Nuptse—which had looked so high from the summit of Ama Dablam twenty-five years earlier, and even higher from the Nepalese Base Camp for Everest—no longer seemed significant. I never would have thought that I would dismiss so summarily the peaks of the Khumbu, among which I had enjoyed such special times.

Perhaps my judgment was numbed by two nights without proper sleep, with virtually no food and little to drink. Perhaps I was also influenced by the fact that I was on the summit of Mount Everest, where height no longer mattered. I certainly had no energy to spare to contemplate routes and possibilities on the surrounding mountains, as I had done from mountaintops on several continents. I was being so economical with my energy that I would not let any of it be taken by jubilation—euphoria could take control once you unleashed it. There were no "dream come true" moments for me. Not yet. Not until I was off the mountain.

For years I had told myself that Everest was just another mountain, but now I could see clearly that it was not. This was a very special place, and I was saddened to see abandoned oxygen bottles and yellow patches of snow where people had urinated. Even the strings of prayer flags frozen into the summit looked spent. There were footsteps everywhere, which is what you would expect after several hundred people had visited.

A few crazy months each year, I thought, and the rest of the time Everest—Chomolungma, Sagarmatha—remained untouched. For those months Everest could support the deadly dreams of people like me, then the monsoon snows would cloak the mountain, and jet-stream winds would blast away the flags and oxygen cylinders. Everest would then become as it always has been: pure, symbolic, immutable.

I completed my 360-degree survey, and saw that Dawa Tenzing was now ascending the final slope. The four of us shook hands. Dorje removed his oxygen mask and smiled nervously. Only twenty-two years old and he had just climbed Everest for the second time. It was the third success for both Lakcha and Dawa Tenzing. I sat down on the lip of the summit, and the thought came to me that this was only the third time I had sat down since we had left Camp Three at midnight. The first stop was for a few minutes when Lakcha and I caught up with Harry, the second when we reached the Third Step, and now on the summit.

I knew that the Russian crew back at Advance Base Camp would be watching the clock, waiting to hear from me. I reached inside my down suit for my radio and pulled the oxygen mask away from my mouth.

With my finger on the talk button, I announced, "Lincoln calling ABC . . . We are on the summit."

Almost immediately Alex answered. "Congratulations! How are you?"

"Good," I said. "Thank you, Alex, for making this possible."

"You are welcome. But you are okay?" He obviously thought the question important enough to rephrase it and ask me again.

"Yes. All of us are well, all four of us."

"How is the weather?" For a few moments I focused upon the extraordinary display of mountains and glaciers beneath me. There were a few clouds, especially to the west, but they were low and insignificant.

"It's a perfect day. Almost no wind at all."

"Very good. Now you must come down."

"Yes, Alex. We are leaving now."

"Good luck, and be fast."

With the radio in my hand, I thought of Barbara and her statement that she did not want to hear from me when I reached the summit, only when I was safely back down. I turned off the radio and tucked it into the pocket of my down suit.

From where I sat, the nature of the final stage of the climb was more obvious than it had been on the way up, when some sections had been hidden from view. I could see almost in its entirety the one-way track traversing below the crest of the ridge. Within a few weeks the path would be buried beneath banks of snow, leaving no sign of the pilgrimage that had been made along this highest of all ridges.

As my eyes traced the route, climbers began to emerge from the easy-angled but shaded rock-face onto the small level area. I did not want to get trapped on the summit by a dozen climbers coming our way. I immediately suggested to Lakcha, Dorje, and Dawa Tenzing that we head back. Dawa Tenzing requested a photo, and so I took a shot of the three of them and a shot over the peak of Changste to the Rongbuk Glaciers, which seemed to show the curvature of the earth. There was no summit shot of me, but that was okay; I would ask one of the Sherpas to take a photo at the place just below the peak where the Project Himalaya climbers were now gathering. I knew there was enough room for us to regroup there without disrupting the flow of traffic. It was 9:20 A.M. by the Rolex. We had eleven hours of daylight in which to descend to the relative safety of Camp Two. Compared to 29,000 feet, the air at 25,000 feet would feel like relative luxury. We would be able to lie down and relax.

The weather was perfect, with only a few harmless clouds around the lower peaks and some more solid cover to the west. Everything was good. Everything was going according to plan.

Fourteen

COUNTING CHICKENS

O N MAY 24, Barbara, Dylan, his girlfriend Tanya, and Dorje celebrated Dylan's eighteenth birthday by going out for dinner at Sada Thai, our favorite restaurant, which is tucked away upstairs above the post office in our small Blue Mountains town. Dylan was already involved in politics and had campaigned at several local elections, so he was now delighted to be old enough to vote. But the next day was a school day, so there was no real birthday party, just a good dinner, with a cake and candles back at home.

As a teacher, Barbara also had to be at school the next morning—but in Sydney, which meant a very early start. She was ready to go straight to bed, but first she checked the phone messages. As she had hoped, there was a message from me, my voice excited but breathless from the extreme altitude. I said there was perfect weather at Camp Three, that our plan was to leave for the summit at midnight and that I felt really strong. It was the best possible set of circumstances for an attempt at the summit. Barbara relayed my message to Dylan and Dorje, and although they knew accidents happen on Everest, they could not have appreciated the extent of the dangers I still faced. The difference between this Everest expedition and all my other big climbs was that this time I was climbing with three Sherpas and using supplementary oxygen. This just had to be safer, Barbara thought, and she went to bed telling herself that I would be fine.

. . .

THAT NIGHT Barbara was not the only person who had my summit bid on her mind. On the other side of the world, at the Tibetan Base Camp, Mike and the Harrises had each taken a walkie-talkie to their tents in case I made a radio call during my final push to the summit.

The previous day Mike had arrived from Advance Base Camp, with Richard and Christopher following on yaks. Christopher had been advised by Andrey not to walk at all, as a precaution against another collapse. Two days earlier, Richard had hurried back to check on his son and had twisted his ankle. After twenty-four hours of rest he was still unable to walk, so he was on a yak's back as well.

The mood at Base Camp was definitely one of imminent departure. A few days earlier David Lien and the Norwegian mountaineers, Petter, Johnny, and Frode, had set off on the long drive to the border at Zhangmu, eager to put the hardships of the last two months behind them. Safely back from the summit, Noel Hanna and Lorenzo Gariano were eating up big. It was not just post-expedition hunger. They were gathering strength for their epic cycle journey over the Tibetan Plateau, down through Nepal and across the length of India to the coast at the Bay of Bengal. Kirk Wheatley was doubly pleased with his ascent of Everest—he had now climbed each of the Seven Summits, which meant never in his life would he have to go near another mountain. Henrik Olsen was also celebrating the completion of his Seven Summits quest but was by no means through with adventuring. For the moment, however, enough was more than enough. Slate had arrived at Base Camp a day ahead of the other climbers who had summited on May 21 but was content to spend the extra time at Base Camp so that he could head out with the team.

Mike was up early on the morning of May 25, wondering how my climb had gone during the night. There had been no word from me, so he continued with the chore of sorting his film gear. Others were packing up as well. Some climbers had already stowed everything except their sleeping bags and the few odds and ends they would need for their last night at Base Camp. Landcruisers were booked for an early departure the next morning. Only Harry, Thomas, and I were not part of the plans. The film gear was in the communications dome tent, and there was nothing unusual about

Maxim Onipchenko being in the nearby radio tent. However, it was only by chance that Mike heard my voice broadcast on the radio. Totally lucid, I was thanking Alex for making it possible for me to reach the summit. Maxim's taciturn nature was legendary among the climbers and Mike wondered whether or not he would have passed on the news.

Mike immediately alerted Richard and Christopher of my success. He attempted to ring Barbara at home. When he could not get through, he rang Simon Balderstone. Simon is chairman of the Australian Himalayan Foundation, of which Mike and I are directors, and Mike was sure that Simon would know how to contact Barbara.

THE NEXT MORNING, on the early train to Sydney, Barbara was thinking about the time difference between Australia and Tibet. By the time she walked through the gates of SCEGGS Darlinghurst, she calculated, it would be 8:00 A.M. at the girls' school and 6:00 A.M. in Tibet. Provided conditions had remained ideal, I would be only a few hours from the summit. The fine, cloudless Sydney day helped reinforce her mood of hope.

On the opposite side of Sydney's famous harbor, Simon Balderstone was busily working at his desk at Manly Cove. Not long after 11:00 A.M. he picked up the phone and heard Mike's excited voice at Base Camp: "Lincoln's on the summit!" Simon had not even been aware that I was making my final climb today. Both of them laughed, then Mike asked him to convey the news to Barbara. The only question Simon asked of Mike was whether I was okay. Mike assured him that I was in good shape and that by now I would be on my way down.

Because it was a Thursday, Barbara was not in class but at a history department meeting. When the phone rang and it was passed to her, she was surprised to hear Simon's voice.

"Hello, Barb!" he said. "It's Simon. Mike just rang me from Base Camp to say that Linc summited this morning."

She was silent for a moment, then answered, "That's fantastic!"

"The weather's good," Simon continued. "He reached the summit at nine A.M. Tibet time and he's got all day to get down. Everything is going really well. You should tell the girls when you get back to class," he added. "It is a bit of history, after all."

Barbara hung up the phone and announced the news to her colleagues. They were a close-knit team and had been following my progress, so they were all delighted.

"It's great news, isn't it?" said department head Jenny Reeves, watching Barbara's face.

"Yes, it is, but now's just as dangerous, when he's coming down. I hope there'll be a message when I get home."

AFTER WORK, on her way to the railway station, Barbara wondered who she should ring with the news, and a few names immediately leaped to mind. First she called my father, who laughed with surprise and pleasure.

"At least he's got that monkey off his back now," she said, and he agreed. Although Al Hall was never one to say much on the phone, he was sure to be dialing a few people that evening.

Barbara then rang Louise Southerden, who was acting editor at *Outdoor Australia* during my absence, so that she could spread the word among my workmates. Her last call was to Greg Mortimer and his partner, Margaret Werner, at Aurora Expeditions. Greg picked up the phone and whooped with delight when he took in the news. He ran downstairs and excitedly told everyone in the office that I had summited Mount Everest. As my closest friend, and one who had been through the 1984 expedition with me, Greg understood more than anyone else the significance of my climb.

Barbara knew that those few calls would send the news rippling through different and sometimes overlapping networks, and although many of our friends and family members would have liked to have known immediately, Barbara did not feel like talking about it anymore. She only wanted to spread the news when she could add that I was safely back down at Base Camp.

IN TIBET, everyone had finished packing. Those with nothing else to do spent their time outside taking their last photographs of Base Camp and of their fellow climbers. Others, constantly hungry after the huge demands of the climb, were in the mess tent drinking cups of tea or coffee and attempting to get to the end of the seemingly endless supply of biscuits.

Maxim had passed on the news that Thomas had been forced to turn around 150 vertical feet below the summit. He was descending well, with Harry, Passang, and Pemba guiding him down.

Mike, Richard, and Christopher were occupied in their own ways, but for the next few hours each of them carried a walkie-talkie. They were relaxed and realized that it might be a while before they heard from me. It was a beautiful day, and they could see no reason why I would not be descending safely with my Sherpas as company.

THAT EVENING Simon Balderstone dropped off his son Fergie at football training, then went to a nearby café in the Sydney beachside suburb of Dee Why to work on a concept document for politician Peter Garrett. Before becoming involved in politics and indigenous issues, Simon had been a journalist for many years. His journalist mates knew he was chairman of the Australian Himalayan Foundation and realized that he was the best local source for information about David Sharp's prolonged death on Everest, and so for a week now he had been fielding calls. The debate had moved away from David Sharp himself to Mark Inglis and the remarks attributed to him at the time when David was still alive. One such call came through from *Sydney Morning Herald* journalist Phil Cornford. Simon pointed out that inaccurate secondhand information from dubious websites had been picked up by the media and conveyed, thirdhand, as truth.

"There's no proper research here, mate," he said to Phil. "But I can tell you some breaking news I heard direct from Base Camp today. Lincoln Hall summited this morning."

Six other Australians had reached the summit of Everest as well, but Simon just happened to have details about my climb. Phil took down the details, saying that he would include a couple of paragraphs about me. And so it was that the story of my seemingly successful ascent of Everest was launched by the media on the back of David Sharp's demise.

. . .

OUR HOUSE IS ON the edge of a wilderness, which means there are many kinds of wildlife but no broadband Internet connections. Our phone line had been "split," giving us one line for calls and another for the Internet. But when Barbara arrived home two hours after leaving school, one line was taken by Dylan's computer and the other by Dorje's, so she was unable to check the phone messages. She prepared dinner, and after the meal she shooed the boys off-line. The only message was from my sister Julia, demonstrating the network effect. Barbara returned the call, then she decided to ring our close friends Iain Finlay and Trish Clark, whom I had taken to Everest Base Camp in 1982. While Barbara spoke to Iain and Trish, a call-waiting tone announced that someone was ringing her, but she allowed it to go to the voicemail. Iain and Trish were a couple with an emotional take on life, so that when they were up, they were ecstatic—which was how they were when they received the news. Julia had been more cautious.

By the time Barbara had hung up the phone in Wentworth Falls it was after 7:30 P.M. Tibet operates on Beijing time, although Beijing is two thousand miles east of Lhasa, Tibet's capital. Consequently, when it is 7:30 P.M. in Sydney, it is 3:15 P.M. in Nepal but 5:30 P.M. in Tibet. By that time in the afternoon on May 25, Advance Base Camp on the East Rongbuk Glacier would be in shadow, but high on the Northeast Ridge the sun would still be shining.

Fifteen

FADING LIGHT

TIME SOMEHOW FEELS DIFFERENT on the summit of Mount Everest. As the air thins almost to nothing, time seems to thin as well. Watches and multifunction altimeters tick over at the same rate, but time remains only loosely connected to its measurement. Sure, the process is the same—when I stepped onto the summit and checked my watch, it read 9:00 A.M.; when I was ready to leave, it read 9:20. Yet I knew about the slippery quality of time at extreme altitude. The beauty can be so mesmerizing that huge chunks of time—perhaps half an hour or more—can pass themselves off as five minutes. When beauty of all kinds is absent, the bone-numbing cold of a mountain's highest slopes can convert a five-minute block into an hour of suffering. When disaster looms, time becomes immeasurable.

At this point, I spoke to Alex, letting him know that we had summited and were about to head down. I knew all about the urgency of descent. It was a very long way down to the North Col, which is where I would feel safe. I knew that on this route there were time-wasting bottlenecks where less competent climbers would struggle with minor obstacles the rest of us found easy. It was the danger of those human traffic jams that made me decide to head down as soon as I saw the other team of climbers ascending. The longer you spend up high, the more likely you are to stay up there forever.

Moving as quickly and as carefully as I could, I led the way. It was a huge relief to be descending, no longer working against gravity. For the nine hours since midnight, in this outer-worldly place where the air was so thin, gravity should have allowed us some kind of break. But the world only works like that in dreams.

The downward path was easier, yet nothing could hide my tiredness. Each of the last three days above the North Col had demanded a huge output of effort. During that time I had barely slept. I had no appetite for food and could not stomach the amount of fluid I needed to drink. With the summit in the bag, the impetus of striving for the mountain's intangible Holy Grail was lost. Survival was now the driving force, but strangely, survival was not as powerful a motivator as summit fever, the force that keeps climbers struggling upward against all odds.

The long, routine, fixed-rope descent ahead of us provided me with a sense of security, but in reality there were many places along the rope where a fall would be deadly. I was aware of the dangers but still expected to make good time because most of the terrain was straightforward.

The strategy of coming down the final ice traverse before any more climbers headed up toward the summit meant we avoided the first possible bottleneck. As we reached the broad, flat area at the end of the ice ridge, the other climbers followed our upward tracks. The change in direction at this one-way passage was as smooth as if controlled by traffic lights. No words were exchanged, only a feeble wave at most. In this most inhospitable place every nonessential action was avoided. We had stepped aside and now busied ourselves with a few quick tasks—each taking a drink, Dawa Tenzing snapping a photo of me with my small Olympus, Lakcha replacing my almost empty oxygen bottle with a full one from his pack.

We then clipped on to the rope and began the steeper descent of the rock-face. We chose to climb down the broken rock rather than rappel because it took less energy. The climbing was straightforward and secure, thanks to good handholds and ledges big enough for an entire boot. At one point I misjudged the distance to a ledge and overstepped it, falling two feet to the next ledge. At that moment more climbers appeared, intent upon climbing up past us. I stepped down onto a rock shelf, where there was more space. As the climbers moved across in front of me, I looked down at the two bodies that lay not far below among the ruins of their tent, the same two that had shocked me an hour earlier. Absolutely nothing could be done, but I was triggered into moving again to get away from these dangerous heights as quickly as I could.

We followed a sequence of ledges, descending gradually until we reached a long ledge that took us to the edge of the snow. A well-trodden path led us across the snow, below the vertical rock buttress, and out onto the exposed slope of the snow triangle that I had scrutinized so attentively through Alex's telescope from Advance Base Camp. I was pleased to reach the first anchor-point on the snow triangle because from here the fixed rope led directly down the forty-degree slope all the way to the Third Step. We would be able to lose height quickly because the slope promised easy rappeling.

But sometimes promises are broken. My harness was working itself loose, a problem that had developed through the night and now became inconvenient. My thick gauntlets made the job of tightening the straps difficult, but I managed some improvement. I clipped a carabiner on to the rope and set off. The relief I had been feeling at the prospect of easier terrain now seemed to transform into a huge sense of lethargy. I descended 150 feet with my arm wrapped round the rope to provide friction. At the next anchor-point I felt sleepy but recognized the need to descend the rope in a more secure fashion. I attached my descender to the rope to guarantee more controllable friction and, in this way, managed to rappel the next section of the line. But then I needed to collapse in the snow.

Lakcha urged me to hurry, and I expect I did my best to do so. It was at this moment that the slippery, erratic nature of time at altitude manifested. I had been acutely aware of the need for speed, and yet two hours quickly escaped me.

My awareness of time clicked in again when I was near the bottom of the Third Step. No longer could the Sherpas push and pull me down the mountain—which must have been what happened during those hours—because the terrain suddenly became more demanding. Fortunately, I responded almost instinctively to the different terrain, and the response was one of fear. This was enough to trigger me into pulling myself together, for this short section at least. I had no way of judging the difficulty of the drop, as the slope plunged away very steeply beneath the rocky section. Any mistake would have horrible consequences.

The only person I was aware of was Dawa Tenzing, who stood four feet above me on the rope. With his descender in place, he was ready to rappel, but because I was beneath him, I needed to go first. The steep section called for fifteen feet of full-body-weight rappeling, which in itself was not a problem. The problem was that Dawa Tenzing was also a few feet to my left. If I threaded my descender on to the fixed rope and put my full weight on it, Dawa Tenzing would be pulled off balance. The angle of the rope above him and its slackness meant that he would tumble down on top of me, knocking me off the edge before he could arrest his uncontrolled rappel.

I explained this inevitable dynamic to him and suggested that he unclip his descender so I could use the rope without pulling him down as well. He looked at me blankly, obviously unwilling to unclip from the rope that was his only lifeline. Again I explained the dangerous outcome if I were to put my weight on the rope while he was still attached to it. Yet he refused to unclip. I suggested that I detach from the rope and let him rappel first, but he objected to this idea even more vehemently. I suggested that he take two steps to the right so that he would be directly above me and hence would not be pulled off balance when I rappeled. Again he refused. Any of these options would have made for a safe and smooth descent.

Yet Dawa Tenzing could not or would not be convinced. Alex and his team had obviously trained their Sherpas to follow a set of "standard operating procedures," not one of which dealt with our current circumstances. As a last resort, I told Dawa Tenzing that I would unclip and climb down unroped.

"You must not!" he said. "You must not!"

"Don't worry. It's only a short way, then I'll clip back on."

Again he insisted that I stay on the rope, but his unwillingness to consider the options had left me with no choice, so I unclipped my descender.

Although I told Dawa Tenzing not to worry, I was certainly scared as I lowered myself over the lip. The drop was nothing more than some angular boulders stacked on top of each other. Because the biggest boulder was uppermost and overhung the others, I was unable to see what lay below. I stretched my legs downward and felt for footholds with my feet, but I could not judge how large or solid they were. My hands felt as if they were going to peel away from the holds due to lack of strength, so I moved quickly. I found a good handhold to my right, a rock ledge for my left foot and another for my right, then I was down.

I was unaware that minutes previously Dawa Tenzing had witnessed me emerging from a delirious state. He must have been startled when I proceeded to give him immediate and lucid instructions to perform what he considered to be dangerous actions.

I called for him to descend, and he quickly rappeled down. Straightaway I clipped on to the rope. Any grave concerns he may have had about my mental state were no longer relevant, as we were both past the obstacle and safely attached to the rope. The short rocky section ahead looked ridiculously easy from below and had posed no great obstacle during the ascent. Had I turned my mind to my own welfare, I would have realized I was not seeing the world through my usual eyes.

The steep snow slope below the rock was no longer frightening. I could see the fixed rope lying on the snow at my feet and leading across to the gentler slope of the main ridge, a half-dozen strides away. But as I looked in that direction, I was stunned to see that Pemba had appeared, as if out of nowhere. He was at my level, with no oxygen mask, holding on to the fixed rope.

I removed my mask as I approached him. "Are Harry and Thomas behind you?" I asked.

"No," he said, "because Thomas is dead."

I was standing right next to him, so there was no mistaking his words. I was stunned motionless for a moment, then I hugged him and began to sob on his shoulder.

"It's okay," he said. "It's okay."

But it was not okay. Pemba spoke good English, but he did not have the words for this. He did not want me to grieve so openly. He wanted me to be strong.

From that moment I don't remember what took place. I was running low on energy at all levels, and I certainly did not have the emotional energy to deal with Thomas's death. Lethargy overcame me again, and again I had no awareness of the passage of time. And while I was mentally absent from whatever was going on, Pemba, Lakcha, Dorje, and Dawa Tenzing dragged me down the slope. From my own experience of rescuing climbers suffering from cerebral edema, I can imagine what a delirious, unaccommodating person I must have been—staggering a few steps, collapsing in the snow, muttering nonsense, refusing to cooperate.

Shortly before four o'clock, the five of us reached the top of the Second Step. Seven hours of descending had brought me only 500 vertical feet below the summit, with half of that distance gained thanks to the unceasing efforts of the Sherpas. There were other Sherpas present at the top of the step, but I remembered none of them. Perhaps they were from another expedition; perhaps they were simply unrecognizable in their down suits and oxygen masks. My harness had worked itself loose again, and Lakcha helped me tighten it. I was rigged ready to go, but I slumped onto the slope to rest.

Immediately Lakcha said, "No, you've got to go! You've got to go!" He kept saying it, so with his help I hauled myself to my knees and then to my feet. The cliff was vertical, which meant there was no room for mistakes. I checked my harness, my descender, and the rope—everything was in order. At least I could manage that much. Then I started to rappel.

The drop-off begins with a short snow slope. Almost immediately, I was going faster than expected, so I brought myself to a stop. At the lip of the cliff, where the snow slope finished, I faced the choice of climbing down the ladder or rappeling the cliff. I balanced on the top rung of the ladder, and for an indefinite time I contemplated the choices. Perhaps it was my inability to choose that jammed both the workings of my brain and my ability to relate to time. Apparently, I rappeled down the ladder, a third, more time-consuming option, but one that sidestepped the need for me to make a choice.

Later that afternoon I was woken by a voice speaking English. I had spoken very little English since passing Harry and Thomas just above the First Step at about 4:00 A.M. When I'd needed to speak since then, it had been in my broken Nepali. My mind began trying to identify this out-of-place voice.

Suddenly, I realized it was Peter Adamson. I was always ready to listen to what Peter had to say, so I forced myself to wake up more fully. I was lying on my side, wedged into a cleft in the rock and attached to a rappel rope. The rope took enough of my weight to stop me from slipping out of the flared cleft. Peter was out of sight, but his voice came from a rope that dangled down from higher up. My good mate Peter was someone who always knew what to do when in a fix. In fact, the aim of his company, Adventure West, was to show people how to find win-win answers to lose-lose situations.

Others might say that I was currently facing a lose-lose situation, but Peter was here and he always found a solution. I could not have asked for a better person to help me. None of the options looked good, but at least I now knew that I was on the side of a cliff in Australia. More precisely, I was on a volcanic pinnacle rising out of a patch of Queensland tropical rainforest, surrounded by sugarcane plantations on the coast north of Mackay. I had been here many times before with Peter, and it was very likely that Tenzing Sherpa was with him as well. I had done more rappeling and climbing with Tenzing than with any other Sherpa, our adventures split between the Himalaya and Peter's human resource development courses.

Someone was speaking in Nepali, but it was not Tenzing. Peter was calling me insistently. I was in a tough spot, but at least I was in the shade and out of the hot North Queensland sun.

"Lincoln!" called Peter. "Your mind is playing tricks with you."

My mind was groggy. I could hear him, but I did not reply.

"They are trying to help you down. Help yourself."

But still I did nothing.

"Please try to change what's happening in your mind!"

Suddenly I understood. Usually it was me shouting encouragement to the coal miners battling their fear on the volcanic cliffs of the pinnacle. For eight months in 1998, and again in 2002, Tenzing and I had worked with Peter and his small team, turning around the fortunes of a coal mine that had been suffering from the hard times that had hit the industry. Every five-day team-building course in the bush involved a different bunch of miners, and each course had culminated in a rappel descent of the fearsome pinnacle. What was different this time, I now understood, was that Peter was putting me through the course not as a facilitator but as a participant.

"Everyone is trying to help you."

The issue here is trust, I thought. Trust above fear. Peter was testing me, trying to push me to do something that I felt I shouldn't.

"All you have to do is use your rock-climbing skills to get down quickly."

"Okay then."

It didn't feel right, but I did trust Peter. And so I let myself go. I slipped out of the cleft far too quickly, my grasp of the rappel rope too loose. Suddenly I was plummeting down the rope. Instinctively, I pulled the rope into braking mode across the descender. I slowed down just as I shot over the bulge, then I came to a stop, dangling in space. Fear kicked in as I realized this was not a test I had to pass but a fight for my life. I was no longer with Adventure West, no longer in Queensland. Pemba was there, rappeling alongside me. As my rope slipped across the lip of the bulge above, I swung toward him. I thought to absorb the impact by bending my legs as we collided. His feet hit mine and the sharp points of our crampons locked together. As I disentangled my feet from his, I kicked the crampon points on one of my boots into his thigh. My shouted apology was muffled by my oxygen mask. To avoid swinging away from Pemba, I held on to him. He implored me to let go, and I could see there was a danger of our ropes twisting around us, threatening to tangle us together and leave us hanging in space like two insects suspended from a spider's web.

To avoid such a potentially fatal entanglement, I pushed away from Pemba and swung like a pendulum. My momentum carried me just far enough for me to pull myself onto a small ledge, which felt marginally safer than hanging in space. It was obvious I could not stay on the ledge for long, but I did not want to relinquish its illusion of security. Adrenaline had given me a burst of energy when I first slipped from my niche, but it was wearing off and I felt myself fading. My mind seemed to disassociate itself from all decisions, which left me simply standing there, empty.

Then I was able to see myself from somewhere else. My point of view was thirty feet away from the cliff and ten feet above the small ledge where my figure stood motionless facing the rock wall. I was hovering in midair above the huge drop of the North Face, looking at myself like a dispassionate spectator. There was no fear, no need to do anything.

Someone called my name, and suddenly my focus was on the rock one foot from my face. Fear flooded back in. Voices were urging me to swing away from the ledge and rappel down. I glanced around for a way to climb out of my predicament, but that was clearly impossible. I braced myself and leaned away from the rock to rappel. There was little strength left in my hands so I was not able to brake effectively as I slid down the rope. I landed unceremoniously in a heap on what passed for a ledge at the base of the Second Step.

Immediately, Sherpas grabbed me and started pushing and pulling me in the direction we needed to go. I recognized none of them. In my semi-delirious state I wondered why they were hurrying me so forcefully. Now that I was down the accursed Second Step I no longer felt in danger. But, of course, the danger zone for me now was the entire remainder of the mountain. I was higher than all of the summits around me. We were now well into the afternoon, yet I had descended only 600 feet during the last seven hours. We were still a thousand feet above our closest camp, and more than a half-mile away horizontally, with some tricky terrain ahead and less than three hours to nightfall.

My mind was groggy, but Pemba made me see sense. I had to grasp reality and clamber across the rock-face as quickly as I could.

"We must hurry," he urged. "Still very far. We must hurry."

He wore no oxygen mask. I could hear the worried tone in his voice, see the desperate look on his face. At midday he had watched Thomas die and had then climbed up to the Third Step to help me down. He was strung-out and with huge responsibilities.

Suddenly I shared his urgency and decided to make a radio call to Base Camp.

"This is quite an exciting spot," I began. "I'm certainly compos mentis, whereas before I was really freaky. I had this gear to go down there, go down the Second Step. I couldn't even put the bloody gear on. A couple of the guys did it for me. I was out of it then, but I'm definitely into it now.

"These guys have got a huge amount of knowledge in terms of rescuing people. If you want to find the greatest density of rescue people in the mountains, this would have to be it. So we're going pretty well. Keep you posted. You don't have to keep ringing and saying how are we 'cause there'll be times when there'll be a lot going on and there'll be times when there's nothing much going on. Cop you later."

I finished by dropping in those last three words of Aussie slang, complete with their coarse double entendre. Even when I was struggling, I could not curb my tongue.

The radio crackled back. "Lincoln, Lincoln, good to hear from you. This is Kevin at ABC. The problem is your Sherpas are becoming very, very weak and very, very tired, and you only have about three hours of workable daylight left. So please get all your strength. If you don't move, you won't get off this mountain. Come down, Lincoln."

WE FOLLOWED A SYSTEM of ledges. Whenever one ledge petered out, another could be reached by stepping down or around an obstacle. As we moved away from the Second Step, I could see the route ahead for several hundred yards, a well-trudged line of footsteps below the crest of the ridge. The route tended downhill but with little loss of altitude, and that made me worry. We needed to lose height quickly. Five people had already died this season above our top camp, which for us was still at least two hours away.

Pemba was in front of me, with Lakcha and Dawa Tenzing following behind. I was unsure of Dorje's whereabouts, but I sensed he was ahead of us. Pemba stopped constantly, turning to face me and urging me on. Whenever I paused to unclip and reclip my harness sling at a fixed rope anchor, Lakcha sped up the process by reaching from behind and doing it for me. I plodded along as best I could, taking advantage of the cliff above me, resting my right hand against it for balance. But soon exhaustion began to overwhelm my instinct to keep moving.

We came to a rise in the ledge we were following. It was a huge effort to make a few uphill steps, but then a blessing came in the form of an anchor which tied the fixed rope low to the ground. The anchor's special aspect was that it allowed me the chance to kneel while I clipped past it. I dealt with the task of clipping but continued to kneel.

"Jom! Jom!" said Lakcha. "Let's go! Let's go!"

I knew I had to keep moving, but because I was on my knees, I began to crawl. It wasn't easy, but it was easier than standing up. Lakcha grabbed me and pulled me to a sitting position so that I was now facing outward, leaning with my back against the cliff, my feet hanging over the huge drop. Lakcha tried to drag me to my feet, but—out of oxygen and on the go for sixteen hours—he no longer had the strength. I crawled to the crest of the rise in the path and lay there. Ahead I could see Pemba, who seemed to be talking with someone, maybe a Sherpa who was waiting for us, maybe Dorje.

Together, Lakcha and Dawa Tenzing pulled me to my feet. With the help of the cliff-face I stayed vertical. After one or two steps I leaned against the cliff, like a drunk leaning on a wall, and took a few more steps. Then I managed to stagger a few more yards without support. Ahead of me was a slight broadening in the trail, which was an obvious place to rest. A couple more steps and I reached out for the cliff, then slid against it down to the ground. I lay on shards of rock, free of snow. In the late afternoon sunshine, the rock looked warmer than the snow, but at these heights it was just as cold. For now, this spot was where I needed to be. I would rest for a few minutes, then I would continue down. The perfect weather created the illusion that all was well with the world and our circumstances. Dawa Tenzing and Lakcha insisted that I stand up, but I took no notice.

I shook my head and said, *"Ek chin bosneh."* Sit for one moment.

Lakcha called out to Pemba, who came back up along the ledge to where I lay.

"Other Sherpas stay with you," he said. "I must go down. You will spend the night just along from here. Very close."

I knew this was not right. It was still a beautiful sunlit afternoon. I did not want to stay here; I had only stopped to rest. Deep in myself, I knew I had to keep going until I reached somewhere safe. Many times I had descended from the summits of mountains in darkness after burning up daylight hours on prolonged climbs. In 1984 Andy, Tim, and Greg had reached the top of the North Face as the sun set. Tim and Greg stood on the summit as darkness fell, and the three of them returned to me and our camp at 27,700 feet at three thirty in the morning.

Now, on this highest ridge of Everest, I faced yet another occasion when I would have to push myself through walls of pain and exhaustion to reach the relative safety of our camp. Survival was not guaranteed; I would have to fight for it. But what I needed now was a few minutes' rest, then I would climb down and continue through the night until I reached Camp Three. But I could not convey this to Pemba. I could barely speak.

"Very close for you to spend the night," Pemba repeated, and gestured to the place where he had been standing when Lakcha had called him.

The spot was only twenty yards away, where the trail of footprints led toward the crest of the ridge. Although I could not see past that point from where I lay, I sensed there was a drop-off beyond it. The route from the Second Step had been a long traverse just below the crest of the Northeast Ridge, and we had not lost much height. The crest itself was a mass of jagged tors, cliffs, and jumbles of boulders, so the obvious route to follow was where the narrow but easy-angled slabs at the very top of the North Face met the rocky crest of the ridge. The drop-off to the north was steep but not vertical, which made it all the more frightening because you could see exactly how far you would fall—8,000 vertical feet, starting from where my boots hung over the edge. My back leaned against the low rocky rampart that formed the crest of this part of the ridge. On the far side of the rampart the Kangshung Face plunged two miles of height to the glacier below. We were at a very exposed part of the ridge. This was certainly not a safe place for me to spend the night.

"Not far," Pemba repeated, the matter decided. "You must go along just a little way and stay where there is more space."

I did not want to hear what Pemba was saying. Instead, I heard something altogether different. I was no longer capable of distinguishing between the reality of the mountain and the fabrications of my mind, so I was not surprised to hear the pronouncement in a voice I did not recognize.

"There are three women along here and they've got a shelter—you can join them."

Then Pemba spoke again. "I must go," he said. "Sherpas will be with you."

I understood that three women were camped in a little space among the rocks where Pemba wanted me to spend the night, but he was now gone. I could hear women chattering and laughing, but I couldn't be bothered visiting them. I didn't have the energy. I couldn't face the social interaction.

I sensed that other Sherpas were with me, but they could only be Lakcha and Dawa Tenzing, and maybe Dorje, whom I had not seen for a while. There could not be others as the upper reaches of the mountain were deserted. I promised I would stay where Pemba had suggested, but I don't know to whom I made the promise. I could not hear the women now. Silence surrounded me. Wind noise was muffled by the hood of my down suit. The only sound was my own breathing. And then that stopped as well.

I was alone now.

I did not think of my whereabouts at all. The thought that I had climbed Mount Everest did not enter my mind. Of most importance was what I could see. The panorama stole my attention completely. The sun was low in the sky, casting a yellow hue across the upper reaches of the Northeast Ridge. Gone was the black-and-white contrast between the snow and the rocks. The soft light gave texture to the snow and patterns to the rock surfaces around me. The dark rocky ridges of the mighty peaks stood even more proud, parading their sharp, conclusive angles. Clouds appeared high above. They framed not only the mountains, the glaciers, and the sky but also the silence, giving a depth to the landscape that I had never before experienced. There was much to be said for letting time vanish like this. I could see forever, for one thing. I could also see the curvature of the earth. A sight to die for.

Only when the sun left my high ridge was the *tick-tock* of time kick-started again by the cold. The entire landscape was freezing now, pulling the clouds down toward me, pulling the color out of the sky.

I WAS SITTING AT that same spot when a man appeared from the direction of the Second Step, a Westerner with a beard, wearing mountaineering gear. I knew that I was the only Westerner alive and close to the summit of Everest, but I did not comprehend the contradiction of his appearance out of nowhere. He stopped and looked at me but did not speak at all. I did not think this was strange either. Somehow I understood that he had come to make sure that I kept my promise, the promise to go to the place Pemba had said would be best for me. I insisted that

I had kept my promise, but the man just stood there waiting for me to provide proof.

And so I gestured for him to follow me down the narrow path, which now ran alongside a wall built from rough-cut but well-fitted stones. It was a style used for houses in rural Nepal, much like the walls that line country lanes in Britain. The top of the wall remained level, so as we went downhill, the wall became higher. I had to step up onto it to show the man that I had been here before. There were no cheerful women—no women at all—and no sign of a camp. Without speaking, I pointed at the pair of socks which I had placed there, tucked into each other to form a ball, lying on top of the wall. The whole time the man kept his silence and a close-lipped mirthless smile on his face. I picked up the socks and showed them to him, then I placed them back on the rock. This seemed to reconcile any issues between us.

At that point, I sensed that the rock wall was the side of a building and that there could be people inside. The man waited while I headed down the track, with the top of the wall above my head level. I took a ninety-degree turn to the right and continued a few steps along the wall to a doorway. It was big and squarish, but there was no door. Inside, it was dark, but the doorway shed light upon a few stone steps that led to a flagstone floor. I went down the steps. To the left, a second doorway framed a huge wood fire. There were people sitting around the fire, quietly talking and laughing. I turned on my heels and retraced my steps, as I needed to see the bearded man go. He was waiting where I had left him, the same inscrutable expression on his face. I followed him until we reached the place where I had been sitting, then he looked back up toward the Second Step. I was not capable of realizing that the only people left above me on the mountain were dead. Without a backward glance, without another footstep, the man disappeared.

Alone again, I realized how cold I was, even though I was wearing my down suit. I decided to revisit the room with the fire. Light was fading as I hurried down beside the wall. I turned the corner only to find that there was no doorway in the wall. I continued past where the doorway had been, panic rising within me. I rounded the building's next corner, which led me back uphill. There was no doorway there either. I continued up beside the wall. Boulders blocked the way, so I scrambled over them and onto the roof of the building, which was also built of flagstones, although the blocks were bigger than those used for the walls. Nowhere was there an entry or exit. I lay on the rough-hewn slabs, hoping there would be some heat transmitted through the rock from the fire inside. But everything remained as cold as ice. There was no joy to be had here.

Dusk was upon me, so I scrambled back onto the path that I had originally followed. My socks were no longer there. I returned to the spot where I had sat to watch the end of the day. There were no colors now, only whiteness swallowing the gray shapes of the mountains across the empty valley. I thought of setting up camp, but my pack was gone. In it had been my oxygen, my thermos, my two headlamps, my spare gloves, my ice axe, and my Australian flag. The whiteness came even closer. Soon the only things that were solid were the narrow ledge I sat upon and the gray tooth of rock against which I rested my back. I thought about climbing the tooth, which was only five or six feet high, but where would it take me?

I sat where I was and thought about how simple life is when there are absolutely no options. I lay down among the rock shards, with my knees brought up to my chest and my hands in my groin. I felt the need to rest, rest in peace. Darkness was not far away. Snow began to fall.

Sixteen

TIME TO KILL

FOURTEEN MILES FROM Base Camp, near the head of the East Rongbuk Glacier, Alex Abramov was up early at Advance Base Camp. He was monitoring as best he could the progress of those few of us still high on the mountain. During the night I had forgotten about the radio nestled in an internal pocket of my down suit. At first light, Lakcha, Dorje, Dawa Tenzing, and I had drawn well ahead of Harry, Thomas, Pemba, and Passang, but it had not occurred to me to make a progress report to ABC until we stood on the summit at 9:00 A.M.

A snail's pace is the norm for those lucky enough to be approaching the highest point on Earth. Although Thomas had been feeling strong, his seriously impaired vision forced him to trudge even more slowly. Suddenly, other factors came into play. The summit was in sight for Harry, Pemba, and Passang, but Thomas's already compromised vision now worsened to almost total blindness. He stopped responding to the directions given to him by Harry and Pemba, and he almost stepped over the huge drop of the Kangshung Face. Harry knew there were no second chances this close to the summit. Shortly after my call to Advance Base Camp, Harry radioed to say that he and his team had no choice but to retreat. So, 150 feet below the summit, the four of them turned for home—which in every sense was a very long way away.

By the time Harry began his call to ABC, I had tucked my radio back into the pocket of my down suit. I continued to descend without realizing that Harry and his team were not far in front of me and my Sherpa mates. I was never to see Thomas again. In fact, I came close to never seeing anyone again. Cerebral edema, one of the great evils of climbing at extreme altitude, had struck me suddenly. At ten o'clock in the morning, on the easy-angled slopes of the summit pyramid's snow triangle, I had become a casualty. Less than a hundred vertical feet below the summit, I had posed a huge problem for Lakcha, Dorje, and Dawa Tenzing.

A sea of lethargy had overwhelmed my mind's ability to think of what I should be doing. The thinnest air on the planet seemed to weigh more than rocks at the bottom of the ocean. Occasionally, I had managed to shrug the weight away long enough to experience what was happening—a dangerous mix of hallucinations amid rare moments of wide-eyed lucidity.

At Advance Base Camp, Alex moved between the radio and the telescope, anxious to know what was happening up high. Base Camp was listening in. Also at ABC, Mingma heard from Lakcha that I was having serious difficulty, and that he, Dawa Tenzing, and Dorje could only move me very slowly down the slope toward the Second Step. There were times that I would descend of my own accord, but very slowly. Most of the time I just lay in the snow, refusing to move. In desperation, they kicked me, but I did not seem to notice.

Mike, Christopher, and Richard were stunned to hear Harry on the radio stating that Thomas had died. They learned that at the bottom of the Second Step, as Pemba was swapping Thomas's almost empty oxygen bottle for a full one, Thomas announced, "Pemba, I am dying!"

He collapsed and slid down the slope, and although he was attached to the fixed rope, his weight carried him ten feet or so beyond the narrow track. Harry was unable to get Thomas upright until Scott Woolums, guide for the Project Himalaya team, came to his assistance. Thomas certainly appeared dead; his face was ashen and showed no discernible signs of life. Alex asked Harry to record the event by taking photographs of Thomas.

When Thomas was confirmed dead, Alex went into serious damage control and asked Harry to send Pemba up to help me as well. Pemba had climbed Everest six times and showed plenty of initiative. Hopefully, he would be better at convincing me to cooperate because he spoke very good English.

This was the first time that Mike and the Harrises had heard I was in trouble, and they were shocked and puzzled. They feared the worst, even though they knew I was with three strong and competent Sherpas. Mike, Richard, and Christopher spent the rest of the day in the communications tent, a small space, waiting for developments. Others dropped by from time to time, particularly Slate and Noel.

PEMBA HAD CLIMBED TO within 150 feet of the summit, and now he had been asked to return to that height. Thomas's oxygen mask had malfunctioned not far below their turnaround point, so Pemba had given Thomas his own mask. Now that Thomas was dead, Pemba did not want to reclaim his mask. It was still warm, and Thomas had been his friend.

Pemba had little difficulty surmounting the Second Step for the second time that day. By the time he reached me, I was near the bottom of the Third Step. To Dawa Tenzing's horror, I had unclipped from the rope and climbed solo down the final section. Although I had run out of oxygen, it was a rare moment of lucidity for me, not the crazy act that it seemed. But there were plenty of crazy times to come.

I clipped on to the rope again, and the next minute I was lying in the snow, talking to myself, saying, "There are three black girls up there; I want to go up!"

Then I wanted to jump off the top of the Kangshung Face. Pemba stopped me from making the leap and noticed that I had pushed my oxygen mask away from my face. The 7Summits-Club expedition had a stash of oxygen near the Third Step, so my bottle was replaced with a full bottle turned up to a high flow-rate. I needed the oxygen, but it did not make me more cooperative. I kept pushing the oxygen mask aside.

"Please, Lincoln," urged Pemba. "Take this mask."

So I decided to wear the mask for a while. Once again I seemed to want to jump off the Kangshung Face, perhaps because in my dreams I was always flying. The Sherpas slowly dragged me down the mountain, hindered by the fact that I kept wanting to go back up.

Pemba radioed Mingma Gelu at Advance Base Camp, and his message was translated to Luda, who radioed Richard Harris at Base Camp.

"Richard, this is Luda. Do you copy? Over."

"Go ahead, Luda."

"Richard, do you know the condition of Lincoln? So, now he's a bit crazy because he is holding on to the rope. All three Sherpas are trying to drag him down, but he's very stubborn. He's fixed to the rope, and he's afraid that the rope will end and he'll fall down."

"Can you get the Sherpa to put the radio to his ear so that we can talk to him, please?"

"Okay, you want Sherpa to give radio to him and you want to speak to him."

But I would not listen. Finally, the Sherpas tied three safety ropes to me while I bucked like a stubborn yak. Exhausted by the struggle, I lay in the snow, which made me much easier to manage, although at 26,000 feet it was very hard work for them. The four Sherpas pushed and pulled me down as if I was a sled. My harness had worked loose again, so during a rest I took it off. It was an awkward task, but they managed to put it back on. Near the Second Step I thought I was at the North Col, which was actually a vertical mile below.

"Where is my soup?" I asked. "Where is my tea?" When the Sherpas tightened my harness at the top of the Second Step, my condition seemed to improve and I appeared to remember that this place had significance.

Pemba put his radio in front of my face and pressed the talk button. For the first time since we had left Camp Three, my voice was heard at Base Camp.

"I'm doing the lethargy for about four people," I slurred. "I don't know if you remember what it was like, but, boy, was it hard to move. And, in fact, I just opened my first eyeball."

The volume lessened as I turned away and asked, "Where are we?"

"At the Second Step," said Lakcha.

"We're still at the Second Step," I relayed. "It's bloody tough up there. Climbing the step was not so hard, but there were some issues. Then I just collapsed, the whole bloody thing. But an amazing place."

I mumbled that my camera wasn't working properly, then coughed.

Mike took the microphone. "Lincoln! Just keep going on. You've got four Sherpas there who respect you a lot, and they're doing everything they can. . . . Do you want to talk to me some more? Over."

I was struck by a sudden coughing fit.

"Do you copy?"

After one more cough, I said, "Did you ask, 'Did you copy?' or 'Did you cough?'"

There was a pause as if they could not believe my question, followed by relieved chuckles. My sense of humor did not seem to be in as bad shape as the rest of me.

"I'll be fine," I continued. "Thanks for the well wishes—to everybody. I guess the ones at home . . ." I was puffing hard and had to start again. "I guess they're the ones who are being tortured, but the ones here know what that torture is really like. I don't know what time it is, but I'll talk to you when I can. Okay. Thanks. Bye."

Mike began to speak desperately, "Okay, Lincoln, we're doing all we can and we're standing by. If you ever want to talk to us again, just get the radio to your ear. Just think of your family, and it's the last hard bit, but there's plenty of support there."

There was no reply from me.

Then I heard another voice. "Lincoln, this is Kevin at ABC."

Yes, it was his voice.

"You get yourself down. Get yourself down now, my friend, because we all miss you, and we all want you down safely. So get here now, Lincoln."

Alex's voice was unmistakable, even though it was only two words repeated, "Go down! Go down!"

I still stood at the top of the Second Step, but again I was overcome with lethargy, partly because I was continuing to refuse the oxygen. Maybe there was a message coming from deep in my psyche that true climbing of mountains is achieved without oxygen. If that was the case, then there could not have been a worse message for my brain to be serving up.

Pemba rappeled down the first section of the step, then, with the help of Lakcha, I rappeled over the lip—very slowly—until, at the top of the lower section, I found a cleft into which I could squeeze myself. It was not secure, but it was good enough for me to sleep in. The Sherpas could not move me.

At Base Camp, Mike and Richard kept calling me on the radio, but it remained switched off in my pocket. Acting on a demand of Mike's, Mingma Gelu radioed Pemba with a request to hand me his own radio.

"Mike wants to talk to you," said Pemba. "Please talk to him."

He held the radio to my face, and almost instantly it spoke to me.

"Lincoln," said Mike's voice. "Your mind is playing tricks with you, and you are trying to fight the Sherpas. They're trying to help you down. Help them, help yourself—for your family's sake and our sakes. . . .

"Please try to change what's happening in your mind to become more clear. Everyone is trying to help you. . . . There's lots of oxygen. All you have to do is use your rock-climbing skills and the help of the Sherpas to get down quickly."

I did not really grasp his meaning, but I knew that I had to move. I let myself slide down the rope, but it was too fast. Fear kicked in. I had not been feeling fear, but now it was overwhelming me. I slammed into Pemba, who instantly rappeled to the narrow ledge below. Then I found myself at that ledge as well, the fear dragging me back into the real world.

Pemba sensed this and handed me the radio.

"This is quite an exciting spot," I began. "I'm certainly compos mentis, whereas before I was really freaky. I had this gear to go down there, go down the Second Step. I couldn't even put the bloody gear on. A couple of other guys did it for me. I was out of it then, but I'm definitely into it now.

"These guys have got a huge amount of knowledge in terms of rescuing people. Like, if you want to find the greatest density of rescue people in the mountains, this would have to be it. So we're going pretty well. Keep you posted. You don't have to keep ringing and saying how are we 'cause there'll be times when there'll be a lot going on and there'll be times when there's nothing much going on. Cop you later."

The Sherpas began hustling along the narrow ledge, and with their help I somehow passed the sections of blank rock.

The radio was blasting, "Lincoln, Lincoln, good to hear from you. This is Kevin at ABC. The problem is your Sherpas are becoming very, very weak and very, very tired, and you only have about three hours of workable daylight left. So please get all your strength. If you don't move, you won't get off this mountain. Come down, Lincoln."

Then there was a different voice.

"Okay, Lincoln, come on. It's Richard." His voice was hoarse and full of urgency. "They're all waiting here for you—Dorje and Dylan and Barbara. They're all worried about you. So you just give it your best and keep coming down so you can talk to them, mate."

The Sherpas did not give me a moment to rest. I staggered some of the way along the rough trail, but my body was too heavy and my eyelids felt like lead. At the times where I could not stand, I was dragged and carried. We reached Mushroom Rock, where I was allowed to rest, and that was all I wanted to do.

Beyond Mushroom Rock the route became more difficult. It was terrain down which I could not be pushed, pulled, or carried. Only beyond the First Step would the route again be manageable for me and my rescuers in my current condition. The Sherpas had no choice but to leave me there. The only decision was who would stay with me.

Pemba had to go down, as he was partly snow-blind and his leg was injured by the accidental kick from my cramponed boot. Dorje was totally exhausted and headed down with my small digital camera, which would hold some kind of record of what had gone before. When Pemba came to leave me, he thought I was dying—a sight he had already witnessed once that day. I was looking in the direction of Mount Everest; my eyes were open but vacant.

Lakcha and Dawa Tenzing stayed with me, trying to rouse me, but they were exhausted by the effort of bringing me down from 28,800 feet to 28,000. They had no oxygen, no food, and no drink. My breathing had dropped to four or five breaths per minute. I did not respond when I was poked in the eye.

Dawa Tenzing made a call to Advance Base Camp. "Alex, you must tell us what to do. Otherwise we will die."

It was a very hard decision for Alex. At Base Camp the team was desperate for an answer as well. The consensus was that I would not want Sherpas to die because of what happened to me.

"It's very difficult for me, but Lincoln doesn't move. If Sherpas don't move, they will also die near Lincoln now."

Russell Brice arrived at Base Camp with a weather report. "By seven o'clock tonight you should have wind speeds of fifteen miles per hour. . . ."

Alex's voice came through to Lakcha's radio and to everyone at Base Camp.

"Okay, okay," he began. "Now I will say: Sherpas will leave Lincoln. First cover him with stones, and then go down."

There was silence at this now expected announcement.

"You've got a long night ahead, guys," said Russell. "I don't think I can do much."

"Thanks, Russell," said Richard.

But then Mike thought of practicalities.

"Russell, we need to get your advice about what happens if the worst happens to Lincoln. What we need to do, officially."

"Yeah, I can help you with that," said Russell. "I've done it, four times during this expedition for other people, so I'll help you with that, no problem. It's just a letter—you write it and get the Sherpas to sign it, saying that's where they saw him last. Then you need his passport and some photos, and take it to the TMA."

We had seen the Tibetan Mountaineering Association when we arrived at Base Camp. It was a building where the road stopped, on the same hillock as the Mallory and Irvine memorials, only set farther back.

"I'll help you there, no worries," continued Russell. "I know the guys there, and they know me. But Alex must have done it already for Igor. I helped Alex, and I'm sure Alex won't mind me helping you."

BACK IN AUSTRALIA, only moments after she finished talking to Iain and Trish, Barbara remembered the call-waiting tone she had heard. When she checked the voicemail, there was a message from Cheryl Harris, asking Barbara to call her, please. The message had been left at 7:30 P.M. Sydney time. She returned the call with her heart beating fast, having sensed that something was wrong. Cheryl told Barbara the latest news—I was still very close to the summit and in difficulty. Cheryl added that radio contact had confirmed I had three Sherpas accompanying me.

Barbara told the boys but reminded them that there was not necessarily anything to worry about. She then rang Julia again to let her know that I was not in as good shape as it had seemed. She left a similar message for Greg Mortimer and Margaret Werner. Half an hour after

Barbara's conversation with Cheryl, the phone rang again, but this time it was Mike, saying that radio contact had been made again and he had heard me speak lucidly. It seemed I had overcome my problems, as I was moving faster. Everyone at Base Camp felt encouraged.

Circumstances can change very quickly in the mountains, as Barbara knew all too well. My fortunes could turn to the good or to the bad. As the minutes ticked past, her anxiety grew. At Wentworth Falls it was a cold night at the beginning of winter, so she sat near the fire. Meditation seemed the best way to deal with her worries. Soon warmed by the fire, she silently led her mind into meditation, where the focus was on the present moment. Suddenly she was startled by a kind of vision—she saw a blinding white light, and within that bright space I was putting my arms around her. The vision became frightening when she could physically feel me embracing her. She was shocked out of her meditation. Perhaps this was really happening—perhaps this was my death.

Shaken by the experience, Barbara realized that she would simply have to wait to see what unfolded. She was in the middle of Salman Rushdie's *The Ground Beneath Her Feet,* so she picked the book up and began to read. One of the main protagonists had the ability to experience a parallel universe, but Barbara found herself reading about death and loss, so she had to put the book down. Soon after that, at around 9:45 P.M., the phone rang.

"Oh, Barbara . . ." Mike began, but then he faltered.

No, she thought. No. I can't listen to this.

But Mike continued. "Barbara, I don't know what to say; I've got terrible news."

"Mike, you don't need to tell me."

"I'm so sorry," he said, his voice very distressed, "but Lincoln passed away about twenty minutes ago. From what we know, he would have passed into a coma and died peacefully."

Then there was silence. And Barbara said, "Thank you, Mike, for letting me know."

She just wanted to get off the phone.

"Is there anyone I can ring?" he asked. "Anything at all I can do for you?"

"No, not at the moment. I think I'll just go."

That was the end of their very brief conversation.

Barbara sat down on the couch for a moment—our red, green, purple, and pale blue leather couch was a demonstration model which had showcased the different colors that could be ordered. It was a one-off that I had bought from friends ten years earlier, for Barbara's birthday. I had it hidden in the shed until the dead of night, when I carried it single-handedly inside to surprise her in the morning. Everything around her now would hold memories. She called Dylan and Dorje, and when they sat beside her, she told them that I had passed away. Our now three-person family sat there on the couch, holding hands, stunned into silence.

Dylan asked if he could tell Ped, his friend of a dozen years, and his girlfriend Tanya. Barbara nodded, so Dylan headed to his room with his mobile. Dorje went to his room—ashen-faced.

Barbara rang Julia and could do nothing but blurt it out: "Lincoln is dead!"

Julia gasped. "I'm so, so sorry," she said, her voice breaking up as she spoke, my father listening in the background. "I'll come straight up in the morning."

Barbara had left a message for Greg and Margaret and was waiting to hear from them. Already she had had enough of talking to people, so she preempted the call by ringing them again. Greg answered the phone, so she told him upfront: "Lincoln has just died."

"No, no, no, no," he kept repeating. As he did so, Barbara could hear Margaret starting to cry in the background. Greg could not believe it and asked Barbara how she knew. When she told him the news was directly from Mike, the shock was beyond terrible. They said that they would come up in the morning.

Even though she felt she should ring Trish and Iain, Barbara could not handle any more phone calls. How could she tell people something that she couldn't believe herself?

I had explained to Barbara many times how easy it is to die this kind of death. Whether from hypothermia or cerebral edema, it is pitifully, inevitably easy for mountaineers to drift off into unconsciousness, never to wake up. She thought this was what was happening to me—that I was not yet dead but was completely powerless to do anything to save myself.

She thought that soon I would be dead and that there was absolutely no way she could prevent it.

She walked down the hall to check on the boys. Dylan had rung Tanya and was lying facedown on his bed, his mobile to his ear, sobbing. Dorje was lying on his bed, facing the wall, quietly racked by emotions he never knew existed.

Barbara went to bed. She usually turned off her electric blanket before she went to sleep, but tonight she felt so cold she left it switched on. She tossed and turned all night, not really sleeping, worrying things through. What she had to do, who she should tell, what needed to be done, in a practical sense, the next morning—all of these thoughts surfaced between fitful bouts of sleep. Despite the electric blanket, she remained cold for the entire night—just as I did, high on the mountain, on the other side of the world.

BY DAYBREAK Barbara was sleeping soundly, but she was woken up by a dream which gave her a strong feeling that I was alive. I was walking toward her slowly, wearing an ancient fleece jacket that I had worn on my first trip to Antarctica, and smiling at her as I approached. The moment of joy as she woke from the dream was instantly replaced by a moment of despair, which faded to deep sadness, because Barbara would not allow herself to feel despair. She got up, made a cup of coffee, and forced herself to have a piece of toast. She knew she needed some kind of sustenance to give her strength for the day.

One of the plans she had made during the night was to send two e-mails. She sat at her computer watching the screen come up. The first e-mail was to Jenny Reeves at SCEGGS, telling her how I had died, and that she would not be in to work next week. The second was to Blue Mountains Grammar School, informing the principal that Dylan and Dorje would not be at school. These were the first small steps toward dealing with what had happened.

Dorje got up soon afterward, and Barbara told him how she had been woken up by a dream.

"I dreamed Dad is alive," she said. "And I've got this sort of hope that it's all a mistake."

At 8:30 A.M. she rang Marion Walker, Dorje's violin teacher, because that day he was to have had a music exam in Penrith, the city on the plain at the base of the Blue Mountains. Marion assured her that arrangements could be made for another time.

Barbara tried to encourage Dorje to eat something, but suddenly our two dogs were barking at the gate. Barbara expected it was Julia, but in fact it was our friends Ken Beatty and his wife, Alison Lockwood, who had dropped their two boys at school after hearing the news from Marion, Alison's close friend. Barbara met them at the gate, and as she spoke, she became aware of how hollow she felt when she said anything about what had happened to me.

They gave her big hugs, and Ken shoved a scrap of paper at her and said, "This is my mobile number—if there's absolutely anything at all we can do, please ring."

It was an awkward moment, an unsatisfactory parting, but everything about the encounter was unsatisfactory, except for the love. Barbara shut the gate behind them, the feeling of hollowness and emptiness only increasing. Alison and Ken's arrival showed how quickly the news was spreading through the Blue Mountains community.

Despite her dream, Barbara was beginning to accept that I was dead. If I had been left for dead the night before, there was very little chance that I would be alive after twelve more hours had passed.

Barbara had been dreading ringing Trish and Iain after having given them the good news the evening before. Iain answered the phone, but his voice was unrecognizable, as though someone was strangling him. Only a few minutes earlier he and Trish had heard about my death from Jan Cristaudo, who had been told by Margie Hamilton, manager of the Australian Himalayan Foundation. Barbara could hear Trish sobbing uncontrollably in the background. They were obviously too upset to talk, so they agreed to speak again later.

Margaret and Greg arrived, and Julia soon after. It was good to have them there, partly because they knew Barbara and me better than anyone else but also because they provided distractions.

Greg did not believe it either, that I was dead—Barbara could see that in him. But the facts were too real to be denied. Greg certainly understood that a night in the open at 28,000 feet without oxygen was a death sentence, especially as I had been declared dead before the onset of night.

Margaret sat on the exposed sandstone slab outside the front entrance with Dorje, talking with him quietly. She had been at the births of both Dorje and Dylan and had witnessed the most significant milestones in their lives, but this was a milestone that she felt no young son should have to endure.

Dylan had been in the shower, but when he came outside, he and Margaret immediately hugged each other.

"I'm a chip off the old block," he said, his voice trembling with emotion. "I'm the man of the house now." He hugged Margaret again, then repeated his declarations.

Inside, in the living room, Julia and Barbara hugged and cried. Both women were strong in a crisis, but with this one, only Julia could talk about what needed to be done. She asked Barbara to find our life insurance papers so that she could lodge a claim. Soon Julia was sitting by the phone talking to the insurers, finding out what kind of proof of death was necessary and dealing with other practical issues.

Late in the morning, Peter Horton-James, Joey Clarke, Camilla Rickards, and Clinton Boys arrived in school uniform, having just attended a memorial service held for me at Blue Mountains Grammar School. The four friends sat on the lookout rock on our western boundary. Dorje's friend Cameron Boys arrived later.

Roley Clarke rolled up, as did Ben Maddison. Roley could stay only a short time, but Ben stayed longer. Neither had much to say. Barbara sat inside for a while by the fire with Ben.

Julia spent most of the day dealing with the many phone calls, relaying messages from friends and family, making herself Barbara's buffer against contact with the outside world. No one could know what Barbara and the boys were going through. As the day opened up, Barbara's hollow, empty feeling grew stronger and stronger.

THE PREVIOUS DAY Greg had been alerted by longtime climbing mate Zac Zaharias that I was in trouble on the mountain—the product of some kind of rumor mill. Greg and I had been declared dead together in the past, so he would need solid evidence before he took any notice of the claims. Barbara's call during the night brought evidence enough.

That night Greg had rung other members of the 1984 expedition—Howard Whelan and Colin Monteath, who had worked with Mike Dillon filming our climb, and Geof Bartram, who was hit by cerebral edema at 24,000 feet but had been strong and bold enough to descend alone. By the time Greg came to ring Andy, it had been late at night, so he'd left the call until the morning.

The other person whom Greg had rung early on May 26 was Simon Balderstone, who lived less than a mile away. Simon had received the awful news from Mike at Base Camp at 10:20 P.M. the previous day, Sydney time. Mike had been in tears, having just spoken to Barbara. Greg and Margaret had hardly slept at all that night; nor had Simon. Greg's early morning call to Simon was to determine strategy; they decided that Greg and Margaret would drive up to our Blue Mountains home, while Simon stayed at Manly to handle the media. He was well aware of how ruthless the press could be when there was a story involving dramatic death and a grieving family.

And while Simon's main focus was on protecting Barbara from the media, he was also trying to find out the source of the rumors that were beginning to emerge suggesting that I might still be alive.

The press believed that we lived at Blackheath in the Blue Mountains, so that was where they headed, arriving four years too late. Their next move was to besiege Glen Nash, who ran the Katoomba-based Australian School of Mountaineering. With a name like that, they assumed Glen must know about me. Sure enough, for a year or two I had worked as a rock-climbing instructor for ASM, but that was many years ago. Glen could tell them very little about my misadventures, but as he had climbed Everest's subpeak Changtse, he could give them accurate background information. He also knew who would know, and soon he was out of the hot seat.

ON THE MORNING OF May 26, Glen Joseph was sitting at his desk at Spinifex Interactive when Martyn Pot came down to speak to him.

"Glen, I need to show you something."

"Can't it wait? I have to make a phone call."

Martyn knew that Glen's life consisted of phone calls.

Glen ran the company, and most of his work was tying up deals, then finding the creative knowhow to make the projects work.

"No," said Martyn. "I really think you should see it now."

With those words, he reached across to Glen's computer and began typing a Web address. Martyn had been receiving Richard Harris's e-mails from Base Camp, and he uploaded the news to the Christopher's Climb website. In the process Martyn had discovered other Everest websites, and it was one of these that he was showing Glen. The page he opened stated that I had been left for dead after failing to climb down from the summit of Mount Everest.

Glen was shattered. He and I had talked through a program of walks we would do in different parts of Australia over the coming year. Much of the time his company ran on autopilot, so Glen was able to get away, and when we completed each walk, I would write it up for *Outdoor Australia*. It was a set of adventures that both of us had been looking forward to very much.

Glen sat at his desk for half an hour, saying and doing nothing. Then he rang Annabel, his wife, who was out and about, with the news that he was going home, despite the fact it was only nine thirty in the morning.

Back at his rambling house at Coogee, Glen returned to the Internet. He was amazed at how full it was with Everest stories. Every time he refreshed a page, more people would be adding to forums. David Sharp's tragic death remained a hot topic, and now I was a subject for speculation and ill-informed judgment. Glen had seen enough. It was then that he remembered the piece of paper I had given him at the finish of our Royal National Park walk on March 31, a week before I flew to Kathmandu. On that piece of paper I had typed my wish list of the six walks we would do. We had both decided we needed to spend more time together, and my list was my commitment to the program. Suddenly, Glen realized that the well-folded piece of paper was the only memento he had of our times together, and he had thrown it out of his wallet the day before.

Friday morning was garbage collection time, so Glen quickly called Michael Clay at the office and asked him to retrieve the paper from the bin under Glen's desk.

Clay rang back. "Sorry, Glen," he said. "Your bin's empty."

"Must be in the skip. Clay, please, could you . . . ?"

"You want me to look in the skip!"

"Please. It's important."

So the luckless Clay went through the big metal bin out on the street, thinking he was looking for a needle in a haystack.

Ten minutes later he leaped out of the skip, rang Glen, and triumphantly announced, "Lincoln's memory is alive but with a few extra food stains!" Glen vowed to complete the walks in my memory.

SOUTH OF OUR HOME, the wilderness extends as far as the eye can see. It is a very different kind of wilderness from that of the Himalaya but with the same uplifting quality. Usually we welcome the solitude, but that morning Barbara had been pleased to have our closest friends gathered around, their presence making her feel less empty. But now, later in the day, she was able to be alone. With just our two big dogs for company, she followed the track toward the lookout. As soon as she was far enough away from the house, she began to talk to me.

"I don't know whether you can hear me, Lincoln," she began, "but this wasn't how it was meant to be. We were going to grow old together, and we've got so much to live for, and so much to do here, and I just don't know if I can do it on my own."

She was voicing some of the thoughts that had been troubling her during the night. Would she be able to keep our wonderful thirty-seven acres? Could she make the effort to do so in my memory? Or should she give up and move on? "I had hoped that eventually, when we were old enough to die, that I would go first so that I wouldn't have to deal with the loss of you."

She had to tell me these things, even though her rational mind was telling her it was too late.

Seventeen

CLOAK OF DARKNESS

THE WHITENESS was so pervasive that I could not determine the time of day. It must be morning, I decided, because I had no memories of what had come before. Often I awake from a night's sleep disoriented after dreaming of being somewhere else. This time I was definitely somewhere else, but I did not know where. All I could tell was that my world consisted of mountains. Fresh snow covered the ground. Five hundred feet below my ridge-top vantage point the valley leveled out, indicating to me that I was a long way from the deep valleys and high peaks of the Himalaya. White mist limited my view to a few hundred yards, but what I could see fitted the characteristics of an exposed ridge in the Snowy Mountains of southeastern Australia, gentle ranges that are the domain of hikers and cross-country skiers, not mountaineers.

It did not occur to me that what I perceived as the valley floor might in fact be a layer of clouds sitting more than a mile above the Kangshung Glacier and stretching from Everest's Northeast Ridge all the way across to Makalu. Instead, I had firmly placed myself in the Snowy Mountains, where I felt with some degree of confidence that everything would work out fine for me. On the rolling hills around Mount Kosciuszko, I had taught myself to ski, and on the nearby slopes above Blue Lake, I had learned to climb the short, steep ice gullies between cliffs that offer good summer-time rock climbing.

As soon as I thought about hikers and skiers, I became aware that other people were nearby. The precipice immediately in front of me was frighteningly steep, impossible for me to descend, but I could see people as dark shapes against the snow where the angle eased. Rows of rock walls lay across the slope. Some of these I interpreted as being the backs of low stone cottages—otherwise, where could the people that I saw take shelter? I could see them in groups, busy with small tasks and chatting to each other, but I could not hear a word. Although the nearest group was a hundred yards away, sometimes the face of a figure would come into focus. As soon as I attempted to put a name to the face, it dissolved into formless anonymity.

There was no shelter and nowhere to sit, so I brushed a small rock clean of its snow. I sat there, hunched up to stay warm, and watched the people below me. One of the faces, small and distant, recurred enough times for me to recognize it as belonging to Michael Dillon. Mike and I had spent a lot of time together as we traveled toward the mountain, sharing hotel rooms in Bangkok and Kathmandu and a string of lodges and dormitories across Tibet. At Base Camp, Mike's tent was immediately in front of mine. All of these points of intersection may have helped me see his face. I took heart from his alert eyes and broad smile. If I could locate Mike, I would be able to escape from the cold as well as the silence and the solitude. Mike would be able to show me around because it was his habit to get up early, head out with his camera, then appear at breakfast and tell me where he had been. He would know the lay of the land.

I watched the figures moving, a few of them walking by with some kind of purpose. I sensed that my sister Julia was here as well. I could not glimpse her face—she was farther away than that—but I had to find her and tell her that by tomorrow morning she must locate a hut where we could have a fire. Then I would go down to her and bring Mike with me, and the warmth of the fire would be so much better than sitting on rocks in the snow.

I decided to look around for firewood. There are trees in the Snowy Mountains—stunted, twisted snow gums with multiple trunks shading summer flowers—but I could not see a single one. I thought that the heavy snowfalls of the winter must have buried them in deep drifts. My ridge-top must have been above the treeline, but I kicked at shapes in the snow anyway, hoping to reveal some firewood in the form of fallen branches. All I found were more rocks. I sat down again and let myself doze off to sleep.

When I awoke, it was early the next morning. At least, I assumed it was morning because I found myself in the same place surrounded by the same eerie whiteness. Again I looked for somewhere different to sit, but nothing about the scene had changed, except that now I could see no people. But I sensed that Mike and Julia were still nearby. I sat on my cold rock and thought about Julia. I needed her presence because she is an organizer. She is a lawyer at work and a troubleshooter at home, juggling life with her partner and three sons under twelve. Our dad lives nearby. Our mother died of cancer a half dozen years ago, and now Julia holds us all together, always remembering birthdays and arranging family holidays—usually somewhere along the coast south of Sydney to make it more convenient for Michele, our elder sister, who lives even farther south. The cold reminded me that I had been unable to gather firewood. My failure in that respect led me to accept that I would not find Julia.

Time must have passed, but I did not sense its passage. The white other-worldliness had gone. The reality of my situation began to manifest as I felt the familiarity of darkness surrounding me, the first darkness I had experienced for what seemed like days. There were no stone cottages, no Julia, no Mike, no firewood, no hope of fire. I was alone. I could sense that people had been with me, but they had left on their own important journeys. I found myself in a small shelter sitting cross-legged on grass that had been laid on the dirt floor. It was the most basic of structures, a low hut with shaped timber uprights and a hastily thatched roof. Even though I was sitting down, there was very little headroom. Behind me was a wall of rough-hewn planks, but the sides were open so the occupant could keep watch in all directions. I was aware of these features despite the darkness. I took the shelter to be a goat-herder's shack in Nepal, and that made sense because I knew that the last words spoken to me had been in Nepali. It seemed that I was making some kind of progress because now I had a crude shelter and grass to sit upon, and yet I had no sense of where I was progressing from or to. I seemed to be endlessly watching and waiting.

I was aware of an expanse. There was only the slightest breeze, but the air was so cold that it chilled me. I could see many lights in different directions, just pinpricks indicating distant houses and settlements. Everything else was pitch-black. There must be a track or a road, I thought, that led to each of those houses. The tiny lights were welcoming but only for those who knew where they were going. When dawn came, I would hunt down the path to the nearest house. With that comforting plan in mind, I let myself drift back to sleep.

Suddenly—after I don't know how many hours—I awoke with a feeling of great fear. In one sense, nothing was different; I was still sitting cross-legged on a ridge-top high in the sky. Disoriented, I stretched out a gloved hand. I felt nothing. I removed the thick insulated gauntlet, and with my bare hand I scooped up a granular substance. It flowed through my fingers, but there were no tactile messages for my mind to decode. Then I realized that my fingers were frozen and that what I was handling was snow. I tried to feel my toes, but they were completely numb. Frostbite had struck, and the full force of the truth struck me at that moment: I was exhausted, frostbitten, and alone on the summit ridge of Everest. I had begun the decline, which would finish with me freezing to death.

The pinpricks of light that I had coveted were not distant houses welcoming me. They were the stars in the sky, and the only welcome they could offer me would be to heaven. Physically I was already there, surrounded by the cosmos, the highest person on the planet, and set to be the next Everest statistic. This was not how it was meant to end. This was definitely not how it was meant to end.

The horror of this realization snapped me into complete lucidity. I knew I had to escape from this awful predicament. My body was not in the best of shape, nor was my mind, but that was of no consequence. The vital point was that I take action, however bad my condition might be. I had to return alive to Barbara and the boys. This mattered to me more than anything else, more than my own death. If I let myself die, I would not notice my own passing, but the foursome of our family was too joyous and complete to be allowed to disintegrate into pain, despair, and endless thoughts of what might have been. I knew that death would be so easy for me now. All I would have to do was close my eyes and let myself slip away from the cold and the loneliness, as too many others had done these last weeks on this same deadly ridge. But for me, at that moment, death was not an option.

I was not in denial by repudiating death; I was not attempting to conjure up some outrageous idea of survival in the hope that it might happen. Hope had nothing to do with it. The odds were stacked against me, and the body count was proof. My only chance in such desperate straits was total belief. I had to live these next hours, next days—however long it took—with the certainty that I would survive.

In Sydney in April 2006, as I prepared to leave for Everest, I had renewed out loud to Barbara and the boys my commitment to coming home. I had repeated it silently to myself weeks later when I stood beneath Everest, wondering what it would demand of me.

And now I knew. Everest wanted everything I had, every last scrap of commitment, of determination, of belief. The focus of my life from this point onward was to be with Barbara, Dylan, and Dorje again. Some might say I was deluded, shrugging away the guilt of shattering our family while fooling myself I could do the impossible. But I had learned many years back that the impossible was not always so. I had been on other mountains when events went so horribly wrong that the question was not whether I would die but when. Each of those times, despite the odds, I came through alive. There may have been some luck involved, but luck is of no use unless you have a never-give-up attitude.

The only way for me to survive the remainder of the night was to maintain two things—my core temperature and my wakefulness. I needed strategies for each. My pack would provide valuable insulation from the snow, and inside it were my down mitts. In its top pocket were heat pads, which could provide up to twelve hours of warmth, produced by chemical reactions. In the darkness I felt for my pack, but it was nowhere to be found. My oxygen set would have helped my frostbite and my mind, but it was long gone as well. There was no sign of a mask or a regulator or a cylinder. The pack and the oxygen may have been a few feet away, but I did not know where the edge of the precipice was. The darkness was total.

My only option now was to conserve the heat my body produced. I continued to sit cross-legged, my arms folded across my chest, my hands crossed not far below my neck, my head tilted forward. This position was the best for keeping my vital organs warm. I wriggled my numb fingers constantly. I could tell they were moving, but the tips felt wooden, totally without sensation.

On other unplanned bivouacs, when it had been either impossible or unwise to sleep, I had spent the night singing. But here I had no breath to spare, and my mind was empty of songs. I felt that even humming would eat up some of the energy I needed to conserve. Deprived of oxygen, my mind had already played tricks with me and was likely to do so again.

Staying awake would be my biggest challenge. I would have to focus on something concrete, and the obvious choice was my body. I maintained my cross-legged position and swayed rhythmically from side to side. The movement kept my blood pumping through me. Soon I found that the variation of rotating my upper body felt better, clockwise then counterclockwise. With my shoulders, I traced small erratic circles, as though stirring my upper body with my spine. There was no need for precision behind the actions—they were just something for my mind to hold on to. I repeated the sequence again and again.

During years of serious meditation, I had experienced different levels of consciousness, but here on the mountaintop I did not want to go any deeper. I did not even want to think about where those other levels might take me. Instead, I clung to the grossest form of mind control, the only one I could manage in my weakened, oxygen-starved state. I set my mind to watch, feel, and steer my movements, and as time ticked by, they became as familiar as well-practiced tennis swings—backhand, forehand, backhand again.

In happier times, less close to death, when meditating I liked to focus my attention on my breath. As the minutes pass and I am drawn deeper into a meditative state, my attention rests longer on the spaces between inhalation and exhalation—that is where the perfect stillness lies. But up here on the mountain I was not looking for stillness. The process of breathing is an automatic one, which happens whether you observe it or not. The danger of attempting a breathing meditation in my current state was that my mind could easily be aware of my breath and yet not focus upon it. Before I could stop it, my mind might drift off, bouncing from meaningless thought to meaningless thought, keeping my breath in the background, forgetting the need for watchfulness, forgetting that my battle was to stay alive.

Even with my easier routine of observing my movements, my mind still managed to steal away, grabbing onto random thoughts. How long it would be until sunrise. What an inconceivable distance I had put between myself and my family. I dragged my mind back to the rotations, to the counterclockwise sweep of the forehand, the clockwise grace of the backhand. They were only small circles, really, but I gave them grander names. The process was simple, with nothing except the reversal of direction to separate one rotation from the next. Soon this became inconsequential as well, leaving me with no need to remember anything at all.

And so I have no clear memory of facing death and then rejecting it. But I did have an experience to which no name can be given.

Toward the end of that night, I found myself on a hill, which I somehow knew to be in Poland, although I have never visited that country. It was dark and I was sitting on a grassy knoll, still waiting and watching. Despite the darkness, I knew I was looking out over treeless rolling hills, all of which lay below me. I was wearing a cloak made of the finest wool; it was thick and warm and all-encompassing. The drape of the cloak made it exceptionally comfortable, although it was not designed for sleeping in, and I had difficulty finding the best place to tuck my hands.

The night sky began to weaken and fade, so I knew that dawn was coming. I looked around for Barbara. I had not seen her, but I knew she and I had been traveling together somewhere in the recent past. Light came quickly, but Barbara was still nowhere to be seen. The cloak was heavy enough for me to be undisturbed by the wind that had picked up as darkness turned to dawn. Although it had invested me with a sense of completeness, the cloak was not mine to keep. I knew I had to return it. I knew without turning my head that it belonged in the building behind me. With the coming of light, I could now see that the cloak was a gray color, and its unusual cut made me think it was ceremonial. As I slipped out of it, I noticed that the hood formed an integral part.

With the cloak in my arms, I turned around and began to walk. There was a slight drop from the knoll, then a gentle rise as I approached the building, which I sensed was some kind of house because it had a welcoming aspect. It was only twenty yards away, but the first light of dawn had not been able to reach it, which meant I had to walk back into the night. Despite the darkness, I was able to find the few steps which led up to the porch. There was no need for me to ring the bell. To the left of the closed door was a row of wooden pegs. Instinctively, I knew which peg the cloak belonged on, so I carefully put it back in its place. It was the only cloak on the row of pegs.

I turned to face the light, conscious of the gloom behind me. Soon I was back on the knoll, where there was still no sign of Barbara. I thought that perhaps she was never meant to come to this place, and I must take this part of my journey on my own. The sky had brightened considerably in the few minutes it had taken me to return the cloak. The hills were as bare of trees and houses as I had envisioned them to be, but there was a wide path that began beneath the knoll where I had spent the night and continued into the shallow valley. It dropped out of sight but then reappeared on the hillside beyond, curving upward to the rounded crest of the final hill.

I surveyed the scene briefly and then began to walk, setting off with no destination, not knowing what the future would bring but eager to be on my way at last. The walking was effortless. I felt only the sense of making the journey and not the passage of time. I found myself cresting the final grassy hillside to be greeted by a freezing wind.

Suddenly, there was a sharply different reality, as though I had stepped between worlds. I stood upon a narrow snow-covered space where the coldest touch of sunshine reflected from the peak above. In front of me was a steep and icy mountainside, which dropped into a dark valley far below. Behind me, where the grass-covered hills had been, there was only a precipice so enormous that it was beyond belief. Whatever the place was that I had been traveling to, I had arrived.

Eighteen

AWAKENING

ON THE EVENING OF May 25, my fate was sealed. At Mushroom Rock, high on the Northeast Ridge, I lay motionless on the snow. It was obvious to Pemba that I was close to death—so close that I might have already passed into the next phase of the life-death-rebirth cycle. As a Tibetan Buddhist, he was aware that over the next three days the different levels of consciousness would leave my body.

Pemba himself was in very bad shape. Wounded by my accidental crampon-kick to his leg, drained and desperately thirsty because he had given all his food and water to Thomas Weber, he was now feeling the effects of snow blindness after a full day with no eye protection in bright sunshine. The pain was like having chilies in his eyes. After twenty hours on the go, most of them without oxygen, Pemba looked at me and decided he wanted to die as well. But then he remembered his family and slowly began to make his way down to High Camp. Dorje followed, carrying with him my camera, the only records of my final climb.

Dawa Tenzing and Lakcha stayed with me at 28,000 feet for another two hours, attempting to rouse me in whatever way they could, including poking me in the eyes. Both men were totally exhausted, having done absolutely everything within their power to keep me moving and—when movement was no longer an option—to keep me alive. Darkness was drawing near, and from 7,000 feet below at Advance Base Camp, Alex instructed them to retreat to High Camp. Dawa Tenzing was also snow-blind and has no memory of how he made his way back to High Camp. But the camp was not a sanctuary—it was dangerous for the exhausted climbers to spend the night at the extreme height of 27,000 feet, particularly when severely dehydrated, yet they had no energy to go any farther down.

The Sherpas were sadly familiar with altitude-induced deaths on the mountain, and they saw that the only difference between my body and those of David Sharp, Vitor Negrete, Igor Plyushkin, Jacques-Hugues Letrange, and Thomas Weber was that mine was not yet frozen.

Alex had instructed them to cover me with stones, in the way that stones had been placed over Igor, but it was not possible to do so at Mushroom Rock. The ridge at that point was a solid spine of rock, capped by a six-foot-wide snowbank tilting upward to the lip of the Kangshung Face. One of the cornices overhanging the lip had broken away, revealing a vertical precipice and a dizzying drop of 9,000 feet to the Kangshung Glacier. The pedestal of Mushroom Rock itself was six feet high, and beneath it the North Face sloped away steeply. Only a few shards of rock lay exposed at the edge of the snow. There were no stones that could be used for my burial.

AT BASE CAMP that evening Mike, Richard, and Christopher were in a state of shock and did not talk much. Richard started smoking heavily, which he had not done for years. Christopher listened to music. Mike's therapy was to busy himself with necessary tasks. He began with the issue of informing the authorities, but as Base Camp manager, Maxim decided he should handle that particular job. In my tent Mike located the notebook which had my insurance details written in a prominent place. He then began to pack up my belongings—not the most joyous of activities—and the tent that had been my Base Camp home for the last two months.

The plan had been for an early start, but the 7Summits-Club convoy was not ready to leave until ten o'clock. As the Landcruiser bounced across the rocky flats, Richard talked about returning next year and building a memorial to me at Base Camp. When Mike looked back at the mountain, he had never seen it more beautiful, so beautiful it was almost luminous.

. . .

LATE ON THE MORNING of May 25, Greg stood outside our house in Wentworth Falls. He remained there for a good while, taking in the spectacular view. The fresh, cold air did not soothe his emotions or ratify his disbelief, but his mind did become less clouded. When he came back inside to the living room, he found that the warmth from the slow-combustion stove, and the body heat of the people standing and sitting where they could, was anything but comforting. Instead, there was a heaviness in the room, a dank and close intensity from the deathly emotions of trauma, shock, and disbelief.

He immediately wanted to go back outside, but he also wanted to be a part of it. As one person consoled another, there were glimmers of humor, gentle ways of maintaining solidarity. At a different level there was a need to conduct rational conversations with people who were ringing up with questions or condolences. These were largely handled by Julia, who was sitting on a low stool that had been made by Roley Clarke and given to Dylan on his fourth birthday. Greg took advantage of a silence between phone calls to place a call to Base Camp. Christopher picked up the phone; he could only theorize about what had befallen me. Foul oxygen was one possibility, he said, and a faulty oxygen regulator was another. It was touching that human fallibility was not suggested.

Barbara thought of one phone call that she wanted to make herself—to Ang Karma in Kathmandu. When they spoke, she asked him if he would perform the appropriate Buddhist ceremony, one that needed to be completed within a certain time of my death.

There was a silence, and then Karma spoke with a hesitancy in his voice that Barbara had not heard before. "I can do that," he said. "I will miss his friendship. He was a good man."

TOWARD MIDDAY, Margaret Werner drove to the Wentworth Falls shops and returned loaded with supplies. She set about making leek and potato soup, and when it was ready, she laid out bread and cheese and a few extras, creating her usual irresistible spread. For many years Margaret had run the Bay Tree Teashop at Mount Victoria, which at the time was heavily patronized by Blue Mountains climbers needing a post-climb feed before the two-hour drive back to Sydney. But today Margaret's leek and potato soup was a post-climb offering, which reminded everybody that for one of our number, there would be no more two-hour drives to Sydney. Or anywhere.

A few people left at lunchtime, but others arrived and Barbara felt obliged to welcome them with cups of tea. This ritual was performed despite how Barbara felt. Her usual focused generosity was absent, not that anyone expected it from her. Instead, the tea-making was a default mechanism, so that she could escape from how she was feeling. People kept bringing food, a substitute for words they could not speak.

Late in the afternoon harpist Dawn Egan arrived with a huge chocolate cake; the beautiful music from her harp would only have brought tears. "I am famous for my chocolate cake," she announced, her gentle voice dispelling any thoughts that she was bragging.

During this busy period someone had turned on the outside light, but the globe had blown. It was a necessary light because there was no other on the outside of our house, and it was a rough path to the gate. Our friend Paul Stephens busied himself trying to fix it, but he soon realized it was a bigger job than he imagined. He told Barbara that he would be back the next day to repair it for her properly.

By this stage the kitchen was overflowing with soups and food, curries and cakes. Our Tibetan mastiff, Norbu, whose head was conveniently at dining-table level, felt that there was so much food that he could take a big bite of chocolate cake without it being missed. But of course the deed was witnessed.

In his poem "First Things First," W. H. Auden wrote, "Thousands have lived without love, not one without water." At our place at Wentworth Falls, no one was going without food, and even the one who no longer lived was loved.

AT MANLY THAT MORNING Simon Balderstone's day had begun with a phone call to Greg Mortimer, asking him to check with Julia that all relatives and other people who should know of my demise were informed before the news hit the media.

He also rang Susie Badyari, general manager of World Expeditions—the trekking company that both Sue Fear and I had worked with over many years—with a similar request in mind. The day before, he had rung Susie with the news of my success, and now he needed to tell her what he knew about my death, partly for her, partly so she could pass on a correct account of events. Both of them were in tears.

The proof of my mortality naturally turned their thoughts to Sue, who was still climbing high on Manaslu, at the very end of the season.

"I'm really worried about Sue," said Simon.

"Why?" asked Susie. "Because of her last e-mail?"

"Yes," said Simon. Sue's most recent dispatch from Base Camp had been full of uncertainty, which was quite uncharacteristic. She wrote that she had "never seen the weather so crazy." There was virtually no one else on the mountain, and she was unsure whether or not to make another attempt. It was a worrying set of circumstances.

Simon had sought to shield Barbara from the press, but interest in the story of my death was growing because of the startling announcement that I had been found alive. Climbers believed it impossible for anyone to survive being left for dead in the open at 28,000 feet. The handful of climbers who had lived through bivouacs at those extreme heights had remained conscious, had been able to talk to each other, and had kept themselves breathing. Only two or three had managed to survive alone, and none of these had been lying lifeless with cerebral edema. The odds were stacked against me, so if there were stories of me being alive, they needed to be proved indisputably. Others had been left on the mountain—if someone had been found alive, it was not necessarily me. And even if the stories proved to be true, what state was I in? And would I be able to survive the descent?

Simon hoped desperately that it was true but saw it as a dangerous rumor. If it was true, there were still too many ways for me to die to risk exposing Barbara to the heartache that would come with the crushing of resurrected hope.

He rang Greg and Margaret to warn them of the breaking story and cautioned them that at this stage it could not be regarded as fact. As he reminded them, the press was prepared to believe anything in the cause of a good story.

The story of David Sharp became even more appealing to the press when there was a possibility that after being left for dead, I had been rescued. It would be the happy ending that David Sharp had not been blessed with. The cloud of argument about climbers passing by Sharp as he died could be given a silver lining. My rescue would be an example of the triumph of altruism over the selfishness of ambition.

Friday was the day that Margie Hamilton worked with Simon on Australian Himalayan Foundation matters, but instead of her foundation duties, Simon asked her to come to his home office to help deal with the impending crisis. Christine Gee, another of the directors, also arrived. Simon was furiously attempting to nail down some hard facts about what had happened to me so that he could pass the details on to the press. He wanted them to be publishing and going to air with facts rather than fantasy.

Queries were coming not just from the press but also from members of the Australian Himalayan Foundation. Others had realized that the foundation's website might be a good place to find answers. An obvious task now was to create a news page that could provide accurate information.

At this point, Jenny Hunter, Simon's partner in life, became involved. Jenny took all the incoming calls on Simon's mobile so that Simon could return calls on the landline according to priority and relevance.

He was able to establish that most of the information was coming from a South Australian website that had links to Jamie McGuinness, whose Project Himalaya team had been camped next to us at Advance Base Camp. The information was absolutist, stating in black and white that I was alive, and yet farther down the page, it said that it was not certain I was alive. Simon was stunned. This level of reportage was the source of the media stories that were beginning to make headlines around the world.

Simon rang Wentworth Falls and, as he hoped, Julia answered the phone. He got straight to the point.

"I shouldn't really be telling you this," he said, "but there are half-cocked news reports that Lincoln might be alive."

"Really?" asked Julia.

"Yes, but I have no idea if they're anything more than rumors. But we're trying to get confirmation from the mountain."

"In that case, I won't mention it to Barbara and the boys until I hear back from you."

"Yes," he said. "That's the best approach. We need to establish to our own satisfaction that the facts have been corroborated and it's confirmed that Linc is alive and in good enough shape to be likely to stay alive."

"Okay," said Julia. "I'll make sure no one who arrives announces the good news until we know it is good news."

GLEN JOSEPH had spent the whole day at home, handling queries from his staff by phone. By late afternoon he was glued to his computer screen, watching the story unfold. He was flicking between three different sites. One had put forward the possibility that I might have survived the night. A posting appeared on a blog that I was definitely alive, but Glen knew better than to put faith in a blog. But there it was on the *Sydney Morning Herald* site at 5:01 P.M., May 26. The headline read EVEREST CLIMBER "STILL ALIVE," and the report included a photo of me taken from the back flap of my biography of Sir Douglas Mawson.

GREG AND MARGARET left Wentworth Falls at 5:00 P.M. because Greg was booked to fly to St. Petersburg only twenty-four hours later. Margaret's phone rang as they drove. It was Simon telling her that there were more indications that I was alive, and they should come direct to his home office because the media would soon be going crazy. When Greg and Margaret reached Manly, not long after 7:00 P.M., Simon explained how the media seemed more convinced that I was alive, but the problem was that the sources were the same unreliable websites. So their first priority was to contact someone at Base Camp who could speak directly about the situation as it had occurred. It was a long shot because almost all the Everest expeditions had packed up and gone home. While the Sherpas packed up the camp, there was only a skeleton 7Summits-Club staff in residence.

NOT LONG AFTER Simon's warning call, Julia received her first inquiry about the rumors. It was from Mary-Anne Marshall, who had visited earlier in the afternoon with her husband, Ian, son Aidan, and daughter Charlotte, who was Dylan's age. Ian had designed and updated the Christopher's Climb sponsorship document and had been following the expedition's progress. After seeing Web reports that I was alive, Mary-Anne had been in two minds whether or not to call.

"There are those reports," Julia admitted, "but no one knows how much truth is in them. I haven't told Barbara, so please don't say anything."

THE NEWS OF MY DEATH arrived at the Australian International School in Singapore late on Friday morning, Singapore time. Johanna Nutall took Barbara's ex-colleague Helen Toppin aside, saying, "I've got to tell you something before you learn of it by any other means."

Helen was shattered to hear the news, but she realized that Dorje's two closest friends needed to be informed privately. Both Rowan Cocks, Australian, and Jonathan Joseph, Jewish Singaporean, had been frequent weekend sleepover guests at our apartment, so we knew them well. While I was away on Everest, Jonathan's family had holidayed in Australia, with Jonathan staying at our house for a few days.

When Rowan's mother, Elaine, arrived at the school, Rowan and Jonathan were taken out of class. Helen and Elaine had remained close friends with Barbara, and they had to control their sobbing before speaking to the boys. Rowan was very practical and was concerned about Barbara, Dorje, and Dylan but was able to return to class. However, Jonathan was deeply shocked and needed to be taken home.

The teachers thought that Dylan's Singapore friends, being three years older and more mature, would be able to manage better.

Every Friday afternoon at the school there were drinks in the main common room. The news of my death had already spread among the staff. Many of them of course remembered Barbara. I was not altogether unfamiliar to them either, as I had spoken to several classes about glaciers, Antarctica, and the Himalaya. I had also given a presentation at an assembly, and I had brought Sue Fear to speak at the school while she and I were working on her book. The teachers who knew us treated the afternoon as a wake, and drinks loosened a few teary eyes.

Half an hour after drinks began, Peter Bond, the principal, made his weekly announcements, among them the fact that I had been found alive on Everest. The wake became a celebration, and much more was drunk than was generally the case at Friday afternoon drinks. Sandra Salamacha, a teacher who had lived in the same condominium complex, was heard to remark, "Only Lincoln Hall could do something like this to us."

Meanwhile, Jonathan had been on the Internet, the electronic tool which perpetuated Dorje's international friendships. Dorje logged on to his MSN online chat not long after 5:00 P.M. Sydney time, 3:00 P.M. in Singapore. Jonathan immediately wrote to him: "Check this out! Your dad's not dead!" Jonathan directed him to the *Sydney Morning Herald* website, where there was a picture of me, a detail from an expedition publicity shot taken at Taronga Zoo. The headline read: LINCOLN HALL FOUND ALIVE.

"Mum! Mum! Come here and look at this!"

Julia heard the call and intercepted Barbara, explaining that news was out that I might be alive, but that lots of people had died and the survivor might not be me. Barbara listened but could not stop the sudden feeling of hope that rose within her.

She hurried into Dorje's room and looked at the photo of me on the screen.

"It's such a nice photo of Dad," she said to Dorje, "but we can't be sure it's true."

"When will we find out?"

"I don't know. I'll have to ask Greg."

"Barbara, it's true," Greg said when she called. "There are reports, but we're trying to verify them. Someone has been found, but there are all these other people who've been reported dead. We don't know for sure whether it's Lincoln; we haven't been able to speak to anyone at Base Camp."

FOR FIVE OR SIX HOURS, people had been arriving at the house, most of them optimistic, only to be told that celebrations were not yet in order. As he had promised, Paul Stephens returned to repair the outside light. He was armed not only with his tools and stepladder but also with a huge amount of food cooked by his wife, Janet. As he worked on the electrical fault, he talked to Barbara about a range of topics, none of which had any relevance to all the current circumstances.

Barbara looked at him as he talked, wondering why he was speaking to her about things like that when her husband was still believed to be dead. As a doctor, perhaps Paul was simply adapting his bedside manner to this stepladder situation, attempting to distract Barbara from her emotions, but the hurt was too deep and too real.

But, in fact, Paul was already convinced that I had been found alive, and because he had immediately commenced the repairs outside, Julia had not managed to brief him on the matter. The food that Janet had cooked was not intended as a comfort but as celebration of my survival. She had almost included a bottle of champagne but decided that perhaps it was just a little too early for that.

FOR THE 7SUMMITS-CLUB CLIMBERS, it was a full day's drive from Base Camp to Zhangmu, with only a brief lunch stop at Tingri. They arrived at the Tibetan border town at 6:00 P.M., which was the first opportunity for Richard and Mike to set up the sat-phone. Richard called Cheryl Harris, and his wife told him about a report that I had been found alive. At first he dismissed the news as nonsense, because that morning the Russians had been unequivocal about my death.

At 9:15 P.M. Sydney time, Mike Dillon in Zhangmu rang Simon Balderstone, who immediately began telling him the optimistic reports that were coming through to Australia.

"Any way that you can contact Base Camp, mate?" asked Simon. "We've got to confirm this. The news we're getting is all rehashes from websites. We need corroboration."

From Zhangmu, Mike managed to get through to Luda at Base Camp. She had spoken directly to Doctor Andrey, who was now treating me at the North Col, where a medical tent had been set up. I had frostbite and signs of cerebral edema and was manifesting a shock psychosis. The details were convincing.

Simon put the phone down and turned to Greg and Christine. "It's true," he said. "Linc's alive. It's amazing that he is, but he's alive."

. . .

THE KITCHEN WAS STILL full of food and the dining table still piled high. The Marshalls had returned, as had Roley Clarke, this time with his wife, Robbie. Julie Clarke and Richard Neville were there as well. In such circumstances nobody knew what to say to one another. Dorje, Dylan, Tanya, and Cameron decided to watch *Lord of the Rings: The Fellowship of the Ring.* There were a dozen people sitting there, watching the fantasy saga set in a different world. Somehow, the mood of the film—the incredible drama and violence, and then the sense of redemption and hope—seemed to resonate with everyone present.

The epic movie had just finished and the credits were beginning to roll when the phone rang.

Barbara had been standing by the wall, next to our huge wooden carving of Krishna holding a five-headed serpent. She snatched the phone with her now-customary anticipation and dread.

It was Richard Harris calling from Zhangmu, his hoarse voice announcing, "It's true, Barbara, it's really true! It's Lincoln!"

So she put down the phone and jubilantly exclaimed, "It is him. He is alive!"

Then everyone was hugging and kissing.

After the excitement had peaked, the phone rang again. It was Greg with a more serious message, "Barbara, it is Lincoln, but he's only been given a fifty-percent chance of surviving. Simon has just been speaking to Mike, who had just talked to the Russian lady."

"Luda . . ."

"Yes, Luda. It turns out that he's in a really bad way. But he's lasted this far, which is incredible. And he is with the doctor now."

Greg's update instantly dampened the brief moments of celebration. However, now that everyone knew that I was alive, there was a strong conviction that I was going to make it.

PRAYERS BEGAN TO BE said that evening. There was no prayer meeting but many phone calls to Barbara. Some people, such as Greg and Slate Stern, had never quite accepted that I was dead. Barbara had never truly believed it either, as Robbie Clarke had perceptively remarked. However, Robbie and Roley had themselves set up a small shrine on their hall table. At their home in the coastal bushland of northern New South Wales, Iain and Trish were keeping a candle burning, and next to a Buddha statue and a small vase of flowers lay their signed copy of *White Limbo*, my first book, which I had given them twenty years ago. Most people had believed there was no way I could have survived overnight that high on Everest, so when the news came through that I was alive, for the time being at least, it definitely felt like a miracle.

People were phoning Alison Lockwood, saying, "We know you know Lincoln, and we're praying for him. We've lit a candle for him."

A committed atheist herself, she summarized the mood with the comment, "Atheists are praying and cynics are lighting candles."

There was an amazing, indefinable feeling throughout that Friday evening, a gathering of belief that grew from a mixture of influences. The harshest of these was the shock of Greg's message that I had only a fifty-percent chance of survival. Against such odds, leaving it to chance was too dangerous. Among everyone assembled, and our other friends scattered across the country and the world, there was a feeling that if everyone could believe in me, then I would make it through. There is no rational method of establishing belief. Hope can be a precursor, but belief has to be allowed to come from within.

TRUE TO HIS PROMISE, Ang Karma had made the preparations for the Tibetan Buddhist ceremony. The statue of the Buddha, photo, prayer books, offering bowls, and incense were in place, as always, on the altar in his meditation room of his Kathmandu home. He had tracked down an appropriate photo of me on the Net, and had printed the image in color. There was nothing else he needed—except for the frame into which he would put my photo. He left the house to buy a frame that was fit for the occasion of marking my death, but when he returned home with it, his wife, Kunga, told him that I had been found alive. Shortly afterward, when Barbara rang with news of my survival, Karma was in a much happier state of mind. She said she was sorry to have put him to such unnecessary trouble. It was no trouble at all, he said. The frame could be used for a happier purpose—another photo of the Dalai Lama would be a good choice.

AT THE TIME of my demise, Dick Smith was in the United States buying a Citation CJ3. As it was a new $9 million jet, he wanted to take a test flight before handing over the check. In Wichita, Kansas, Dick was taxiing out to the runway when his cell phone rang. Normally he would ignore such a call, but as it was from Marilyn, his secretary back in Sydney, he picked up the phone.

The first words Marilyn said were "Lincoln Hall has died on Everest."

As the patron of the Australian Sceptics, Dick always examined the evidence behind any claim that hadn't been proved, but because he knew the huge risks involved in an Everest climb, this time he did not question the news. The death of his friend Rob Hall near the summit ten years earlier, plus the eleven other Everest deaths that season, had clearly demonstrated the dangers.

Dick tossed up in his mind whether to continue with the takeoff. For the moment he decided to say nothing to Pip Smith, his wife, who was sitting behind him. They got airborne and he flew up to 42,000 feet. While flying across the vast Midwest, he was supposed to be checking whether the aircraft was acceptable, but the news had distracted him. When he brought the plane back down to the tarmac at Wichita, he realized he had not taken in all the details of the flight. But he bought the plane anyway and ended up flying it back to Australia.

As they taxied toward the hangars, he said, "Pip, there's some very sad news. I've just been told by Marilyn that Lincoln has died on Everest."

He felt sick and could not sleep that night. The next day they were checking their e-mails, and there was a message from our mutual friend Anne Ward, from Kununurra in the north of Western Australia. The very brief message read: "Have you heard? Lincoln's alive!"

Through his company Dick Smith Foods, Dick was the major financier of our expedition. Over two decades or more he had funded many expeditions, most during his years as chairman of the Australian Geographic Society. Often the funding was in the form of small grants, but occasionally he would fund entire expeditions. As the supporter of so many dangerous undertakings, he realized that one day, on one of the adventures he had sponsored, someone would die. That day came with my death on May 26, but his perfect record was restored when, early on the morning of May 26, I looked up and greeted my rescuers.

Nineteen

THE *WHITE LIMBO* GUY

WITH THE SUN ABOUT TO RISE, on the morning of May 26, Dan Mazur and Jangbu Sherpa were startled to find me alive, sitting cross-legged on the crest of the ridge at 28,000 feet. In the semi-light between dark and day, they spotted a yellow object wafting in the breeze. At first Dan thought it was a wind-damaged tent, but as he and Jangbu approached, it became clear that it was the empty arms of my yellow down suit. And wearing the suit, in a rather ineffectual fashion, was me.

During the twelve hours since I had been left for dead, I had not spoken. My brain, my tongue, my lips, and my mouth took a few seconds to coordinate themselves.

"I imagine you are surprised to see me here," I managed to say at last.

And they were indeed.

Myles Osborne and Andrew Brash had caught up to their two SummitClimb companions. When Myles heard those words, he thought that he himself must have said them, or that he was hallucinating, because there was no way that someone in as bad a shape as I was would be able to speak that articulately. Myles could see that I was without oxygen, without a pack, without even an ice axe. Perhaps I was a very experienced climber, he thought, who had been taking a power nap in the middle of some very challenging feat. Otherwise, how could I seem so coherent?

When Andrew saw me, he found himself moved to tears because

it seemed inevitable that I would die and that he and his three friends would witness the process. Andrew's assessment appeared to be right on the money. I had taken my arms out of my down suit, which is why it was flapping in the breeze. I had also pulled off the gloves I had been wearing. The red balaclava that my mother had knitted me many years ago was lying at my feet.

Dan was busy trying to work out what was going on.

"Do you know how you got here?" he asked me.

"No," I replied. "Do *you* know how I got here?"

"No, I don't . . ." He tried another tack. "Do you know your name?"

"Yes," I said. "My name is Lincoln Hall."

"You're the *White Limbo* guy?" interjected Andrew.

"Yeah, I'm the *White Limbo* guy."

"What does that mean?" Dan asked.

"It's the book he wrote," said Andrew, "about the Australian climb of the North Face in 1984."

That piece of history was not relevant to Dan's assessment of my state.

"Where do you live?" he asked.

"The Blue Mountains."

"Where are they?" asked Myles.

"They're in Australia," I said, "near Sydney."

Despite my ability to speak in full sentences, Dan and the others were worried. My words were clearly no indication of what was going on in my head. My eloquence in the limited-vocabulary world of 28,000 feet was like a car engine revving on high but not in gear, making all the right sounds but going nowhere.

Jangbu had seen it all in his years as a climbing Sherpa. As a long-time guide and climber, Dan had seen a lot as well. Jangbu maintained his Buddhist equanimity, but Dan, Andrew, and Myles were asking themselves what on earth this guy was doing there. The weather was perfect and the summit was only a few hours away. Why did he have to be here on this particular day, at this particular time, when all four of the Sum- mitClimb team were feeling strong?

They were angry to have encountered such a situation, but it was obvious to all of them that something would have to be done. In the short term, I had to be prevented from removing the gloves I was wearing. To them it seemed crazy, but in fact I was removing the gloves because they were not mine. My own were a pair of thick, cozy Black Diamond gauntlets, orange in color, but the pair I kept rejecting were thin dark gray overgloves that offered very little protection. It did not occur to me to mention this to them. Maybe someone had exchanged their overgloves for my gauntlets when I had been dead, because in that state I had not needed them. Perhaps I had taken them off and they had blown away.

There were three possible reasons why I had pulled my arms out of my down suit on this bitterly cold morning. Even Andrew, a Canadian who was accustomed to the cold, could not get warm. The first possibility was that I was in the last throes of hypothermia, where a person dying from cold feels warm; the second was that cerebral edema was still muddying my mind and sensations. The third was that, by taking my arms out of my down suit, I felt I was handing back the Polish cloak.

For Dan and his team, the problem was what to do now. They knew I was a member of Alex's 7Summits-Club expedition because Alex had spoken proudly about having me on board. Dan pulled out his radio and called Kipa, the SummitClimb cook at Advance Base Camp. Kipa's radio was kept on 24/7, so he responded quickly. Dan asked him to rouse Alex or one of the other Russian guides, but the Russians were sleepy and none of them would believe that I was alive. On a perfect day for climbing, this was a very frustrating situation.

Dan decided to contact Phil Crampton, who had been turned back by the cold about an hour before I was found. Two weeks earlier Phil had incurred frost-nip while bringing cerebral-edema sufferer Juan Pablo down to safety from the base of the Second Step. Dan radioed Phil, who easily located the 7Summits-Club Sherpas at High Camp. They were still shattered from bringing me from near the summit all the way down to Mushroom Rock. Phil was very persuasive, so they quickly accepted that I was alive. However, they were too close to death themselves to be able to go back up to help me, but they did convince Alex that I was, in fact, in the world of the living.

There were 7Summits-Club Sherpas already climbing up the mountain, but their purpose was to strip the camps of tents, sleeping bags, stoves, and any personal belongings that had been left behind. None of them were wasting battery power by having their radios turned on. At the end of the season, with no climbers around, the climb up to Camps Two and Three was a routine day out in the mountains. No input was required from Base or Advance Base Camps, but Alex needed to let the 7Summits-Club Sherpas know that a rescue was under way.

Luckily, Jamie McGuinness, the manager of the Project Himalaya team, whose climbers I had overtaken on my way to the summit, also had Sherpas packing up camps. At Alex's request, Jamie radioed a Project Himalaya Sherpa already high on the mountain, asking him to contact the 7Summits-Club Sherpas.

Meanwhile, the five of us stayed put. There was still more work to be done to stabilize my condition. Myles gave me his bottle of warm Gatorade, as he felt I needed it more than he did. Dan had with him an experimental oxygen set, as well as a regular one in case the experiment did not work. He let me use the regular oxygen set and took the experimental set himself. Dan also gave me two Snickers bars, which I pocketed, as I was not interested in food.

There were many things I was not interested in at that time, such as where I was and why. Already behind me was the question and answer session. I felt no special gratitude toward Dan, Andrew, Myles, and Jangbu, because at that point I did not understand the sacrifice they were making on my behalf. I was not at all concerned that Roby Piantoni and Marco Astori, two Italian climbers, had passed by in the direction of the summit not long after the SummitClimb team had arrived. One of them carried an oxygen cylinder, the other did not, but that was their business.

I did not understand that my sense of balance was compromised and that, as a result, my mind had placed me on a boat. As a mountaineer, my survival depended on superb balance, and so it could not have been me who was rocking and swaying—it could only have been the substrate beneath my feet. My memory bank had referenced Antarctica, where several summers in a row I had looked out across a sea of icy mountains from the pitching and rolling deck of a boat. In reality, I was swaying toward the dangerous lip of the Kangshung Face, with Dan gently but firmly persuading me to stay put.

. . .

MY JOURNEY FROM POLAND brought me to a boat, but I had to hurry. As I boarded, the vessel was pitching under my feet, so Dan reached across and grabbed me by the shoulder.

"Only just in time," he said. "Sit down—quickly, or you'll fall off."

I moved to the edge so that I could enjoy the view, but Dan pulled me back again.

"You have to stay back here," Dan insisted, "otherwise you could easily go over the edge."

I said nothing, but I sat where he suggested and thought about how cold it was. The wind cut through me like a knife. One of Dan's team tied me by the waist to a blue rope, presumably so I would not get knocked overboard if we hit rough seas.

When the sun rose higher in the sky, warming me in the process, I realized that I was not on a boat at all but on an aircraft of some kind. I was sitting in the open with only sky above, so I could see very well that no boat could ever be as high as this. The place where I sat sloped at an angle steep enough for me to think that I could easily slip off the plane, had I not been tied to the blue rope. The natural position for me was to sit facing outward, down the slope. I wanted to look in the other direction, but the sun was much too bright for me to see anything at all, which was a pity. Undeniably spectacular as the panorama was in front of me, I would have liked to see the view from the other side of the aircraft. If I ever joined Dan's tour by airplane again, I would definitely bring my sunglasses so that I could see what lay beneath us on the other side.

The shadows seemed to be changing more quickly than the movement of the aircraft, which seemed odd. I wondered how we could be flying so slowly. Surely the aircraft would stall at this speed? Then I remembered other times I had looked out of the window of passenger jets at the leisurely change of the landscape, despite the incredible speed of the jet. Obviously, our aircraft was flying much more slowly than a jet, otherwise we would not have been able to sit on its sloping snow-covered open deck. The other clue to our slow speed was the complete silence and only the slightest breeze.

. . .

I MUST HAVE fallen asleep for a short time because when I came to, I was lying half propped up by the sloping snow, next to a rough rock pillar that looked like a giant mushroom. The snow was even brighter here, and because I was sheltered from the wind, I felt quite hot.

Dan told me to stop fiddling with my oxygen bottle because I might waste the oxygen. Andrew and Myles were sitting nearby, talking about the summit and the fact that there was no time to climb it now. They wondered whether I would be well enough to get down the mountain alive.

"I hope so," said Andrew.

"So do I," I immediately volunteered.

Myles and Andrew kept saying that they were struggling to stay awake. More in tune with reality than I was, they noticed two figures climbing up toward us, so they picked up their backpacks and walked slowly around the rock pillar and out of my sight. Maybe climbing down was the only way they could stay alert.

"You will have to wait," said Dan.

"Where have they gone?" I asked him.

I did not catch his answer properly, but I somehow understood that Myles and Andrew were again boarding the boat, which was moored nearby, and would be heading up the fjord. When they got close enough to Mount Everest, they would climb it.

I could not see the boat or the fjord because the rock pillar was blocking my view. In any case, the sun was reflecting so brightly off the snow that I had to keep my eyes more than half-closed.

I sat with Dan and Jangbu for a while. I asked how long it would be before the others returned from their climb.

Dan said, "You won't be seeing them again today."

"When will we go?" I asked.

"Not too long now," he replied.

He was right. Two Sherpas appeared. One of them spoke good enough English, but the younger one said nothing at first. What I did understand was that they were not happy because they had carried oxygen for me from eight-three. By eight-three they meant 8,300 meters, or 27,000 feet. They were speaking about the altitude of our High Camp. I could remember this much information about Mount Everest.

"*Matthi tsokcha tapailai,*" the younger Sherpa said, with irritation in his voice. "You have finished the summit."

That was right. I had climbed Mount Everest. But why the anger? There was a conversation between Jangbu and the Sherpas who had just arrived. They were speaking too fast for me to pick up a word, but they continually mentioned "eight-three." I decided that they were angry because my need for the oxygen was put ahead of theirs. I assumed they had planned to use it to climb to the summit, whereas I needed it because I was very weak and tired. It was the end of the season so it was only now that they had a day's spare time to climb Mount Everest. But instead of the climb they had been told to take me and the two oxygen cylinders back down to eight-three. I could understand why they were unhappy.

I thanked them for bringing the oxygen to me and told them both that I was sorry but that I was very tired after my climb and I would not be able to climb down without the oxygen. The tension between us seemed to lessen. We began to walk down around the mushroom-shaped rock, but I was very unstable at first, balancing myself against the steep rock wall.

I could not say good-bye to Dan or Jangbu because I was now below the pedestal. Loud radio traffic, with both transmission and reception in English and Nepali, was keeping them fully occupied.

THE EMOTION IN the voices of the two Sherpas lifted my consciousness out of its airplane- and boat-filled reverie. I had furnished my reality with the first thoughts that settled in my mind because I did not have the mental energy to look any further. But now the two Sherpas were talking about climbing down with me, which meant I could no longer lie daydreaming in the snow. Without registering the transition—as it was merely a lessening of my hallucinatory state—I had grasped the dangerous reality of the present moment. I was high on Mount Everest with a long way to descend. Now I was definitely aware of where I was, but irregular waves of hallucination were still passing through my mind and fogging it.

For the whole four or five hours that I had waited with Dan, Jangbu,

Myles, and Andrew, I had been in a hallucinatory world. I had recognized Changtse and Cho Oyu and the sweeping white curves of the Central Rongbuk Glacier, but my mind had made me see them from a boat or a plane rather than from high on a ridge-top.

Whatever had happened to me on Everest, it had been powerful enough to push the events of the recent past into the inaccessible recesses of my brain. My mind could bring forth only a limited number of memories for me to use as reference against my current situation. It was like looking into a mirror and seeing someone else's face—my mind went into emergency mode, accepting the first match presented to it rather than the most likely one.

WHAT ACTUALLY HAPPENED that morning had been relatively simple. Dan, Jangbu, Myles, and Andrew had found me close to death. The bare facts were that they had provided me with sufficient oxygen and fluid to enable me to stay alive long enough to enjoy the warming, restorative power of the sun, amplified by its reflection off the snow. They had alerted the leader of my expedition to the fact that I was alive. Whether or not I had been dead the day before was immaterial because I was definitely not dead now.

The revelation sparked a rescue mission, the first expression of which was the arrival of the two tired and unhappy Sherpas, one of whom was carrying my pack, now empty except for an ice axe, a full oxygen cylinder, regulator, and mask.

Of course, there were no fjords. The only waterways here had been frozen rivers of ice for millennia. Andrew and Myles had not set off to climb to the summit but had begun the long descent of the mountain as soon as they saw the two Sherpas climbing up to us. The Sherpas had never intended to climb to Everest's summit that day. Instead, there was the grueling task of bringing me down the mountain. The baton had been passed.

PART THREE

RUNNING ON EMPTY

Twenty

THE DEVIL'S SPADE

A S SOON AS I BEGAN to descend with the Sherpas I was pulled sharply back into the reality of climbing at 28,000 feet. Because I had been on the crest of the ridge all night and had climbed this section in virtual darkness on the way up, I was unaware of the narrowness of the route across the sloping North Face. Immediately, I understood why my Sherpa companions of the summit day had been unable to bring me any farther down.

At this point of the climb, the Northeast Ridge forms a rocky spine, and where that backbone meets the top of the North Face, there is a system of narrow ledges that requires careful negotiation, especially when a climber is in a weakened state. I was able to walk and to clip my carabiner past the anchors, but it was difficult with my frostbitten fingers. During my time at Mushroom Rock I had become aware of my frostbite, but treating it was a task for another time. What I really needed to do was descend as quickly as possible so that my fingers could be thawed out properly. The cold was the cause, of course, but the mechanism of damage was the fluid in my tissue expanding as it froze. That expansion caused the cells to explode, and if that tissue was thawed and then became refrozen, the damage would be much worse. I had now descended less than 1,000 feet from the summit, although the horizontal distance had been twice that far. With another 7,000 feet of altitude descent to Advance Base Camp, I needed to manage my frostbite carefully; if I didn't, I could lose all my fingers.

And while I could clip my carabiner past the anchor points, it was a slow process, so the young Sherpa in front of me began doing it for me most of the time. Although we were cutting across the top of the face, we were losing height as well, which was good news. What did disturb me was how far we had to descend, and I was already exhausted. At least my mind was processing this information properly, rather than feeding me some crazy hallucination instead. I knew now it was going to be a very long day.

Suddenly, the network of narrow ledges that we had been following came to an abrupt end. Ahead of us was a vertical drop.

"First step," said the older Sherpa, who was behind me.

I did not understand what he meant, but he gestured at the drop-off and repeated the words.

"First Step."

This time I got it. We had arrived at the top of the cliff called the First Step. As we were descending, for us it was the last of the three famous steps. On the way up, I had found the First Step to be encouragingly easy. In normal circumstances this would be a simple rappel, but in my weakened condition, the prospect frightened me. Boats and airplanes were long gone. I was completely aware of where I was and what I had to do. But because I was exhausted, it was not only in my physical movements that I had to summon strength; I could not let my mind waste any energy either. Any memories I had of what had happened over the last few days were not accessible to me, but that was not important because my only concern was the descent. When resting at Mushroom Rock, my mind had the time and space to wonder about what the view would have been like on the other side of the "aircraft." But here I focused on rappeling over the First Step.

Immediate action was called for—I was alert enough to recognize that. I was not going to get any stronger, so the sooner I completed the rappel the better. The young Sherpa attached his descender to the rope and then dropped over the edge. The kind of descender we were using was standard for almost everyone on the mountain. It was known as a figure-8 because the alloy device was shaped like the numeral. There were two ways to attach the descender to my harness. If I wanted to travel fast, I threaded the rope through the larger metal circle, and if I wanted to go slowly, I threaded it through the smaller circle. Once the descender was clipped to my harness, I could not swap from fast mode to slow mode without unclipping the descender and the rope from my harness. This would be a dangerous maneuver because during the swap-over I would not be attached to the rope at all. On this expedition to Everest, every time I had used my descender to rappel, I had used the fast option, mainly because my thick Black Diamond gauntlets provided extra braking power if I needed it. Using the larger circle, I attached my descender, leaned out over the edge, and began to rappel.

The Sherpa had stopped six feet below me, but when I saw the steepness of the drop below him, I knew I was in trouble. I pulled up immediately, just above him, with my head now just below the level of the lip. The older Sherpa squatted above, watching and waiting for his turn.

The problem I now faced was my frostbitten fingers. The cliff beneath me was steep, so all my body weight would be on the rope. Frostbitten flesh has none of the resilience of healthy flesh. If I continued the rappel, with the minimal protection of the thin gloves, the rope running through my fingers would destroy the frozen flesh, giving them no hope of recovery. The damage to my hands would also make it much harder and more dangerous for me to complete a descent that we had barely begun.

I needed to swap my descender from the fast option to the slow one, and the sensible way to do this was to haul myself up the ledge, which I could easily reach. It would be a huge effort.

As I started to move up, both Sherpas asked me what I was doing. I briefly explained my problem.

"No. You must go down," said the older Sherpa.

"I can't go down until I change my descender. *Mero haat hiung-le kao. Tolu janne ani egdam kartara.* My hands have been eaten by the snow. It is too dangerous for me to go down."

They dismissed my explanation.

I tried again. "I come up only to fix my descender. Then I go down."

"No, you must go down now."

"Not until I can fix my descender."

"We must hurry. You must go down."

It was a stalemate. They would not let me climb up and I refused to go down. Without the argument, I would have been past the obstacle in five minutes, maybe ten, given my weakened condition and damaged hands.

I explained that I had been climbing for thirty-five years, since before either of them had been born. I had taught hundreds of people to climb and to rappel. I had climbed mountains that no one else had climbed. I knew what I was doing. I needed to move up just for a few minutes, then I would go down.

That speech only made them angry.

The elder Sherpa mocked me and laughed. The younger one started to shout at me. His English was poor and he was in a rage because he obviously felt I had belittled him. But desperate situations require desperate measures. Unfortunately, my desperate measures had only made things worse.

The young Sherpa held my rope tight so that I could not move up at all. His mate laughed at the scene.

I was getting worse than nowhere. I had to remain calm and look for the way out. Then I saw it—to my right was a second rope, a white one, which I could clip my harness to while I swapped my descender. That way I would not have to go up at all.

The Sherpa above saw me reach for the rope. He instantly whipped out a knife and with one savage slice he cut it clean in two. The piece I was holding dropped down onto my hand. He smiled at me triumphantly.

I was absolutely astounded.

At that moment Roby, the Italian, appeared, and he was stunned to encounter the roadblock on the ropes.

"Go down!" he shouted.

"I have to change my descender," I replied vehemently, but my voice was so hoarse that he may not have heard me. "And this Sherpa has just cut the rope!"

Roby glared at the three of us.

"I have climbed Everest without oxygen! I must get down or I will die!" And with that remark, he grabbed a bunch of old ropes and swung down past us, hand over hand.

The young Sherpa was holding the blue rope so tight that there was no way I was going to be able to remove the descender from it and make the vital adjustment. What was so frustrating was that the procedure was normally so simple.

I was not going to give in and sacrifice my hands. I realized there was another way to protect myself.

To the young Sherpa, I said, "I will go down, but I will go down first." He grimaced in refusal.

"You want me to go down?" I said. "Then let me go down first."

"Okay," said the Sherpa above me.

Now the young Sherpa did what I had wanted to do—he unclipped his descender and put it back on the rope above me. Because he had no need to moderate his speed, he did not adjust it. I realized that he had decided to disagree with everything I said. But I did not want him to sabotage my rappel, which he could have done had he still been beneath me. I readied myself to rappel, and as I began, I pulled the rope across underneath me so that I was slowed by the extra friction as the rope slid across my backside. The technique went a long way to reducing the strain and damage to my hands.

When the young Sherpa saw what I was doing, he immediately rappeled down after me, shouting, "No! No! Stop! Stop!" He was objecting because I was not following the one-method-only procedure he had been taught.

I did not stop until I reached the bottom of the steep section. I had achieved my goal—I had protected my hands—and, as far as I was concerned, our dispute was over. The young Sherpa obviously did not think so, but his companion showed no signs of his feelings.

I had taken my oxygen mask off during our dispute, which must have lasted half an hour, and I could now feel the effects of oxygen deprivation. I took my ice axe from my pack to use as a walking stick and donned my oxygen mask. The adrenaline produced during our altercation had left me feeling drained. My rule at high altitude has always been never to get flustered, but this time I had blown it.

A significant amount of snow had fallen overnight. The fixed rope remained obvious, however, and there was a line of footsteps left by Dan's team and the Italians from when they had climbed up. Despite the tracks, the deep snow made the going awkward. For what looked like several hundred feet the track was virtually level, cutting across the North Face. I felt impossibly weak and I could walk only very slowly. Every twenty or so steps I had to stop and lean on my ice axe to rest.

Immediately the young Sherpa began to hassle me.

"Fast!" he urged. "Go fast!"

Of course I was going as fast as I could. The fourth or fifth time that I rested on my axe he came and snatched it from me.

"Now you just walk. No rest."

I objected but to no avail. The Sherpa behind me laughed. I attempted to follow the tracks, but with nothing to help me balance I kept falling onto the snow. When I landed in a drift of deep snow from which it was difficult to extract myself, neither of them would help me up. They smiled and watched me flounder.

I struggled to my feet and begged for my ice axe back. This seemed to be what they wanted, to have me begging. I begged readily—I didn't care, I just wanted my ice axe returned. But the young Sherpa kept it.

"Go," he said, waving the axe in the direction ahead.

I staggered onward but grew weaker with every step. In the hope of breathing more oxygen, I held my mask to my face with my hands.

"Fast, go fast," he said.

I kept walking and I kept falling in the snow, but I could not go any faster. Then he raised my ice axe as if to strike me.

"Yes, go fast or I hit you."

"No, not that," I pleaded. "You need to help me, then I can go faster."

He gave no answer but turned on his radio and talked into it rapidly, smirking and glancing at me as he spoke. It was easy to see that he was bad-mouthing me. That was fine if it kept him from attacking me with my ice axe.

I was falling over more frequently, and I began to wonder if soon I would not be able to get up. I could not bear to think about what might happen then.

I begged them to let me walk in between them, one Sherpa in front, one Sherpa behind, with each of them keeping tension in the rope so that I could use it to balance.

"This way I can go faster . . ." I began again.

The young Sherpa interrupted immediately, saying, "No kissy-missy, sweetheart deals. Just go."

The two problems I faced were poor balance and the weakness of my legs. The only way I could stay upright for more than a dozen steps was to walk more slowly. By concentrating on each step individually, I could ease my weight onto my leg, which allowed me time to bring my leg muscles into play and to be conscious of my balance. With that leg stable, I could repeat the process. Decades of trekking and climbing with heavy packs had given me very strong legs, which operated as if on autopilot. I used to enjoy running down steep, rugged trails, jumping between levels, watching my feet put themselves where they wanted to go, with me only consciously intervening to avoid a slippery surface, or when instant damage control was needed. But now, with my mental functions impaired by exhaustion and hypoxia, each step through the shallow snow felt like walking on a balance beam.

I trudged onward in this fashion, with my left hand holding my oxygen mask to my face and my right hand free on the uphill side so that I could protect myself when I stumbled. Mercifully, the terrain was level. I would not have been able to take an upward step.

This slower mode of walking was effective, but it riled the young Sherpa. I tried to explain, but he would not listen, and I suspected that he spoke more English than he understood and in these circumstances it made him feel inadequate.

I turned to speak to the older Sherpa. "If I can go slowly, then I can keep going. But if I try to go fast, I fall over. Too much time wasted."

"No kissy-missy, sweetheart deals," pronounced the younger Sherpa.

That phrase again. Where did he pick it up? What did that mean? Deals? What kind of deals?

"Go quickly or I hit you."

Then a cold chill came over me, different from the cold of the snow I had been floundering in. From the recesses of my mind came the warning that Sue Fear had given me about banditry at high altitude. Suddenly I was very, very scared.

The shock drained me and I crumpled to my knees.

He raised the ice axe and swung it at me.

"No! No!" I cried and threw my forearm up to block the blow, but it never came.

"Go!" he said.

I struggled to my feet and staggered forward. I forgot about controlling my legs and my balance, so after only a few steps I stumbled again and collapsed in the snow.

"Go," he said again, threateningly, as if he were training a dog.

"I can't. I have to rest."

"No rest," he shouted, "or I hit you!"

I shook my head, then he raised the axe as if to strike, but I was too exhausted to lift my arm in defense. Out of the corner of my eye, I saw him swing at me. This time he followed through and struck me hard across the back of my ribs. I stared in horror as he swung the axe again, aiming at my head. I threw my arm up, and the metal shaft slammed into my upper arm. Instantly, I rolled out of the way.

"Now you go!"

Slowly I stood up, my heart thumping. He was a madman. The blows had been delivered without restraint. If I had not blocked his second swing, it would have whacked my skull and cheek with sufficient force to knock me out. And had I been knocked unconscious in my weakened state, I would surely now be dead.

He stared hard at me, with no regret apparent in his expression.

I was physically drained, but my survival instinct had snapped into action and with it came mental energy. I would have to play my cards very carefully, except that he and his partner held all the aces, all the trumps. It would have to be a lay-down misère.

The young Sherpa took a step toward me, lowering his voice as he said, "You tell no one. You see what happens. You don't want trouble."

I watched him carefully and said, "No, I don't want trouble."

That would be my key.

"You need to walk fast."

"I will walk as fast as I can. I do not want trouble."

The incident had brought clarity to my mind or as much clarity as was possible at this height. I needed to make progress. I needed to avoid angering my tormentor, and I needed to get among some other people as soon as I could.

During this whole episode, the older Sherpa had said virtually nothing, which was far from unusual at these heights, where every breath mattered and speech was a waste of oxygen. His silence was not surprising, but his lack of interest in the tyranny of his young friend could only be seen as complicity. I knew I could not seek from him the voice of reason.

My pace slowed as my body metabolized the oxygen that had accumulated in my muscles while we had "rested." I was still holding my oxygen mask to my face with my frostbitten fingers in their clumsy lightweight mitts because I was unable to fasten the elastic strap.

The young man came toward me and gestured at my oxygen mask. "You love that mask. Maybe I take it from you and you walk quickly." He pretended to grab for it and, as he had wished, I jerked away from him. "Too much time with your oxygen."

Then he weighed the ice axe in his hand and said, "Anyone coming, you say nothing, or I hit you many times."

My heart sank. A few hits would be enough to stop me from saying anything ever again. I kept walking, then I realized that the threat had real meaning.

I heard another voice and turned to see Marco Astori, the second Italian, approaching us at twice our speed. The demeanor of both Sherpas changed to one of welcome. Marco had seen that I could walk unsupported but must also have noticed how badly ravaged I had been by the mountain. I said nothing, sticking to my instructions. Marco offered the Sherpas his oxygen cylinder, which was almost empty and which he was no longer using. They said that they had enough oxygen for me but I did not want it. Marco walked on.

I had desperately wanted to call out to him, but the attitude of Roby when he had stormed down the First Step made me fear that Marco, too, might choose not to get involved. Certainly he did not give that impression, but if I spoke out and he rejected my claims, I feared that once he was out of our sight, I would be beaten again.

I was prepared to take what I had to in order to stay alive, but it would have been so easy for the young Sherpa to overplay his hand with the ice axe. I felt sure that he had no comprehension of how deeply exhausted I was. He treated me as if I was lazy and therefore not worthy of respect, whereas I was holding myself together by a thread so fine that it made a spider's web look like a tugboat's towline.

As Marco disappeared from view, I regretted my silence. If we encountered anyone else, I decided I would throw those lowly misère cards down on the snow and let fate decide the final hand.

I began to trudge through the snow again, thinking that the Sherpas must now be confident that I was their tool. As we walked, they demanded various things from me as a reward for my rescue. We talked about money, we talked about cameras, and we talked about not saying a word to anybody. I said yes to everything.

There was a new buoyancy in their step as they chatted to one another. It seemed to me that we had entered a new phase, and I wondered whether they were enjoying the calmness before my death or merely the exploitation. I preferred that it not be both.

Of course, I had no money. I only had the empty pack they had brought with them so that I could carry my oxygen equipment. Anything they could get from me would be in the form of promises, promises I would not keep. Death had been trailing me for too many hours now for me to get excited about it, but I did not want to give these men the opportunity to take others to the point of death in order to exploit them.

Ahead of us, I could see the crest of the ridge, where a number of people were gathered. This was the point where the long traverse of the Northeast Ridge finishes and the fixed rope leads down the Exit Cracks and through mixed rock and snow to High Camp. Judging by their size, the Sherpas—they could only be Sherpas—appeared to be still 200 yards away. Fifty yards ahead, the North Face bulged slightly, obscuring all but the final section of the traverse to the rappel point.

If I could make it past the bulge before my two Sherpas attacked me again, I would be close enough to shout for help. The only problem with this plan was that my voice had been reduced to a hoarse whisper. I burned with frustration, but at that moment a figure began approaching us purposefully. I hurried, and as a result, I stumbled and fell to the downhill side of the slope. I was only too aware of the huge drop beneath me. The young Sherpa approached me, and I feared that he might unclip me from the rope and dispatch me with his boot. Instead, he repeated his chorus, "Get up. Go fast."

Safety was within my grasp. The man striding toward us was too close for them to abuse me anymore. He spoke to me directly. "Why are you so slow? Very fast when we climb to summit, but now too slow."

It was Lakcha, and I could not have been more pleased. He was strong and forthright, straight down the line. I was still on the snow and I waited until he was right next to me. As I moved to stand up, I made a sudden grab for my ice axe, and the element of surprise allowed me to snatch it from the young Sherpa.

"Naramro manche ho! Janne, janne!"

Bad men! Let's go!

I attempted to leap to my feet but in the process tripped over the fixed rope and fell backward. My mountaineering boots, with the sharp crampons that had wounded Pemba accidentally, were now in the position to wound with a purpose, plus I had the ice axe. I clambered to my feet and hurried across the slope, with Lakcha at my heels. I was worried that either one of us would be axed in the back, until I remembered that I had the axe.

"Chito! Chito!" Quickly! Quickly!

This time it was Lakcha urging me on. I was not sure if he believed that the danger I conveyed was real, but he certainly knew that I was in such bad shape that I needed to lose height quickly. There were rocks among the snow, so I had to watch where I was putting my feet as I ran. It was the slowest running I had ever done in my life but by far the most exhausting. I looked up to find that we had reached the rounded snowy crest at the top of the Exit Cracks. There were four or five Sherpas waiting, exuding a completely different ambience. They were obviously pleased, not so much because of where they were but because my arrival meant that all of us could now descend to safety. However, the burst of energy that had allowed me to escape had been completely spent, to the point where I could do nothing but sit at the top of the fixed ropes. All the Sherpas were encouraging me to start down the ropes, but it was only when my two "companions" appeared that I was motivated to move.

THERE WAS NOW SAFETY in numbers. Lakcha led the way at a fast pace, and because it was downhill, I thought I would be able to keep up. All too soon I began to flag. The Sherpas who had been spread out above me were now directly behind me. Lakcha reduced his speed. It did not occur to me that all these Sherpas were here because that morning I had needed rescuing. Most of them were already on the mountain to retrieve all the

7Summits-Club equipment from the upper two camps, and the only reason they had climbed up from High Camp to the crest of the ridge above the Exit Cracks was because Alex wanted them to be at that place for my rescue. And they were in good spirits, even after the long climb, because they had seen that this was no longer a rescue but an assisted descent, which required virtually no effort from them.

From the Exit Cracks, the fixed rope led more or less straight down the slope, which meant that my progress was governed by gravity. And while gravity helped, the fact that the mountainside was not very steep meant I could keep most of my weight on my feet, which was much easier on my frostbitten hands. The steepest terrain was in the first thousand feet from the Exit Cracks.

After we came down through the cliffs, there were still boulders and rocky obstacles. I found it very hard to balance, partly because soft snow had built up around the boulders, obscuring some of them completely so that I was never quite sure whether any given footstep would be firm or soft and deep. The hardest part for me was clipping my carabiner past the anchors because I had to bend down, which meant I then had to raise the weight of my upper body again. That had never been an effort for me in the past, and this showed me how weak I had become.

While still on the rocky section, I tripped over the fixed rope twice. The second time was more dramatic, as I tumbled over a three-foot drop, slipped down another slab, and slammed into Lakcha. Luckily, I hit him with my shoulder and not with my crampons. However, I had managed to land on my back, and the soft snow made it impossible for me to right myself. Even though I was upside down, I enjoyed the rest. Two Sherpas pulled me upright and I was on my way again, but not before the Sherpa behind me clipped a short rope to the back of my harness so that he could prevent me from falling forward if I slipped. All of us were wearing down suits with the hoods pulled over our heads. I was the only one not wearing goggles or sunglasses, so I found it very hard to recognize anyone. But Lakcha's gold tooth was unmistakable. Among the people above me were my tormentors, but nothing was said by them.

The descent of a big mountain always seems endless, but with Everest it was like descending three mountains at once. The first mountain brought us down to High Camp. At 27,000 feet, the camp was less than 600 feet below the Northeast Ridge, but the short rappels and the snow-covered rock conspired to draw out the process, and once again halluci-nations came into play.

I was no longer in fear of my life, but I was still aware of the dangers. The steep terrain had demanded concentration, and I was now begin-ning to feel how much energy that mental focus had taken from me. High Camp was the beginning of the long snow slopes, which demanded focus on balance and awareness of the terrain underfoot. In places there was only a thin layer of snow covering the rocks, a combination which required extra care. Such ground looked deceptively straightforward, and with the added danger of long distances between anchor points on the fixed rope, a slip could have had very serious consequences.

It was a beautiful afternoon and I was aware of it. I was severely dehy-drated and running on empty, and yet I could look beyond my desperate state to the magnificence around me. There was a trap in this because the beauty made the place feel benign—which was a long way from the truth.

The second of the three mountains was from High Camp to Camp Two at 25,000 feet. Again, long snow slopes allowed relatively fast decreases in altitude, but there was a mix of steeper, rocky ground which slowed me down, partly because my oxygen mask made it difficult for me to see where I was placing my feet. This had been an issue every time I pulled the mask over my face, but now that I was impossibly tired, the obstructed view had become more of a nuisance.

The five or six Sherpas who had come down from the Exit Cracks with me had stopped at both High Camp and Camp Two to strip them of gear and tents. Their loads were heavy, and their occasional playful com-ments became less common. A more serious mood existed, as we were all aware that we had to get down to the North Col before dark. There remained a very long way to go.

The last of the three mountains was from Camp Two to the North Col—a long and tiresome descent of 2,300 vertical feet down the snow-covered North Ridge.

The change in energy among us added a somber tone to the descent. My mind again became vulnerable to hallucinations but nothing as

otherworldly as the mountainside village, the bearded man, or my journey with the cloak. The boat and the airplane were products of my mind's
attempts to find familiarity and security in an incomprehensibly dangerous situation—in other words, a fantasy world.

But now my hallucinations bordered on paranoia. The beating and
abuse I had suffered below the First Step triggered in me a perception
that the Sherpas had split into two rival groups. The Sherpas who had
beaten me had gathered allies, and they were aligned against Lakcha and
his team, who were with me. A competition was to be held at the North
Col, with fatal consequences for the losers. I was the catalyst, but as a
Westerner, I was immune and the dispute was now between Sherpa and
Sherpa. As we descended, I found examples of booby traps at anchor
points, as well as delaying tactics and sabotage. At last I had to stop and
beg for mercy, that the competition must be abandoned and the animosity must be dissolved. Perhaps some resentment had built up toward me
because I had slowed down the entire group, and I had tuned in to that
emotion. But now that I had spoken to them all, with great passion and
distress, about the pointlessness of the plotting and the needless violence,
the atmosphere changed completely. It must have been obvious to all the
Sherpas that my rantings were pure craziness, the kind that led to climbers jumping off mountaintops. The mood of animosity that I had sensed,
which may not have existed for anyone but me, evaporated.

I now felt free to air my other grievance, one that had roots in fact. I
spoke of privileged Westerners and how embarrassed and ashamed I was
when I saw foreign climbers treating Sherpas as servants. If these mountains belonged to anyone, I said, they belonged to the Sherpas and the
Tibetans who lived here, to the people who respected the mountains and
their spirits through their prayer flags and *pujas*. Then I sat in the snow
and cried.

I would never have made the speech about disrespect had both my
mind and my emotions not been at the cracking point, now that I was
close to the end of my ordeal. I had bottled up my reactions to the examples I had seen during my two months here, burning inside at the implied
superiority demonstrated by a few Western clients—only a few, but
enough to taint the water and make Sherpas close their hearts. There was
guilt there, as well, because of my own privileged position.

. . .

THE SUN WAS BEGINNING to set, turning the entire mountain a pale pink. I watched the shadow overtake us, watched it chase the tinted snow up the slope, the intensity of the color growing as it rose. The edge of the shadow pushed the pink snow upward, compressing it, finally squeezing a whole mountainside of color onto the glowing red of the summit. Small wonder that we wanted to climb to those sacred places.

Darkness came quickly now, exaggerated by my every action being slow. We had reached the final, easy-angled section of the snow slope leading down to the North Col. I could manage only fifty yards at a time. I was torn between resting while I stood to save myself from the effort of standing up again and sitting in the snow because it took the load off my legs. The radio was crackling, and it was in the hands of the silent partner to my abuse. But that seemed past us now. Alex was calling, demanding that we hurry. He did not want me out after dark.

I asked for the radio and pressed the talk button. "Alex, it's Lincoln. I'm okay but very tired. The Sherpas are making me move as fast as I can. So don't blame them."

"The important thing is that you are alive," he replied.

This seemed too obvious to state, but Russians often have their own way of looking at things. At that moment, of course, I did not appreciate the subtext.

We kept plodding down the hill. Darkness was upon us for the last hundred yards. I had been dreading the final section into camp. The lowest dip of the North Col harbored no tents, as it was consistently a very windy spot. Tonight we were spared that indignity, but another awaited me. From that low point I began an exhausting climb of fifteen vertical feet up a gentle slope. Because it was uphill, I had to rest after every few steps, but all my rests were standing ones. Much as I wanted to collapse in the snow, I felt I owed it to the Sherpas to remain upright, now that we were so close to the camp. At last I reached the crest and the first of the tents, but I still had to trudge the last hundred feet to the 7Summits-Club camp.

As I pulled up outside the mess tent, now an improvised hospital, I felt incredibly hot. Hands began to remove my oxygen set, my pack, my crampons, and my harness. I wanted to stay outside; I wanted to lie down on the snow to cool down before going into the stuffy tent.

I struggled vigorously against the hands that drew me inward, but there were too many of them and I was carried inside. Two of the card tables had been taped together to create a makeshift bed. A mattress had been placed on top and I was made to lie there. Immediately, I stopped struggling.

Perhaps it is not so hot in here after all, I thought, now that the stove in the vestibule is turned off. Perhaps I was suffering the last, most dangerous stages of hypothermia.

As I lay there, Andrey quickly checked my pulse and blood pressure. I begged for a drink but was allowed only a few sips at a time—a cruel gift in my severely dehydrated state.

The Sherpas helped me slide into a sleeping bag and then laid me down again. An oxygen mask was placed on my face, and I snuggled in to make the most of the opportunity to relax. Before I understood what was happening, straps were laid across the table and I was tied in place.

Andrey had been talking to the Sherpas and no doubt had heard about my crazy stories. There was no way he was going to let me escape into the night, wandering off the lip of a cornice, muttering to myself that it was too hot inside.

BACK AT MY JOB in Australia, I had worked with Norbert Gilewsky, a man born in Germany who was in charge of scanning the photographic transparencies for every issue of *Outdoor Australia*. Norbert's father had been in Stalingrad during the Second World War, where—on the last day of hostilities—his shoulder had been blown apart by a mortar. For the rest of his life, Herr Gilewksy had not cursed his misfortune but had thanked his lucky stars. He had frequently declared to Norbert that he had *"dem Teufel von der Schüppe springen"*—leaped from the devil's spade, the spade that dug the graves.

And now I, too, had survived the last day of hostilities. I had leaped from the devil's spade. Compared with where I had been and what I had been through, and even though I was still at 23,000 feet, the descent from the North Col would be like a walk in the park.

Twenty-one

RUNNING ON EMPTY

THE NEXT MORNING, the low roar of the gas stove in the outer section of the tent masked the background noise. As I woke more fully, I became aware that the outer vestibule was busy with Sherpas coming in for cups of tea and whatever was available to eat. I attempted to turn and look behind me, but I was still strapped to the metal tables. The entire camp was to be packed up today, which meant everyone would be busy, so I just lay there until some Sherpas came in to collect bags of food that needed to be carried down. At my request, they undid the straps and I was able to roll onto my side. After a night on my back unable to move, it was a pleasure to change my body position.

More Sherpas came in to gather more stuff. Not wanting to create further obstructions, I just lay there and let them empty the place. Someone handed me a lukewarm cup of tea, which was like an elixir. Andrey had only allowed me to have small sips from the bottom of an almost empty cup, as apparently this was the best way to deal with the severe dehydration from which I was suffering. The entire time I felt desperately thirsty and my throat was constantly dry.

I sat up and carefully wriggled out of my sleeping bag so that I would not tip the tables, then I found my boots underneath. I could get my feet into my boots, but because my fingers were frostbitten, I was unable to do up the laces. I shuffled outside and watched the Sherpas assembling enormous loads. Everything had to be carried down—tents, sleeping bags, collapsible stools, food, stoves, and the big gas canisters—and I was sure no one wanted to make two trips.

I went into the tent in which I had slept on the way up, to check for any belongings I may have left behind. There were a few items of mine and a pair of fleece trousers that belonged to Mike. My approach was thorough and I was thinking quite clearly, so I felt that I would be able to manage the day. I left the tent and decided I should have something to eat and drink, but all the kitchen gear had been cleaned and packed away. My last proper meal had been breakfast here at the North Col on the morning of May 23. It was now May 27. In the last sixty hours I had eaten nothing but two sports gel sachets. Maybe Andrey had fed me something the previous night, but I really could not remember. The worst thing about the kitchen being packed up was that there was absolutely no water.

The weather was perfect, which made me worry about snow blindness. When the two Sherpas had come up to 28,000 feet with my pack, it had been totally emptied of all my belongings. The only things they had brought for me were my ice axe and a single fresh oxygen bottle with breathing gear. I assumed they had not wanted to carry anything other than what was absolutely essential—but in that category I would have put my goggles, or one of two pairs of prescription sunglasses, and either my thermos or water bottle. All of these items had been left behind.

Andrey had been giving instructions to the Sherpas, but now he was ready to leave the North Col. Mingma Gelu led the way, followed by me and then Andrey. I was confident about my ability to walk but was concerned about how, with my frostbitten hands, I would manage rappeling the steep sections of fixed rope. Some of the Sherpas had gone ahead, and even though I was squinting because of the glare, I could see them moving slowly farther down the face under their huge packs.

I descended the ladders across the crevasse at the top of the face very carefully. Because I put my palms on the rungs instead of my fingers, I had no problems. The first fixed rope was steep and very tight, the tightness preventing me from being able to attach my descender. At this point on my previous trips down from the North Col, I had wrapped the rope around my wrist and lower arm because that technique provided enough friction to slow my descent. This time I kept the rope away from my fingers and wrapped it only around my arm. I had expected my biggest challenge would be managing tasks without using my fingers. Although the first couple of steep ropes were demanding, the rest were much easier. Instead, I found that the biggest problems for me now were my lack of energy and the weakness of my legs.

Energy. I no longer knew what the word meant, at least in the physical sense. While my body was completely drained, my brain had switched itself on. As we descended, I talked nonstop, as if someone had given me a truth serum.

Mingma talked back, saying that everyone was amazed that I had survived a night so high on the mountain, alone and without shelter. "No one has survived that," he said.

This morning I could not remember much about that experience. I thought of it as just another night out on a mountain, but at a ludicrous height. I did not want to discuss it. Instead, I talked about my sons and my wife, and our home, and my friends—anything that had nothing to do with Mount Everest.

I was speaking to Mingma in Nepali, but suddenly I realized that Andrey, who was close behind me, would not have understood a word. He may not have been at all interested—it was the Russian style to appear that way at least—but I apologized and then repeated myself in English. Moments later I forgot about English and chattered away in Nepali to Mingma. Then I remembered Andrey, and the cycle continued. When we stopped at each anchor to clip on to the next section of the fixed ropes, I sat and told an anecdote until Mingma urged me on.

Because I had no sunglasses to protect my eyes from the intense glare of the sun reflecting off the snow, I wore one scarf low over my brow and another pulled right up close to my eyes. On the long and simple snow descents, when safely clipped on to the rope, I would close my eyes to keep out the glare. It took a little more energy to descend this way, as I had to take more care with how I placed my feet.

After one particularly long section of fixed rope, I announced, "I need to rest."

"No, no," said Mingma and Andrey, almost in unison.

"We must go down," added Mingma.

Only a few minutes later the snow leveled out. We were at the bottom of the slope, with only the broad névé of the glacier to cross. I clumsily hugged Mingma, then Andrey.

The morning sunshine in the glacial bowl was now unbearably intense. Andrey led the way, with me right behind. The ground sloped gently downward, leveled out, then rose over the slightest of humps. That small rise was almost more than I could manage. I was so hot that I had to ask Andrey to stop so I could crouch behind him in his shadow. My thirst had become almost unbearable. I had not changed any of my clothing since adding a fleece underneath my down suit the night we left for the summit. I was still dressed for the extreme cold on the heights of Everest.

We reached the edge of the névé and rested on rocks that were strewn across the exposed ice. I took off my down suit, slowly, because of my fingers. There were trickles of melt water, but Mingma and Andrey would not let me bend down and suck it up. I said I could not continue without a drink. No one had any water at all, which I could not believe. Mingma radioed Advance Base Camp, which was now only a twenty minutes' hike down the moraine valley and asked for thermoses to be brought up.

Imagine a tap that has locked up, with only a dribble emerging from its spout. The effort required to loosen the tap suddenly yields results, with the sudden release causing the tap to be turned on much too far. Water gushes forth, splashing out of the sink, before the tap can be turned back to a practical level of water flow. My garrulous babble during the descent from the North Col had been like such a tap—when suddenly turned on full, I spouted irrelevant facts, painful wordplays, and meaningless opinions. But as I sat on the rock, I began to relax, the wildness in my mind subsided, and I no longer felt like talking.

Now, as I sat there waiting, facing away from the sun to protect my eyes, my mind dealt only with what was in front of me, and that was a scattering of rocks lying in the snow. As I hunched over, all that was required—not by me but by my state of being—was a flat, chocolatey-brown rock, about the size of an abalone. Slowly I began to close my eyes, to block out everything but the rock, leaning closer as I did so. All I could see through the narrow slits of my trembling eyelids was the brownness. I watched a swirling in the color—not a pattern but a movement—and I sensed the rock was opening itself up to me. At first it seemed that some kind of metamorphosis was taking place, but as I watched, I realized no physical change was happening, only a change in my perception. Rocks were always like this, but my mind had never before slowed down enough for me to be a witness. The swirling movement took shape and rose toward me, which made me fearful, even though I knew it was not alive. It was the kind of anticipatory fear I sometimes experienced when being led into a deep meditation by my teacher, where I became aware of other levels of consciousness that challenged my everyday view of the world.

I drew back, opening my eyes fully as I sat up, and looked at Mingma. Weeks ago, at Advance Base Camp, he had told me that there were gaps in the everyday reality, which, among other things, allowed satellite phone messages to be delivered. He had described an opening through which the messages could come and which afterward would close again. It was a description of the Eastern concept of ether, the fifth element of existence.

"Mingma," I said, "there is movement in the rocks. I can see them opening up."

He nodded in agreement, and although we were talking about rocks and not the sky, he said, "Like for the sat-phone."

TENDI ARRIVED with a single thermos, which was ridiculous given that there were ten of us. He poured warm water into a mug and offered it to me, watching with great concern. I felt in dreadful shape, and I imagined I looked it as well.

"Do you know my name?" he asked.

"Of course," I said. "You are Tendi."

A couple of other Sherpas asked me, and though I knew both of them, I could remember only one of their names. I apologized to the other man with sobs rising in my throat. I don't know why—perhaps it was because I did not want him to think that I saw him as a faceless person in whom I had no interest. But he told me his name and smiled at me warmly, aware that my misadventure had exacted deep consequences.

The same question came again from the edge of our circle, with an edge of hesitancy. "What is my name?"

"I don't know. Forgive me."

The man sitting next to him asked the same question. I gave the same answer but did not cry. Neither of them could hide the relief they felt at my replies. Their packs were loaded high with sleeping bags and other gear, their faces almost black with sunburn. I knew who they were all right, even if I did not know their names. They were the two Sherpas who had terrorized me.

Tendi's water had moistened my throat but did nothing to quench my thirst. We continued on down along the icy edge of the glacier. Its slipperiness was negated by its covering of rock shards. Sometimes there were slabs of rock, which were good to stand on and were perfect for sitting. Whenever Mingma looked around, he saw me sitting down. His solution was to put a loop of rope around my waist, with the other end in his hand, so that while he led the way, he could tell when I had come to a halt. And although he let me stop, he prevented me from sitting down. He knew that what I needed more than anything else was to be in the 7Summits-Club medical tent at Advance Base Camp. Once he had me on the leash, we rested only once, and that was when some of our Sherpas were resting with their heavy loads.

We arrived at the camp around midday, and the height of 21,000 feet felt like sea level. In the five days since I had climbed the mountain, most people had gone. Piles of gear were stacked up, waiting for the arrival of yaks. A few Sherpas at other camps were still packing, but the place was almost a ghost town.

As we walked past the remaining tents, two people stood watching me, only about four or five yards away.

I heard one of them say, "That's Lincoln!"

"Yes, it's me," I replied, my recognition of them very cloudy. "I have to get back to my tent, but just drop by and say hello when you feel like it."

It was only another twenty yards to the much diminished 7Summits-Club camp. Alex welcomed me warmly, and I was pleased to see him as well. I was surprised by the great enthusiasm of Kevin's welcome. I looked behind me to see if there was anyone else, but there was no one.

Kevin and I had always gotten along well. Altitude treats everyone differently, and he had been very slow to acclimatize. He made three or four attempts to reach Advance Base Camp, setting out each time with

Harry, Thomas, and Milan. The first time he had turned back at Intermediate Camp, the second and third times he had continued toward ABC, but nausea and weakness had forced him to retreat. It had taken him most of the expedition to make it to here, and now he was a permanent resident.

"Good to see you, too," I said, but he could tell that I was puzzled.

"The rest of the world thinks you're dead, mate."

THE MEDICAL TENT WAS right near the kitchen, so while Andrey prepared space on the floor to accommodate my arrival, I sat outside on a chair sipping warm lemon cordial. It was sticky and sweet, and I would have preferred water, but it was liquid. Andrey had obviously briefed the cook because the mug was only one-third full. I could have drunk the whole kettle.

As soon as Andrey was ready, he ushered me into the sun-heated hospital tent. My inflatable mat was on the floor with my sleeping bag on top. The thought of lying there on the floor was bliss, and it proved to be so as Alex, Andrey, and Sergey lowered me onto my mat. If I had been allowed to drink my fill—not cold water, I had had enough cold—it would have been paradise.

There was a stuffiness in the tent, and immediately I began to feel hot, so I stripped down to my long thermal underwear and lay on top of my sleeping bag instead of in it. Alex peeled off my socks—another of the duties of my expedition leader—and I could see I had a few frostbitten toes on my right foot. I had learned to cope with amputations on my left foot, so I was not too concerned.

After a quick check-over, the first thing Andrey did was to insert a drip into my arm.

"What's in it?" I asked.

He shrugged his shoulders. "Some things you need," he said, his dismissive gesture confirmed by the way he pursed his lips.

I gathered that he wasn't accepting questions at this time. That was okay; I was quite happy just to relax. His next move was to deal with my fingers, one by one. All of them were numb, but to differing degrees. A strange sensation came to each finger, which I didn't bother analyzing until he got to my right index finger, when I felt the sharp pain of an injection. Pain's good, I thought. Means I've got feeling there.

He continued injecting a vasodilator into each finger of my left hand, to stimulate circulation just below the level of the frostbite.

My hands had thawed by then, but—mercifully—I did not remember the pain of them thawing, which I knew from my first bout of frostbite years before to be intense. The thawing must have taken place during the night, in the deep sleep of exhaustion.

Kevin came though the tent door with his big movie camera whirring, which did not worry me. However, Andrey scowled at him, so he retreated outside, his lens poking through the door flap.

A short time later, Kevin came back into the hospital tent and offered to ring Barbara for me on his sat-phone. It was an offer I could not refuse.

"Tell me the number," he said, "and I'll call her."

I had no difficulty remembering our number, and after dialing it, he held the phone to his ear. Would there be anyone at home? He waited and I waited, and then he began to speak.

"You don't know me," he began. "My name is Kevin Augello, and I am at Advance Base Camp with Lincoln and he wants to talk to you."

Sat-phones often lose their signals and drop out without warning, so with every word he spoke, I was thinking: just give me the bloody phone. But then he passed it to me.

"Hello, this is Lincoln," I said, and waited.

"Who is that?" said Barbara. It was definitely her voice, but she sounded worried or confused.

"It's Lincoln."

"Is that you?" she asked again. "Is that you, Lincoln?"

"Yes, it's me."

"You're Lincoln?" She still did not sound convinced.

"Of course it's me." Then I remembered that my ordeal had destroyed my voice. "It's me," I repeated, but I needed some way to convince her. "It's Lincoln Ross Hall of Wentworth Falls." Then I added, "I hope you haven't started looking for another husband."

"It's you!" she cried, knowing that only I could say such a thing. "It really is you."

"Of course it's me, and I'm so sorry that I couldn't call you before now." I began to cry, but managed to blurt out more. "My voice is shot. I only got to ABC an hour ago. I had no idea everyone thought I was dead. It must have been hell for you all."

She told me not to worry, that everything would be all right. I told her the same thing. We were on the same wavelength immediately, each wanting the other to feel that there was no need to worry. Not now, not ever again.

"I've got some frostbite," I said, "so I might not be coming back with all my bits."

She then said, "It doesn't matter what bits you lose. I'll always love you."

Andrey was now gesturing to Kevin that his time was up. I said good-bye and handed the phone to Kevin. He pushed out through the tent-flaps, and I could hear him talking outside to Barbara.

"Lincoln has just come down with the Sherpas. They spent the night at the North Col. He's now here at Advance Base Camp in the hospital tent, and the doctor is giving him medical attention. There's a good team of people here, and he's out of danger now. Everything will be okay."

Kevin spoke calmly and reassuringly, and I felt so much gratitude that he had been able to bring Barbara up to date. But he was not finished yet.

"I couldn't ring you earlier," he continued, "because I didn't have a number. I even thought of ringing the toll-free number on the Dick Smith Foods peanut butter jar. I figured that, as your sponsor, maybe they could find you."

The drip that Andrey had put into my arm made me feel sleepy, and I soon dozed off. Later in the afternoon I received my first visitors. When Alex entered the tent followed by three men, at first I could not place where they fitted in. Dan Mazur introduced himself again, as did Myles Osborne and Andrew Brash. I was still sleepy and lying on my mattress on the floor. I recognized two of them as the pair who had identified me as I walked into camp. Their names meant nothing to me at this point, but I was happy to talk. Gradually, from their line of questioning me, I realized that these were three of the people who had kept me alive the previous morning. I joked about the boat incident, putting forward my theory that my mind had somehow confused my lack of balance with the instability of the deck of a boat. I found that I had to slow down my speaking because my mouth and my tongue could not keep up with my words. To them, I must have seemed totally wasted, while in myself I felt happy with my evolving set of circumstances. They left after only a few minutes, and it had not even occurred to me to thank them. The only thanks I gave them was a polite "Thanks for dropping by."

I sensed that they felt good because they realized how significant their role had been in my survival.

Dinnertime was very quiet for me because I was lying alone in my tent. I did not eat, either because Andrey thought I shouldn't or because I couldn't accommodate the idea—I can't remember which. I went to sleep, only to be woken by Andrey and Sergey preparing me and then themselves for the night. Andrey made sure that my nasal oxygen feed was working and was securely in place. He checked that I had not brushed the bandages off my hands.

"You can wake Sergey or me in the night for any problems," said Andrey, "but I think you will be okay."

I slept very heavily through the early part of the night, but I was eventually woken by a tremendous thirst. I knew that somewhere in the darkness, within reach, there was one inch of Coke at the bottom of a mug. With my numb hands, I had no hope of finding that holy grail without knocking it over. I tried to produce some saliva, but those glands had dried up two days ago. At last I called out and managed to wake Sergey, who came with a flashlight. We found the Coke, which I drank immediately, then Sergey replaced it with a third of a cup of water. He left me with the flashlight in case of another crisis.

The next morning I felt both better and worse. Solid sleep had recharged my batteries, and my mind seemed clearer. I could comprehend my condition more clearly, but the news was not good. My frostbite did not concern me too much because Andrey had taken it in hand, and I knew that the treatment began with months of waiting. It was dehydration that was driving me crazy. Andrey had given me a good reason why I should take only small sips of liquid at well-spaced intervals, but I could not remember what that reason was.

Kevin arrived with some dried fruit that Barbara had prepared for me at home, as well as some sports gels and CocoChia bars—all booty from my tent. Although he had brought them for me, I felt strangely possessive about them. He laid them all out on the tent floor beside me, praising them like a salesman, but I did not want to eat anything because my throat was too dry.

Alex came into the tent and announced that he had arranged a yak for me to ride down the glacier. My plan had always been to walk all the way back to Base Camp, and I did not want to listen to Andrey's plan.

I interrupted because I needed to talk to him about the Sherpas attacking me. I asked Kevin to leave the tent.

"Look, sorry, mate," I said. "This is something very personal—I just want to talk to Alex."

I began to explain but then made a suggestion. "Maybe Sergey should be here," I said to Alex. "This is something very sensitive to your business, and his English is very good."

"My English is good enough," Alex replied, and he asked Sergey to leave the tent as well. I started to explain my encounter with the two Sherpas below the First Step, but I hadn't reached even the first signs of the intimidation when someone called for Alex through the door. Alex excused himself, and I lay there waiting. When he returned, he announced that my yak was ready for me. This was an announcement I certainly was not ready for.

"But I want to walk."

"You cannot walk," said Andrey, who had come into the tent with Alex. "You also have frostbite on your foot, so to walk would make bad."

I sighed inwardly but accepted the logic.

"Now we make ready for you one yak," said Alex. "We will bring you outside."

That brought to a close any possibility of a discussion that day about my confrontations with the Sherpas.

I HAD NEVER RIDDEN a yak and was not looking forward to the experience. My steed was a medium-sized black beast sporting a good pair of horns and a typical wooden cargo-saddle. This had been modified for human transport by having a thin foam mattress lashed to it. Because my frostbitten fingers were bandaged for protection and it was feared that I would not be able to hold on, I was lashed to the saddle as well. I was not enthusiastic about this approach because I would be in serious trouble if the yak slipped. On the glacier were sections of steep ice, covered in rocks, down which a yak could easily tumble. If this happened while I was tied to the animal, I might as well have stayed on the top of Everest.

Accompanying me were two Tibetan *yakpas* and Andrey, as well as three other yaks carrying my two big dry-bag duffels, along with barrels of rubbish and some tents. The saddle was uncomfortable, but the rhythm of the stride of the yak as it walked was more tolerable than the motion of the camels I had ridden in Rajasthan. I felt out of place as I rode down the hill away from Advance Base Camp. I was a walker, not a rider.

The Tibetan *yakpa* had no English or Nepali, but he was fluent in sign language. Before we hit dangerous ground, he gave me a lesson in yak-riding. The principles were the same as riding a motorbike. It was all to do with leaning the right way. The difference was that bikers leaned into the corners, while yak-riders leaned parallel to the hills. When heading up a steep hill, I was to lean forward toward the yak's head, as this would make it less likely for the animal to tumble over backward. When descending a steep slope, I was to lean backward to make it easier for the yak to balance. The concept was to keep the center of gravity in a useful place and to trust the beast between my knees.

Soon I tuned into the plus side of being a passenger. I did not have to concern myself with where I was going to put my next step or whether I was going to tackle the upcoming hill fast or slow. I did not have to think about anything at all. The animal's long black hair absorbed the heat, and I could enjoy its warmth on my face as I leaned forward, while on the downhills I could take in the view without having to watch my step.

Fourteen miles was a long way to go on the back of a yak, and five or six hours in the saddle was a long time. It was a strange mix of sufferance and comfort, and I pondered how that theme exists throughout life. Philosophy from the Back of a Yak, Lesson One. There were a few times when I was seriously frightened as we headed down long steep slopes. But fear was like a well-worn pair of jeans to me now.

Despite the wooden saddle chafing my backside, the second half of the journey went quickly. As I drifted into a reverie, my mind freewheeled with an open sense of well-being. As we descended to the lower East Rongbuk valley, I admired the steep craggy peaks with their dramatic rock pinnacles and deep canyons. The rugged and challenging landscape elicited different emotions from me than those of the giant icy mountains I was putting behind me. There were no jet-stream winds, no avalanches, no life-snatching blizzards, and no frostbite to threaten me here. The rocky peaks had their own storms, certainly bleak and inhospitable but not deadly. The rugged, snowless landscape was reassuring, almost welcoming.

Of course, all mountain landscapes are immutable and emotionless. There is a purity that exists in the absence of life there, and perhaps it is to make that beauty a part of ourselves that we climb mountains. Looking from afar is not enough. As climbers, we need to sacrifice our comfort, our safety, and arguably our sanity, as a tithe to the mountain. But no matter what homage we pay, we are the losers, spurned in love. A summit reached can be a one-night stand, big on experience but empty of meaning—except to our egos. We need the mountains, but the mountains do not need us. After the summit, I had taken a drubbing—fingers, toes, my voice, and my ego, all sacrificed. There was no longer the obstacle of ambition, and any possibility of the conceit of conquest was vanquished. Although Everest was behind me, at last there was simply me and the beauty of the mountain.

Twenty-two

TOUCHDOWN

THE FRIENDSHIP BRIDGE IS the perfect border-crossing between Tibet and Nepal. Upstream lies the huge gorge that splits the Himalayan range. Downstream lies a lesser gorge, one filled by a seething torrent that smashes against the vertical walls and huge boulders rounded to perfect smoothness by a million years of pounding water. The river begins as snowmelt from the countless Himalayan glaciers that drain from Tibet.

No fences are necessary where the Bhote Kosi River emerges from the upper gorge. The roar of the river is a constant reminder that the bridge is the only route between the two countries.

Late on the evening of May 29, after a long drive from Base Camp, Andrey and I arrived at Zhangmu, the noise of the river beneath us.

THAT MORNING I HAD awoken in the hospital tent at Base Camp. The extra oxygen in the air 4,000 feet below Advance Base Camp had knocked me out like a sleeping draught. Andrey had put morphine in my drip as a backup. The last thing he wanted was for me to revert to one of my fantasy worlds and to walk off to Poland in the night, looking for Barbara. As I lay there, in the morning silence of the deserted Base Camp, an unexpected figure stepped through the door flap.

"Hello, Russell," I said.

"So you know who I am?"

"Of course."

"That's fantastic. After what you've been through, I wondered if you'd ever be the same again."

There was no guarantee that I would be. I had yet to assess the damage.

"Look, I've just checked in to see how you are. I'm leaving for Tingri with the Sherpas straightaway. I've got a storage place there and the guys have got to sort all the gear, and then we'll head to Zhangmu. Let's make sure we catch up there."

"Sounds great. Thanks for dropping by." That phrase again, but at least this time I knew exactly who I was talking to and why.

We had a quick breakfast, and it was not long before Andrey and I were standing next to the battered Landcruiser that was to take us to Zhangmu. There was nothing for me to pack because my belongings were already en route to my next of kin. All I had to do was say my good-byes to Harry, Milan, and Kevin, to Alex, Luda and Maxim, to the two Sergeys, and to the kitchen crew. Everyone except the kitchen staff, both Tibetan and Nepalese, I expected to meet again in Kathmandu. I had set aside some useful items to give as presents to these hard-working men, who received none of the kudos of the climbing Sherpas. Unfortunately, everything of mine, except for the clothes I had worn on the mountain, had already arrived in Kathmandu. Sincere thanks had to be enough.

The Sherpas were pulling down tents and packing gear, but Pemba took time out and wandered over. I had not seen him since he had left me at 28,000 feet. No doubt he wondered what I now thought, given that the last time he had seen me he had left me as dead. I gave him a huge hug, only then realizing how short he was. He had always appeared much larger than that. There was nothing to say except thank you, as he now knew that everything he had done with me and for me had been for the good.

I looked around for the other Sherpas, but the Tibetan driver was already in the Landcruiser, revving the engine. Andrey sat in the front, while I stretched out in the back.

We rattled across the vast flat to the beginning of the road, and we picked up speed as we drove through the shantytown of tents that I had never bothered to explore. I looked back, but the rear window was covered in dust, and what little visibility remained was obscured by the dust churned up by our wheels. I knew that a short way down the valley there were curves in the road where I would be able to see the great mountain. I wound down the window in preparation, and although we were now far away, when the mountain came into view, it looked larger. The close-up views from Advance Base Camp showed only one flank, and from Base Camp, Changtse hid sixty percent of Everest. While on the mountain, I had found the scale incomprehensible. Although the vehicle was already full of dust, the driver insisted I wind up my window.

I had nothing much to say, as I seemed to have learned how to disregard time, which meant there was no need to fill in the silences. On the summit of Everest, I had been aware of the elusive nature of time but only because I had a finite amount in which to complete my quest. Now, on the dusty back seat of the Landcruiser, the passing of time was irrelevant. Its only measure was the discomfort announced by my stripped-down body. At extreme altitudes, there is not enough fuel to keep the body operating. By my third trip to the North Col and back, all my fat reserves had been metabolized. My muscles had wasted away as well. Other natural processes had gone haywire through the lack of necessary enzymes, hormones, and other metabolic processes. It was not surprising that my body ached, and yet the most intrusive injury was the raw patches on my buttocks from the wooden yak saddle. As the hours passed, my discomfort became less of an issue. I was warm, I was traveling, and there was an ever-changing scene at the window. The monotony that had been a feature of our journey to Base Camp now no longer existed. It was almost a shock to arrive at Nyalam because I had been in a state of observing and not ticking off milestones.

We wound down into the Bhote Kosi gorge and began the long sequence of switchbacks that led down toward Zhangmu. The most spectacular aspect of this part of the journey was not the huge gorge with its imposing cliffs—rugged terrain had surrounded us for two months and was no longer anything special. What was different now was the greenery. The flanks of the gorge were cloaked in jungle. We had left behind a world where life was represented by weather-beaten mountaineers, Tibetans, and Sherpas, and supply trains of yaks. There were also birds, deer, and rodents, although these were rarely seen. But now the overwhelming impression was that plants had taken over the world, and it was a hugely welcoming transformation.

It was a strange feeling to be driving into Zhangmu. Only the one road zigzagged down through the town, but it was sealed and all the buildings were made of bricks or concrete. The road was two lanes wide, but there was usually traffic only in one direction at a time because one side of the street was taken up by parked trucks. Of course, there were suicide drivers who drove uphill against the trucks heading down into Nepal with loads of Chinese manufactured goods. Power lines were everywhere, and there were dozens of stores selling the bargains to be found at any border town. Massages were available, with the option of happy endings.

Andrey knew which hotel to go to, just across the road from where we had stayed two months ago. We bumped into Russell and agreed to meet for dinner. In our room I lay down on the bed in my filthy dust-covered clothes, only to be woken an hour later by Andrey, who said, "Now is time for dinner."

I had been so deeply asleep that at first I had no idea where I was, but Andrey was such an unforgettable character that I soon snapped back into our current project, which was to have dinner with Russell. *Project* was the best word to describe the way I was dealing with each segment of life at that moment.

Dinner was good. Russell was sitting with fifteen Sherpas in a restaurant where he was obviously well known to the proprietors. He brought a lot of customers to the business, and they loved him for it. They loved Andrey and me as well. It was strange to be sitting in a proper restaurant again, surrounded by people I didn't know. The three of us sat together, with Andrey saying very little. We had arrived late, and soon the Sherpas had finished eating and headed off to do whatever they did at the end of another hard but successful expedition.

Our food came quickly, and as we ate, Russell talked about how my plight had been perceived. I was stunned to learn that I had been battling against the Sherpas who were with me when I was stricken with cerebral edema.

"You've got to know this, mate," he said. "This is what they're saying. The Sherpas know that people go crazy up there; that's just how it is."

"That's unbelievable."

"It was heartbreaking to listen to it on the radio," he said. Then he went on to say that I had been calling them black bastards. This was unbelievable and I could only suspect that the Sherpas who had bullied me had spread that rumor. I would have to find the Sherpas when they arrived in Kathmandu and hear the facts from all of them.

Andrey abruptly excused himself and disappeared into the street. Russell took the opportunity to talk about David Sharp. Russell himself had not become aware of David Sharp's existence until 9:30 A.M. on May 15, because none of his Himex climbing team had realized in the very early hours of the morning that Sharp was alive—or, rather, that he was in the process of dying. It was when the Himex team descended from the summit in daylight that some of the climbers realized David was alive. Attempts were made to rouse him, but he was obviously very close to death. Members of the Turkish expedition also had to give up their attempts to resuscitate him. Most climbers who came down past David assumed from his appearance that he was dead.

All the Himex climbers had departed from Base Camp over a week ahead of Russell, and during that time the press had descended upon them. Mark Inglis, who as a double-amputee was among the least able to perform a rescue, was pilloried by the media because he initially believed he had seen David alive in the depth of the night. However, the climbers directly in front of and behind Mark have confirmed that they did not see David until their descent in daylight. Mark was a victim of high-altitude confusion. For him the climb of Everest was not only a personal goal but also a way to raise both funds and awareness for Cambodian amputees. He achieved his goal of the summit but suffered severe frostbite as the price.

Russell found himself under fire as the leader of one of the two expeditions on the mountain at the time when David Sharp was dying. In fact, it was Russell who had made it his business to establish the identity of the climber, a search that led him to the camp of Dave Watson, who realized the description matched that of his friend David Sharp. Ang Tshering Sherpa of Asian Trekking, who had organized the logistics for several small teams and some independent climbers under the one permit, was able to provide David Sharp's details. Russell rang Sharp's parents and promised that, en route to Chamonix, he would stop in London to give them David's belongings, as well as film footage of his last day.

I realized that this course of action was typical of Russell's thoroughness. Everything that Russell said on the matter made sense to me. Although I was deeply exhausted, the extra oxygen at 8,000 feet allowed me to process information better. We talked late into the night, stopping only because the hot water was to be turned off in the hotel at midnight. I desperately needed a shower, not only to wash away the grime but also as a kind of ritual cleansing that would signify the end of my ordeal.

THE EVENTS OF the morning began with a rush. It was still very early when we arrived at the same restaurant for breakfast, but most of Russell's Sherpas were finishing up and heading out the door. Russell was hunched over a pile of papers, no doubt manifests for taking mountaineering gear back into Nepal.

The service was again fast, which was something new to me in Chinese territory, and Andrey and I ate quickly as well. Russell arranged for a young Tibetan man who spoke good English to lead us to the front of the line at the immigration post 200 yards down the street. Because of my frostbite and because Andrey was my doctor, we were the first people to be allowed through when the office opened. My pack was only half full, and Andrey's was not much more. His belongings and all the medical equipment would follow in a day or two, on a truck from Base Camp. A black Chinese jeep awaited us, and we drove down the street a few hundred yards, to where the road had been destroyed by a landslide. There appeared to be no real danger, but we had to walk across this section, which included another few hundred yards of undamaged road that zigzagged down the hill toward the Bhote Kosi River and the bridge.

While still at Base Camp, I had spoken to Barbara, who told me that she would be coming to Kathmandu with Simon Balderstone, and that on the day I was to cross the border, Mike was hoping to be at the Tibetan border with the Australian ambassador for Nepal.

"Don't worry," Barbara had said. "Someone will be there to meet you. The press are likely to be there as well. You've got no idea how much interest your story has generated."

I had almost forgotten about that conversation as my weary mind endeavored to cope with an increasing array of "projects." Now I could no longer dwell in my head and only have conversations with people like Russell and Andrey who knew exactly what life was like on the mountain. I would have to face the world and in a very big-picture sense, if the press was going to be there. I felt nervous as I walked to the Chinese immigration point at the beginning of the Friendship Bridge. It was here that the final formality from their side was completed with a stamp on my passport and the passing over of a simple form.

Sure enough, when I looked down the wide concrete bridge, I saw crowds of people on the Nepalese half. Among them were some TV journalists, recognizable by their sound technicians who carried poles with boom mikes. I walked toward them, as that was the only direction available. Suddenly I spotted Mike beaming at me, so I locked my eyes on his as I walked and tried to ignore everyone else. When I reached the halfway point, people crowded around me, asking in Australian accents what had happened to me, how I felt, and what I was going to do now. The only question I answered was that I felt good, all things considered. The severe hoarseness of my voice was a good excuse to say nothing more, so I dropped the volume and whispered, "I really can't talk."

The press seemed to accept the situation, encouraged no doubt by the impression that I was a dead man walking. They followed me into the Nepalese border post, where the ambience was much more relaxed than at the other end of the bridge. Cameras were poked over my shoulder as I signed forms with my bandaged frostbitten fingers. Travelers heading into Tibet were puzzled by the commotion. As I stepped out onto the road, Mike quickly took me aside and introduced me to the Australian ambassador, Graeme Lade.

Bizarrely, I now had to deal with the protocols of diplomacy. Everything was proper, contrary to my appearance. We walked toward a late-model Land Rover Discovery, the ambassadorial vehicle. The ambassador's presence kept the press at a discreet distance. As Mike opened the car door, Graeme told me that protocol required that he had to sit directly behind the driver. That was fine by me.

Protocol also put the press vehicles behind the Land Rover bearing the Australian flag. Soon we were driving down a narrow street, chickens and dogs leaping out of the way and children waving from windows and doorsteps. None of us was in a particularly talkative mood. The ambassador did not need to know the details of my misadventure; he would have read the appropriate briefing papers, with Mike having filled in the gaps. Graeme pointed out the eco-resort where he, Mike, and the driver had spent the previous night. Its big selling point was a hundred-foot bungee jump from a cable suspension bridge, the first in Nepal.

There was a long drive ahead of us, but it was a relaxed journey through what was, for me, familiar countryside. I dozed at times, chatted when I felt like it, but mostly I just watched the world go by. Impatience is not a trait that is of any use on a mountaineering expedition. There are countless opportunities to express it, but they only weaken one's resolve and commitment to safety. But when we crested the rim of the Kathmandu Valley, I began to feel its first twinges. From the crest of the pass, it always felt much farther than it really is to the city of Kathmandu. My first real stirrings of impatience in two months came from the possibility that Barbara had already arrived.

At last we met the ring road surrounding the ancient city. We drove along the section that flanked the airport, and at that very moment the Thai Airways 12:30 P.M. flight from Bangkok flew directly over us, not more than 200 feet above the ground. Barbara and Simon were on board. It was a unique coincidence that made me believe that everything would be okay.

I KNEW FROM BARBARA that she and Simon would be staying at the Radisson Hotel, so that was our first stop. The traffic had been thick as we came through the town, a welcome contrast to the deserted streets during the civil unrest at the time we left for Tibet. Graeme dropped us off, and we thanked him profusely for the long journey he had undertaken to shepherd me home. He may not have realized that I regarded Kathmandu as my second home, although I had talked about some of my trekking and climbing experiences during the long drive. Mike and I were able to grab a quick lunch from the famous Radisson buffet. This was my first opportunity to drink as much as I liked, as Andrey had gone directly to the Vaishali Hotel when we were dropped at the Radisson.

He had arranged with my insurance company for me to visit the International Clinic, and an appointment had been booked. My insurance company was Danish—you have to look far and wide to get insurance for climbing Mount Everest.

We caught a cab to the clinic, expecting that we would catch up with Simon and Barbara back at the Radisson. To my surprise, the press were already there in the courtyard. A much better surprise, when we went inside, was to find Barbara and Simon there ahead of us. A quick exit from the airport, where they were picked up by Ang Karma, had given them a head start. Barbara was seriously overdressed for the pre-monsoon heat, having based her wardrobe choices on our winter visit eighteen months earlier. We hugged and kissed, but only briefly because open displays of that kind of affection are not the way of things in Nepal.

"Are you okay?" she asked, her expression revealing that she felt I was not.

"I catch dinosaurs," I said.

This may have startled Simon and Ang Karma, but Barbara would have understood. A common response of mine when people asked how I was, at a time when things could have been better, was for me to say that "I catch dinosaurs." These words were from a Bob Dylan song, "I Shall Be Free": "I see better days and I do better things. (I catch dinosaurs, I make love to Elizabeth Taylor . . . Catch hell from Richard Burton!)"

I turned to Ang Karma and shook his hand.

"Welcome, Lincoln Daai," he said with a gentle smile.

Simon and I hugged.

"Onya, mate! So good to see you."

I turned to Barbara again, but the doctor was impatiently beckoning me to his consulting room. He gave me a fairly thorough going-over with various instruments, while Andrey made brief comments. From the outside it appeared that nothing particularly remarkable had happened to me. At this time of year, no doubt, a procession of damaged mountaineers would have come through his rooms. It was an unusual consultation, nevertheless, because it had been planned for me to go to another clinic directly afterward—one that Simon had determined had the best reputation for the treatment of frostbite.

We had some spare time up our sleeves before our next appointment, so rather than joining the press and their cameras outside, we sat in the waiting room and talked. Or, at least, the others talked and I conversed in my hoarse whisper.

Barbara kept asking me, "Are you okay?"

I assured her that I was, but I had forgotten what I had looked like in the mirror of the hotel at Zhangmu.

The time came for us to go to the CIWEC Clinic Travel Medicine Center, which meant we had to brave the press. There was only one way out, as far as we could see, and that was directly through the mob. I was amazed at the size of the crowd. A dozen flashes went off; questions came from all directions. It was easier that way because I wasn't refusing to answer any particular questions, just all of them at once.

Ang Karma's driver was waiting to take us to the CIWEC Clinic. The press must have assumed we were heading for the Radisson, which was just around the corner from the clinic, because only one journalist followed us. Once inside the clinic, I was given the once-over again, with a tetanus shot for good measure. Dr. Pandey examined my frostbite, and again Andrey explained how he had handled my injuries. She soaked my hands and my foot in an antiseptic solution, then she called in Shanti, a nurse, to dress my fingers. This process took an hour, and once it was done, I looked like I was wearing boxing gloves. They certainly provided good protection.

Our stay at the CIWEC Clinic had been long enough for the press at the Radisson to get bored and disperse. My next priority was to get away from everyone and to have a bath and a sleep. Barbara was also deeply tired after restless nights of worry. She had seen in my eyes that I had been deeply traumatized, but when we were able to spend time together, her fears that I might have been irreparably damaged were laid to rest. I had frostbite, yes, but I had decided to regard it as a rite of passage.

THEY WERE STRANGE but busy days in Kathmandu. After Ang Karma had dropped us back at the Radisson that first afternoon, he told us that he and Kunga would bring us a dinner of *mo-mos*.

"This way you will not have to face restaurant crowds," he said. "We will come to your room."

"Can you do that?" I asked. "What will the hotel think?"

He raised his hand, palm upward and outward. He needed to say nothing. He knew the people here; these were special circumstances. His gesture and patient smile said it all.

The *mo-mos*—fried vegetable dumplings—were delicious. He knew they were my favorite Sherpa and Tibetan dish.

The next morning Karma and Kunga came with breakfast, a rich delicious porridge. They brought tea in a thermos and toast insulated by tea towels. It was simple food but just what I needed. Each morning they did this for us, making us feel welcome, making us feel at home, eager to rebuild me, with their lovingly prepared food, into the man I had once been.

Another caring routine was the daily changes of the dressing covering my frostbite at the CIWEC Clinic. Dr. Pandey would check my progress, then Shanti would slowly and carefully replace the dressings. It felt almost like a ceremony to me. Regardless of what was happening in the room—Mike filming the treatment or the NBC crew doing the same—Shanti remained unflustered.

The damage was quite distinct now. The outermost joint of every finger was black, signifying dead tissue, and the delineation became clearer every day until it was as distinct as the squares on a chessboard. My thumbs were damaged as well, but I was confident they would recover fully. But the entire big toe of my right foot appeared to have had its final marching orders.

ANOTHER DAILY ROUTINE was me trying to piece together my story. My hallucinations were remarkably clear, as were many of my memories of the climbing—the different camps, the funny incidents, the tragedies staring me in the face. I talked to Barbara about all these things, not as an extended monologue—although there were a few of those—but when incidents came into my head. One anecdote would prompt another that I had forgotten, and in this way I gradually filled out the picture.

Russell Brice had worried me with the stories his Sherpas had passed on to him about my behavior on the mountain when overcome with cerebral edema. We left each other messages at our hotels that we should get together for a beer and a chat. I was not so keen on the beer, but I like my water, so long as it is not cold.

Dan Mazur proved to be a hard man to find. I learned that he was out of Kathmandu and that he would be arriving on a particular afternoon. Details changed and messages went astray, but finally we made contact. We agreed to get together that afternoon at a delightful place known as Mike's Breakfast. I first went there in the early 1980s, not long after the old elephant-keepers' quarters had been converted to a lodge and restaurant. The elephants had long since moved on.

I could barely remember my previous conversations with Dan, but I knew that I hadn't yet thanked him for giving up his chance for the summit in order to save my life. He was a guide and very experienced climber, and he had summited Everest some years earlier, so for him it was not the end of the world. Dan brought with him Jangbu Sherpa, who was keen to see how well I had recovered. It was early days yet, but I was a different man from the one they had resuscitated on the summit ridge. We joked, took photos, and I asked Dan to point me toward Myles Osborne and Andrew Brash. I learned that Andrew was staying at the Kathmandu Guest House, so well known and long established that it is now an institution.

I rang the Kathmandu Guest House and left a message that we should meet. A message came back suggesting that we meet for dinner at a restaurant I had never been to—"just show up if you can," the message said. I was unable to show up because I could not find the place.

I then got distracted by the arrival of an NBC television film crew, which flew in from a project in London. I spent half a day with them, then needed to sleep the entire afternoon afterward. Sleep was one of my biggest needs.

Some people I did not have to chase. Mostly we ate our lunches at the Radisson. There was the convenience factor, as my doctor's instructions were to walk as little as possible, but there was also the fantastic lunchtime buffets. I knew the hotel well because I had spent many nights here over the years as a trekking guide for World Expeditions. Here I could put my foot up on a chair. A procession of the 7Summits-Club climbers came through. It seemed that just before they left Kathmandu they came to see me. Among them were Slate, Ronnie, Henrik, and Kirk—when they had left Base Camp I was dead, high on the mountain.

"I thought it was impossible you could die," Slate told me over lunch. "With the attitude you had and all your experience, I thought it was not possible for you to die."

He speared another potato with his fork. "And I was right—it was not possible."

AS THE DAYS PASSED, I felt stronger, thanks to proper rest, good food, and plenty of love and water. The frostbite was glaringly obvious, but the damage inside was impossible to judge. The trauma I had suffered was still apparent in the wildness of my eyes. Barbara, Simon, and Mike withheld some bad news from me until they felt I was able to cope. Then Barbara told me one morning that Sue Fear had died on Manaslu. The accident had happened while I was riding the yak to Base Camp, three days ago now.

"We didn't tell you because it wasn't confirmed at first."

To say that "I could not believe it" was not true, but I did not want to believe it. When I learned of the circumstances, I thought that the only realistic hope could be that she had died without pain.

Sue and her climbing partner, Bishnu Gurung, had reached Manaslu's 26,781-foot summit on the morning of May 28. They had descended to a snow plateau at 25,000 feet, where Sue broke through the crust of the surface snow and plunged headfirst into a deep crevasse. Bishnu held her weight tightly on the rope for over an hour, shouting to Sue but hearing not one single reply. He endeavored to set up a pulley system that might have made it possible for him to pull her free, but suddenly the snow around the crevasse collapsed, dragging the rope and the anchor in. Bishnu leaped to the side and escaped with his life. He was alone, high on the mountain, and was very lucky to make it down alive.

Barbara told me that everyone had been holding out hope because I seemed to have come back from the dead, so why not Sue? Crazy logic. It is one thing to be a body left on a mountaintop, but altogether another to disappear down a crevasse high on a deserted, 26,000-foot peak, without a trace, without a cry for help.

Sue's death was a missile from left field. There had been so much death on Everest, and I had grieved as best I could for those people—and to ease my own spirit. I tried to rationalize, to find reasons, but there had been only cold comfort, so that in the end I walked gently and could only wash my hands of the tragedies.

But I did not want to wash my hands of Sue. Her intense make-it-happen approach to life had defined her. Whether her spirits were up or down, she had always looked for the next chance or was creating it. There were no more next chances now, and I felt deeply saddened by the fact that she would no longer be bringing goodness to the world.

THE NEWS ABOUT SUE made me only more desperate to track down Myles Osborne and Andrew Brash. Dan had disappeared off the radar, so I could not confer with him, and the message system at the Kathmandu Guest House did not seem to be ideal.

There were other engagements that took up time. I liked to spend my evenings relaxing and my nights sleeping, but it would have been rude to say no to the 7Summits-Club farewell dinner at the Rum Doodle. I arrived late and left early because I knew I would not be able to raise my voice above the noise of the crowd, and that if I tried, my throat would ache. It was a night of vodka and toasts of all kinds, including one to me for surviving and another to the Sherpas for bringing me down. If there were mentions made of the dead, I did not hear them. I wanted to talk with the Sherpas, but it was too festive an occasion, and instead I asked Alex to arrange a time for me to meet with them in more controlled circumstances.

Mike, Barbara, and I had dinner with Russell Brice and a few other Everest luminaries at the Red Onion Bar, Russell's favorite watering hole, which just happened to be next door to the Radisson.

Simon turned up much later, having undertaken to bring back to Australia all Sue Fear's belongings. Since we had arrived, he had been kept busy dealing with the press. I was not all that surprised at the initial flurry of interest. The press could always draw a few column inches from a death or survival story on Everest, and my story had both. There was also Sue's tragic death to add to the mix. However, I was surprised the media interest did not die down. Channel 7 sent a four-person crew to Kathmandu to shoot a twelve-minute interview with Barbara and me, which took place in the garden at the Radisson and inside at the CIWEC Clinic. When Kunga heard this was about to happen, she whisked Barbara away to a beauty salon so that her hair could be styled, her nails done, and more makeup applied than I had ever seen on Barbara. Kunga was more excited about the process than Barbara. Simon commented that she looked like a Nepalese princess.

Simon was also taking care of our travel arrangements, so he walked down to the Thai Airways office on Durbar Marg, the main street running south from the Royal Palace. He wanted to confirm seats for himself, Barbara, Mike, and me and to make sure that Barbara and I had been allocated vegetarian meals. The arrangements were fine for everyone except me. My ticket had been canceled. Simon was stunned, but it was quickly determined that my ticket had been canceled within twenty-four hours of my death. Proving that I was alive was the initial stumbling block. There was a bit of a tussle because the plane was now fully booked, but Simon is good at tussles, and so we all ended up flying business class, which was much better for my frostbitten foot.

MY MEETING WITH the Sherpas took place at the bar overlooking the rooftop swimming pool on the fifth floor of the Radisson. Fifteen Sherpas showed up. Luda and Sergey Kofanov were there with Alex, looking to continue their drinking after the meeting, I guessed. By chance, Michael Kodas, a climber and journalist who had been in the next camp to us at Advance Base Camp, was there as well. It was a good bar, with a great view. Mike was there with his camera to record the meeting so that I could put all the pieces together at another time. Mingma Gelu translated questions and answers, but not every answer was clear and some were contradictory. The two Sherpas who had persecuted me, who had been so relieved when I told them I did not remember their names as we rested on our way down to ABC for the last time, looked like they did not want to be there. I asked them to describe my hostility high on the mountain, and what they gave was a mirror image of events—one of them repeated the motion of swinging with the ice axe but attributed it to me. I raised my arm to show the bruises, but they did not appreciate the implications. There had been only one ice axe.

Alex was sitting next to me, and I asked him, "Have you ever seen anything like this before?"

"No," he said.

"So what do you think?"

He paused for a moment, then smiled and said, "That you are a real man, after all."

A real man in the Russian sense—vodka-swilling, ice axe–wielding, bride-selling. I had to laugh with him.

Mingma continued to answer questions on behalf of the Sherpas, but I only became more confused. I thanked everyone, and then we closed the meeting with some group photos.

WE HAD FIVE full days at Kathmandu, and by the evening of the fifth day I had still not been able to track down Andrew or Myles. I figured the best thing to do was to be at the Kathmandu Guest House at breakfast time the next day, in the hope of catching Andrew before he went out. Ang Karma came with me, and to my delight my plan worked. At a table in the outside eating area, I spotted not only Andrew but also Dan Mazur and Andrew's wife, Jennifer. With them was a man whom I did not know, taking notes.

We were flying to Bangkok that afternoon, so I was not looking for a long conversation. What I really wanted to convey to Andrew were the important omissions from my spaced-out conversation at Advance Base Camp a week earlier. I explained to him that, now that I was thinking more clearly, I wanted to thank him personally for looking after me and for giving up his summit climb for me. It seemed to go down well. The man with the notepad took photos of the four of us.

My next task was to find Myles Osborne. They were able to name his hotel but could not tell me where it was. This was where Ang Karma helped greatly. He spoke to the shopkeepers who were opening up but hit a few dead ends. We hired a cycle-rickshaw in the interests of both speed and resting my foot. Gradually, we eliminated all alternatives and reached another dead end, which was where we found Myles's hotel.

But first I noticed Elizabeth Hawley, legendary chronicler of Himalayan expeditions, at an outside table with Dan's associate, Phil Crampton. I greeted Miss Hawley and introduced myself to Phil.

"Myles is inside," said Phil. "He had a big night at the casino, so he could be feeling a bit seedy."

He called out, and one of the hotel boys appeared. Phil asked him to fetch Myles. It was a few minutes before he arrived—hair tussled, T-shirt inside-out, but pleased to see me.

"So glad to catch you," I said. "I'm flying out in a few hours so this was my absolute last chance. What a rabbit warren these alleys are."

He smiled and said it was good to see me looking much better.

"Thanks to you," I said.

"Not really, you got yourself under way when the time came."

"After you guys kept me alive."

I also thanked him for giving up his summit for me.

That had to be the end of the conversation because I had to get back to the hotel and out to the airport. Karma took a photo of us, and we were on our way.

THERE WAS QUITE a farewell on the steps of the Radisson Hotel. Graeme Lade was there, along with Ang Tshering Sherpa and his manager, Dawa Sherpa, who between them ran Asian Trekking, the very successful expedition outfit engaged by Alex. Ang Karma and Kunga were there, of course, along with Lakpa and Uma, who managed different aspects of the World Expeditions trekking groups that stayed at the Radisson.

Mike snapped a couple of quick photos, then we were bundled into the embassy's van and were weaving through the traffic to the airport.

AS WE FLEW from Bangkok to Sydney, Barbara and I sat at the front of the plane. I had decided to devote the entire nine-hour flight to relaxing completely. My seat was tilted back, my feet were elevated, and I drifted into a deep sleep. When I awoke, Barbara was reading Salman Rushdie's *The Ground Beneath Her Feet*. Back at Wentworth Falls, while waiting to hear if I was dying, Barbara had been forced to put the book down. She had reached a phase of the story that had been full of death and loss, but she was well past that section now.

I turned to my left and looked out the window. The Java Sea looked metallic, a fluid mercury made yellow by the angle of the sun. The sharp-edged shadows of huge towers of monsoon cloud turned sections of sea to the gray-blue color of slate. The clouds themselves could have been progeny of benign nuclear explosions. It was an amazing sight. The sun shone onto me through the window, warming me and making me feel a part of the scene.

It was so beautiful that tears filled my eyes. I began to sob softly, and then without control. The scene was blurred by my tears.

"What's wrong?" asked Barbara, reaching across to hug me. "What's the matter?"

"Nothing," I sobbed. "Absolutely nothing."

At last I could let everything go.

FLOODLIGHTS REFLECTED OFF the veneer of rainwater that lay across the black tarmac as we taxied from the runway to the terminal building. Unlike Singapore, Cairns, or Seattle, Sydney is not a place where it rains very often, so I pondered the odd fact that when I flew into Sydney on an international flight, it usually seemed to be raining. Of course, my assessment may have been warped by my expectation of returning home to Sydney's perfect weather, leading me to take particular notice of the rainy days. Tonight it could have been raining cats, dogs, and gremlins and I wouldn't have cared.

After calling home from Bangkok, Simon had told us that his partner, Jenny Hunter, Himalayan Foundation board member Christine Gee, and my sister, Julia, had organized a pain-free re-entry to Australia. A wheelchair had been arranged for me so that I would not have to walk a long distance within the terminal. There would be a private room where family and friends could greet us, and a strategy was in place to manage the media.

The wheelchair awaited me, and as Barbara pushed me through the crowds that flooded in from the last flights of the night, I wondered what I could say to everyone waiting in the private room. I felt I owed them all an apology for the anguish I had unwittingly caused. Yet they would be delighted to see Barbara and me together again, and to see me as more than a fading picture in a newspaper. At the same time, I felt embarrassed because in my passing I had forced them to reveal how they felt about me. And even if I could articulate something appropriate, I had only the hoarsest of voices with which to speak. I was, however, excited by the thought of seeing everyone. Meeting these special people again would pull me back into the world I had known before Everest; it would be confirmation that life and friendship could now continue for all of us.

After Barbara, Simon, Mike, and I passed through immigration and customs, we were led away from the flow of travelers and taken through an unobtrusive door to the promised private room. There was a strange atmosphere, as if we had arrived at a party in a sterile room with not enough chairs before the hosts were ready. Handshakes were on hold because of my frostbite, but there were hugs and kisses all round. Words did not seem important. It seemed that I was not the only one who didn't know what to say. Light conversation was enough, because—for everyone else at least—the issues had been resolved.

The strangeness of the evening peaked with my introduction to the Australian media. Jenny had once managed the press office for Prime Minister Bob Hawke, so she knew how to lay down the law to the media. My wheelchair wanted to accelerate down the short ramp ahead of us, but Simon kept it under control. The press were in a huddle ten feet away, facing the door as it opened onto a broad corridor. With Jenny standing sternly behind him, Simon wheeled me out. I looked at the press and the press looked at me, and I realized that Jenny must have emphasized my fragility to the point where nobody wanted to utter the first word. Her warnings to the media must have been supported by my appearance—wild hair, wild beard, and eyes so wild they had changed color. Silence was the last thing I expected, so I made an announcement.

"It's great to be home," I said. Cameras flashed and flashed. "Thank you for the enormous amount of support I have received since I came off the mountain. It has been fantastic."

I fielded a question about my health—one question must have been Jenny's cutoff point—and for once the limit was respected.

I thanked everyone again, then Simon pulled me and the wheelchair back through the door. My departure from the press was as unobtrusive as my arrival had been.

THE NEXT MORNING the rain had stopped and it was a beautiful day. Julia had driven Barbara and me across the Harbour Bridge. We had turned eastward toward the coast, and now we drove down past Taronga Park Zoo toward the harbor. The zoo was where Bradley Trevor Greive had arranged the media conference for Christopher's Climb thirteen weeks ago to the day. Excitement and optimism had been the tone of that morning at the zoo, but today would be very different. Our destination was Athol Hall, a beautiful, historic building set within native bushland, which was where Sue Fear's memorial service was to be held.

The hall was packed with trekkers, climbers, guides, and other outdoors people. There were Sue's friends in the media, in the outdoor equipment industry, and those involved with the same charitable works. Old friends and new friends, and of course family. It was a blur for me to be among so many familiar faces. Maybe two hundred people crowded the hall, with even the standing room taken. The only open space left when we arrived was the wide central aisle between the blocks of seats. Again I was in a wheelchair to take the weight off my feet, so I was pushed down to the front row. I did not want to be up in the front. But this was not about what I wanted: it was about Sue, so I made every effort to hold myself together.

It was a beautiful service. The friends and family who spoke encapsulated the different facets of Sue Fear. I had heard the music that was played before, as the soundtracks to the CDs of images Sue had sent me, and so it took me back to those mountain scenes. Many of the images were projected as two separate slide shows by Soren Ledet, Sue's good friend and fellow guide. I could see every mountain in three dimensions because my heart and mind were still so close to the Himalaya.

Everyone was grieving for Sue in their own way. For me there were no concepts that had to be grasped, no visualized ideas. I had fallen in crevasses and rescued people from them. Thirteen days earlier—that number again—I had been stepping past bodies on Everest's summit ridge. And I could understand her spoken wish that if she were to die on a mountain, then her body should be left there. But understanding made things no easier.

Sue had always been one for a few beers and a good yarn, and it was pronounced, correctly so, that she would have preferred us all to enjoy her wake rather than mourn her passing. I saw Grahame Fear, her elder brother, and raising my weak voice as much as I could above the now noisy crowd, I told him how pleased I was that together Sue and I had managed to write *Fear No Boundary,* the story of her life and her climbs. The book was so much more important now, I said, because the inspiration that Sue delivered when she had been alive would be perpetuated in print.

With everyone standing, the aisles were now full of people, so there was no room for me in my wheelchair. Rather than having Barbara pushing me, I shuffled along with the wheelchair in front of me like a shopping cart. Many of our friends were here, but I apologized to everyone with a hug, telling them that we had flown in last night and that we needed to get home to see Dylan and Dorje.

Julia drove us to the Blue Mountains, which from the easternmost part of Sydney is a two-hour drive. Questions circulated in my mind during the journey—"Why me? Why am I the one who is alive?"—but at this stage there were no answers.

OUR TWO DOGS BARKED vigorously when Julia pulled up at our gate, as is their wont when strangers arrive. After only a week away Barbara was not exactly a stranger, but she brought with her a bevy of exotic aromas that ranged from Kathmandu streets to sanitized aircraft cabins. And although Julia had spent two days at our home when it seemed that the worst had happened, there had been so many visitors during that time that the dogs did not recognize her either. As for me, I was obviously a wild man. Quite apart from my long absence, I was different in appearance and demeanor and I was treated by the dogs as a complete stranger.

The barking of the dogs drew Dorje and Dylan out of the house.

"Hello, Dad," said Dorje, hugging me strongly.

It was more of the same from Dylan.

"Welcome home, Dad," he said, and hugged me long and hard.

Then all of us were laughing at Tosca, our big white Maremma sheep-dog, who was skirting around behind me, constantly barking as if I was an intruder.

As a homecoming, it was low-key. It felt strange because Barbara and I had not rushed up the highway immediately to see the boys, who had to remain in the Blue Mountains to attend school, under the care of Barbara's sister, Gaye. By staying in Sydney, I had felt only partway home. I was very glad not to have missed Sue's memorial service, as it brought me some closure to her death, but of course it took the exhilaration out of the joy I felt at returning home.

But now we were here at last, looking out over the wild uninhabited country to the south. A benign fading light led the spurs and ridgelines into shadow, leaving a dark silhouette to separate the earth from the sky. It was a quiet time of day, and finally I was at home again, with the secure, grounded feeling that I had kept the resolve I had made thirteen days earlier—to return alive to my wife, to our boys, to our big noisy dogs, and to the rest of our lives together.

Twenty-three

POSTMORTEM

THE DAY I CLIMBED Mount Everest was the day I died. I lost my life, the tips of eight fingers, a toe and a half, thirty-seven pounds, and two-thirds of the energy I needed to live in my normal fashion. The tips of the fingers are gone for good, as are the toes, but I regained my life, some of my energy, and more than those thirty-seven pounds.

Many people have a problem with the issue of my death, and I must admit that I did at first. I was not able to fathom how I could have survived the set of circumstances I had experienced.

The facts of the matter are that within an hour of leaving the summit of Mount Everest, I was overcome by lethargy. At times I seemed to be conscious, but I behaved erratically, sometimes with great strength. I wanted to climb up the mountain, not down it. I wanted to jump off the Kangshung Face. I continually rejected my oxygen mask and the Sherpas continually made me put it back on. My symptoms were consistent with cerebral edema, which at 28,000 feet is a death sentence.

It was because I had shown no signs of life that I had been left by the Sherpas on the mountain with nothing in the way of life support. When Dan Mazur and his team found me next morning, they considered me to be close to death, which was a considerable improvement on how I had been the night before. When they heard me speak, they had agreed that I had a good chance of surviving.

Because of the frostbite I suffered, and a paralyzed left vocal cord,

I spent a lot of time with all kinds of doctors during the second half of 2006. None of them could tell me why I was alive. It seemed that none of them wanted to ask the question. I know enough about high-altitude physiology to appreciate that the cold should have killed me, that cerebral edema should have killed me, that hypoxia should have killed me, and that if I was somehow surviving all of these, then dehydration should have tipped me over the edge. And maybe that's what occurred. But whichever of these it was, I was regarded as dead.

If I was dead on the evening of May 25 but alive on the morning of May 26, what happened? Some may say that I had not really died. When I first arrived back at Advance Base Camp and was told that everyone believed me to be dead, my first thought was that this conclusion had been reached because I was overdue. Storms, disorientation, and exhaustion often delay climbers. On the biggest mountains, these three causes could easily add a few days to a descent, and I assumed that this was what had happened to me. I was certainly disoriented when I came down, and my sense of time was hugely distorted.

But a chill went down my spine when I learned that, after lying totally motionless in the snow at 28,000 feet for two hours, I had been pronounced dead, with the probable cause of death being cerebral edema. No one that season who had lain down on the Northeast Ridge exhausted, delirious, and unable to move had survived—not David Sharp, not Igor Plyushkin, not Vitor Negrete, not Jacques-Hugues Letrange. I knew myself too well to assume that I was tougher, stronger, or fitter than those men. Like them, I had been declared dead.

Perhaps one difference was that I had learned never to give up. During my second season among the daunting peaks of New Zealand's Southern Alps, when I had just turned twenty-one, my partner Matt Madin and I had climbed Silberhorn, an impressive but straightforward peak near Mount Cook. We gained confidence from the ease of our success on Silberhorn and decided to traverse south along the crest of the range to the summit of Mount Dampier, the country's third-highest peak. All went well at first, but soon the going became tougher.

Hours passed as we struggled up ice that was harder and steeper than either of us had encountered on any mountain during our short mountaineering careers. We had learned to climb in the Australian bushland on granite, which offered the security of superb friction. By comparison, Dampier's ice was hard, slippery, and dangerous. We thought escape would be easier if we continued upward to Dampier's summit and then down the other side, but we experienced no joy upon reaching the summit. The descent to the south was just as hard.

The sun was setting by the time we found a low point in the ridge from where we could descend. We dropped down onto the shady side of the ridge above the Linda Glacier. Instantly we were cold, and hurried to find a safe route down the hard snow of the steep face. At least we had left the ice behind. Darkness came all too quickly, and we still had not found a way down. Every time we descended, the slope below us steepened, and as we peered downward with our headlamps, every option looked like suicide. We were exhausted, with our spirits beaten from constantly climbing in a state of intense fear.

Throughout the night we searched for a way down until finally I felt I could go no further. I sat on a ledge that I had dug in the snow with my ice axe and decided that I would die there. I no longer had the strength to climb up to the crest and reclimb the frightening ridge above it. I accepted that this was my last resting point, that I would freeze to this spot.

It was Matt's turn to scout for a route down, and from near the end of our 165-foot rope I heard him call out.

"I think we can get down here!"

There was an energy in his voice that I had not heard for hours, so I stood up and carefully climbed across to him. The combined power of our two fading headlamps showed that, yes, the face was still steep below us but with a huge mound of avalanche debris piled up against it that lessened the angle and completely filled the huge crevasse that ran the length of the snow-face. An hour later we had descended the avalanche debris and were headed down the Linda Glacier toward Plateau Hut. Twenty-six hours of nonstop climbing had passed between our departure from the hut and our return to it.

Mountain climbers who discover the ways of mountaineering by themselves, rather than by taking guided climbs, find themselves in extreme situations. It is through those narrow escapes from death that climbers learn their limits. At 4:00 A.M. on Mount Dampier's East Face, I had given myself up for dead. It was a serious misjudgment that could have cost us our lives, if Matt had listened to me. The lesson I learned that night was that as long as you can keep moving, you should do so, because you will never know exactly how much you still have left to give.

On several occasions since that night, I have had to dig deeper into myself than I did on Dampier, every time extending my boundaries. We all have survival instincts, but I believe that when those instincts have been tested to the edge there is a resonance within a hidden level of consciousness which allows the energy you need to be pulled from somewhere. On Everest, as nowhere else, I had been determined to survive. Hallucinations were dancing through my mind, but beneath them was a commitment to come home. Perhaps in my case that commitment extended beyond death.

The natural forces on Everest can destroy every last shred of life, and I was lucky to have been spared that maelstrom. The elements could have been much crueler to me on the night that spanned May 25 and 26. Even so, how could I be alive? I can't answer this to my satisfaction, and I don't expect to until I have recovered properly and have had time to explore what happened. In the meantime, I rely on Tibetan Buddhism, where there is an understanding that there are eight levels of death. Judging from the criteria, I passed through the first two of these.

THERE IS A CYNICAL belief among the less informed that consciousness is an entity that is either present or absent and is therefore impossible to manage. Psychologists know that mental activities can take place at a subconscious level, without our awareness. Tibetan Buddhists understand that the subconscious mind has many levels, all of which can be explored through meditation.

Meditation is commonly thought of as a form of relaxation, a calming of the mind, but that is only the beginning. Meditation is the essence of Tibetan Buddhism. It is like exercise, in that you can take a walk in the park or you can be an Olympic gymnast. It can calm your mind, improve your sleep, or disempower your anger. You can also utilize meditation to explore the very nature of your mind. The high lamas of Tibetan Buddhism use meditation to examine the nature of reality. Although a long-time student of Tibetan Buddhism, I remain at the stage of learning to understand my mind. There are many Buddhist meditative practices that can be taught only by a lama initiated into a particular rite, but through that rite, students can experience different levels of consciousness. These are windows into a different aspect of reality.

On Mount Everest in 2006 I chose to meditate at high altitude, generally when I woke in the middle of the night and did not feel like reading. These midnight meditations were times of stillness and may have helped build the framework that kept me alive.

Meditation and hallucination are, effectively, opposites. Meditation is a stilling of the mind where thoughts no longer have control, while hallucination is the mind desperately scrambling for a foothold in a brain that is no longer doing its job properly.

Hallucination was my friend on the mountain. Cerebral edema had me in its grasp and was guiding my behavior, but my subconscious mind was still active. It was my subconscious that threw up solutions to the gaps in my conscious perception. When my sense of balance was compromised, my subconscious offered me a solution by putting me on a boat. The physical reality of being perched on a narrow ridge of the world's highest mountain—and of knowing that my balance was out of order—would have been too scary to contemplate. My misperception did not lessen the danger, but it may have prevented me from panicking. As the morning sun warmed me and Dan's oxygen set resuscitated thousands of brain cells, my subconscious offered me the concept of an airplane because this adequately explained why I was at the cruising level of a jet.

However, not all of the interpretations offered by my subconscious were comforting. It seemed that once my mind was tuned to fear or danger, there were two directions it could take. One of these was the lifesaving reversion to an alert state; the other was a sinking into paranoia. I had experienced alertness when climbing down unroped from the Third Step, and again when the two Sherpas whom Alex had directed to escort me down the mountain refused to let me adopt a safer method of rappeling. The fear of damaging my hands to the point where they could no longer be of use had sparked that particular return to clarity.

But paranoia had kicked in after the Sherpa beat me with my ice axe. I became convinced that the pair of them wanted to rob me and were prepared to kill me to achieve that goal. There was some logic to support that belief—neither of them helped me to my feet at any of the many times I fell down; nor would they listen to my opinions about how best to negotiate obstacles. My paranoia may have been irrational, but my fear was certainly justified. The blows delivered by the young Sherpa were witnessed by the Italian Marco Astori, who descended the First Step after the three of us. In Kathmandu, Barbara photographed the bruises and Mike filmed them by chance during my question-and-answer session with the Sherpas at the Radisson.

It is possible that Alex asked the two Sherpas to do whatever it took to bring me down, although he would have been horrified to think that they would hurt me. Their intimidation certainly motivated me to keep moving when I thought I couldn't. The unfortunate irony was that, had they let me walk between them with the rope pulled tight, as I had suggested, we would have made much faster progress.

Perhaps the Sherpas themselves were not functioning normally. Certainly they did not behave in the considerate and professional manner of every other Sherpa I have worked with over almost thirty years. Ang Karma was shocked when I showed him my bruises. All he could say was that not all Sherpas were good Sherpas.

However, after my meeting at the Radisson's rooftop bar with all the Sherpas who had been with me on the mountain, I realized that this horrible event could not be adequately explained by the simple matter of branding the two Sherpas who bullied and threatened me as bad Sherpas. In my worst throes of cerebral edema, when Lakcha, Dorje, Dawa Tenzing, and Pemba struggled desperately to drag me down from just below Everest's summit, I behaved irrationally and struggled against their efforts to save my life. And while the two bullying Sherpas were deliberate in their abusive actions and seemed to take pleasure from tormenting me, who am I to judge their actions when my own had been so reprehensible only twenty-four hours earlier? The best course of action was to regard everything as water under the bridge, all resentment and confusion washed away. And while I am still shocked at what happened, I now think of the incident dispassionately, and number it as one of many close scrapes with death during those unbelievable two days.

. . .

WHILE I WAS ON the mountain, my hallucinations had seemed to be either comforting or menacing, but I came to realize later that there had been a third category. Everyday consciousness identifies only life or death—not the passage in between—which means the only way to process the event of dying is through an altered state of consciousness.

My experience with the cloak took on new meaning after a Buddhist healer referred me to "The Song of the Pearl." The story dates back to the writings of Thomas, an apostle of Jesus. It describes a journey, a quest, and, most important, a cloak. At the completion of the quest the traveler is welcomed home and enfolded by a luxurious cloak, "the splendid robe of glory." Even in my altered state of consciousness, death remained too abstract to be directly embraced or rejected, so its all-encompassing finality was represented by the cloak. My interpretation of this is that I had been drawn into the first and second levels of death, as described in the Tibetan texts, and that the scene on the Polish hill took place at a level of consciousness where my mind could still intercede. From here I was able to turn back from my spiral through the levels of death. By returning the cloak I had chosen to continue to battle for my life.

ANYONE WHO HAS BEEN at altitudes above 27,000 feet knows how desperate it is to survive at those heights. By normal standards, climbing at extreme altitudes is very slow, even when using an oxygen apparatus, so invariably climbers set out for the summit of Mount Everest in the middle of the night. Vision is limited by the bulky oxygen mask and by the narrow beam of a headlamp. Speech is also difficult because of the masks, and in any case, every breath is too valuable to be wasted on words. There is a fear of the unknown in a strange place where anonymity is the norm. Figures by the path are either resting or resting in peace; often it is impossible to tell which. Sometimes the figures are not sure themselves, and their slide from life to death can pass virtually unnoticed.

My name has become irrevocably linked to that of David Sharp because, ten days apart, both of us were thought to be dead but then shown to be alive. The big difference was that when the sun rose and warmed me, I was given drinks and oxygen by Dan Mazur and his team, and from that point I was able to walk. When the sun rose on David Sharp, it did little more than show just how close to death he was. Efforts to help him were made by several people, and some sat with him in tears, each of them realizing that his death was inevitable. With the difficult terrain, the capabilities of the climbers on the mountain, and the states they themselves were in, rescue was impossible.

The media soon learned that forty people had walked past David Sharp in the earliest hours of May 15, as he lay alive but unmoving on the trail, and that he was dead by May 16. There was an outcry against the heartless ambition of climbers who would tag the top of Everest at any cost, including the price of the life of another. David himself was criticized, from afar, while he was dead or dying, for wanting to tackle the mountain on his own terms, in a simple, unencumbered way.

My own survival led people to think that David Sharp's death could have been avoided, but there were many differences between our two situations. The view of the press was simplistic: I was rescued, therefore I survived; but David Sharp was not rescued, therefore he died.

In fact, my rescue took place above 28,000 feet, when Lakcha, Dorje, Dawa Tenzing, and Pemba brought me down from near the summit to Mushroom Rock. These men gave me the opportunity to survive. That opportunity was then extended by Dan, Andrew, Myles, and Jangbu, who stopped to help me and gave up their summit chances. The subsequent "rescue" by the two Sherpas was beyond the control of Dan and his team, and proved to be more dangerous than no rescue at all.

As anyone who has floundered in deep water would agree, when you yourself are close to drowning, it's near impossible to save someone so exhausted and full of water that they can no longer float. In the case of David Sharp, there was no mountaineering equivalent of a surf lifesaving team. The most popular alpine climbing destinations in the world have trained rescue squads, but in the high Himalaya—the world's most dangerous mountains—there is none.

David's death was certainly a tragedy. Years ago I spent hours next to an injured climber, waiting for a chopper to arrive and airlift him from the base of the cliff. The man was in a coma, and I was unable to do anything for him; nor could the climbers with me. At least we were living presences by his side. Had I been able to sit for that same number of hours with David Sharp high on Everest, I might well have died myself—that is how marginal life is up there. Above 27,000 feet you can easily die when doing nothing, which is why some call it the death zone.

There was what I would call immoral, sensationalist reporting about the death of David Sharp, and scapegoats were found and lynched in newsprint and newsreel. Even my own situation, with its happy ending, was manipulated for dramatic effect to make better television. One of the problems was that the mainstream media took most of their information from a few Web reports from climbers at Base Camp who had little concern about the accuracy of their words. What they said was treated as fact and interpreted by the press as it wished. This hype meant that the press expected my story to showcase conflict between me and Alex, and me and the Sherpas who could not revive me. Nothing could be further from the truth.

In Kathmandu an Australian television crew interviewed me and Barbara for a segment to be broadcast on the Channel 7 show *Today Tonight*. At the time of the interview, I had thought that everything had gone well, with the drama of my exploits requiring no embellishment.

One of the questions *Today Tonight* had asked was: "Did you know that Alex told the Sherpas to leave you for dead?"

"Yes," I had replied, without any indication of distress or disapproval.

However, the editor or segment producer had spliced in a different answer, one that I had given to a completely different question, presumably because they wanted some extra drama.

The first I knew of this was back in Australia, when Barbara, Dylan, Dorje, and I were watching a videotape of what had gone to air. There was footage of climbers in the mess tent at Base Camp listening to a radio conversation between Alex and the Sherpas.

It began with Alex saying, "But now Lincoln is very bad. If possible, send one Sherpa up to help Lincoln. He is near dead also."

Next came voiceover from the interviewer, with footage of Alex at his telescope peering at the mountain.

"This, we are reliably informed, is the voice of expedition leader Alex

Abramov from Everest Base Camp, instructing the Sherpas to leave Lincoln and return."

I was now on camera being interviewed with a surprised expression. Hesitantly, I said, "Okay . . . That is news to me. . . ."

Again there was voiceover from the interviewer: "This is the first time Lincoln has been made aware of Abramov's orders."

But I knew from Alex that I had been declared dead. My comment had concerned another issue altogether, and I immediately told my family as much. The question to which I had actually responded, with obvious surprise, had been: "Did you know that Alex told the Sherpas to cover you with stones?" This was a totally different issue, and I had been stunned to learn that my death had been so definitive that a burial of sorts had been arranged.

"You know the man well," said the interviewer. "You must be pretty disappointed in hearing him say that. You're sitting here alive and well, admittedly with a bit of frostbite."

"Look . . ." I began.

But the interviewer threw words at me.

"Shocked? Angered? Offended?"

"I guess I'm a little bewildered," I said, meaning that I was bewildered to learn that a pile of stones was to have been my grave. "I need to talk to Alex about that."

"I would think so!" pronounced the interviewer, and the audience would have thought that I was bewildered because I had been left for dead.

At the time of the interview, Alex had not yet told me about the burial plan, which in the end had turned out not to be feasible or indeed necessary.

Obviously, the truth was not being allowed to interfere with a good story. They already had the good story, so I assumed that they had wanted to convey a sense of conflict between Alex and me or that he had attempted to keep the truth from me—neither of which had any basis in fact.

Alex had done everything he could to save me. Fifteen 7Summits-Club Sherpas had been on the mountain to strip the camps of tents and other equipment, but Alex had redirected most of these men to help with my rescue. As it turned out, this number of Sherpas was unnecessary because I had been able to walk down the mountain.

With the mainstream media deliberately creating misinformation, it was not surprising that amateur Web reports from the mountain and elsewhere were riddled with inaccuracies and (hopefully) unintended slander.

BUT THE MEDIA IS a double-edged sword. Good stories were also published, by journalists who had done their research and analyzed points of view before presenting their version to the world. Invariably, these were stories that were overviews of what took place on Everest in April and May 2006. What happened to me was certainly one of the stand-out events of the season, but because I could not give many interviews, the articles usually included only summaries. The journalists who wanted more detailed information resorted to the initial garbled reports of my misadventure.

The part of my story that could be told without any input from me was that I had been declared dead high on the mountain, that I had been left out in that state overnight, and that I had been discovered alive in a weakened but remarkably lucid state. No one who had been left for dead at that height had survived. These were a unique set of circumstances, which added a feel-good factor at the end of an Everest season that had first caught the eye of the press because of controversy and tragedy. I was happy to provide that feel-good element.

My apparent death and survival led to headlines not only in my home country of Australia, where a media flurry might be expected, but also around the world. The headlines included words and phrases such as "Miracle Man," "Lazarus," and "Dead Man Walking." There were plenty of photographs of me taken by the few climbers still around when I descended from the mountain, as well as those taken by Dan, Myles, and Andrew. The media in the United States was very keen on the story, partly because Dan was an American who could tell the story firsthand. He found himself regarded as a hero, and I was certainly prepared to support that view. As a Canadian, Andrew Brash received similar treatment in his hometown of Calgary. Myles Osborne was British but was studying at Harvard and spent much of the rest of 2006 researching his dissertation in Africa. The beams of the limelight did not highlight his contribution as effectively.

Meanwhile, I was consciously avoiding the attention. Simon Balderstone handled all media inquiries for me because I simply did not have the energy to face the press.

However, one opportunity arose that was impossible to refuse. An NBC crew had filmed us in Kathmandu and invited us to appear with Dan Mazur in New York on the *Today* show and *Dateline,* both hosted by Matt Lauer. Dylan and Dorje were invited as well and were excited until they realized that it really was a "flying visit," with almost as much time in the air as on the ground. When they did the math, they decided their social engagements for the upcoming weekend seemed more appealing. Barbara came, of course, as part of the story and to look after me, while Simon looked after everything else.

The long flights that took us from Sydney to New York were the ideal way to relax. There was absolutely nothing else I wanted or needed to do but lie back and let my healing continue. When we landed at Los Angeles, my wheelchair and bandaged hands brought us special treatment, which allowed us to sidestep the huge line and be the first on board the flight to New York.

A black stretch limo waited for us outside JFK Airport. I hobbled toward this well-polished symbol of opulence and chuckled when I realized the vehicle was a Lincoln. I was also laughing at the absurdity of the whole experience and at the distance I had traveled—not the physical distance of our travels but the inconceivable divide between the world's greatest mountain and its greatest city.

Our first interview, for the *Today* show, required an early start. Matt Lauer was very easy to talk to, and our time on air was over before we knew it. The segment was received very well, according to Simon, Barbara, and Dan's partner, Liz, all of whom had been in the audience. Back at the hotel on Central Park South, we relaxed by sitting down to breakfast next to the windows. It was good to get to know Dan in more relaxed circumstances. We shared a similar deadpan sense of humor, with ridiculous comments building upon each other until we broke up laughing. Barbara and Liz were instantly on the same wavelength. Initially they collated the advantages and pitfalls of men who were mountaineers, but they quickly moved beyond that subject.

We were surrounded by New York, of course. One day we set out across Central Park to the Metropolitan Museum of Art. It was a crowded and colorful journey because it was the annual Puerto Rican Day Parade, when a million Puerto Ricans march through Manhattan. Barbara and Simon took turns pushing me in my wheelchair, with the detours set up because of the parade doubling the distance we had to travel. As fate would have it, a Hatshepsut exhibition was showing at the Met. This was a delight for Barbara, who has a master's degree in Egyptology. Hatshepsut had been one of the few women to rule as pharaoh, and her wealth and importance was obvious from the ancient artifacts on display.

Many of the exhibits were made of gold, and that reminded me of Tibet, where golden statues of Buddha and associated deities were once a feature of the monasteries. Both Egypt and Tibet had been plundered of their riches, Tibet only in the past sixty years. At least Tibet still has its mountains.

It was midday in New York, which meant the whole of Tibet would now be covered in darkness. Less than three weeks ago I had sat at Mushroom Rock in that same darkness, with snow swirling around me. I had faced the horror of death, alone and at the cruising altitude of a jumbo jet. Soon I would be at that height again but with Barbara and Simon, on a United Airlines flight.

I continued to marvel at the wealth and beauty of the three-thousand-year-old treasures. The mass and demeanor of the museum itself spoke of the wealth of modern America, with New York as its showpiece.

In one cabinet that displayed ancient body decorations, I spotted some finger and toe coverings, lying at the front of the display as if they had been laid out ready to wear. They were made entirely of gold and shaped like replica fingers and toes, complete with golden nails. There were two full sets. I called Barbara over.

"Look at these," I said. "They're exactly what I need."

My fingertips were dead, black, and mummified—not that different from the fingertips of pharaohs who had been prepared for the afterlife. I had almost passed through to an afterlife without the help of gold, so it was difficult for me to argue for it now. And besides, among the replica Egyptian ornaments and gold jewelery for sale in the museum shop, there were no golden fingers.

EPILOGUE

THE LAST SATURDAY of February 2006 was the day I had begun my training for Everest in earnest. My legs had been fit for running but not for going up and down steep slopes—which is the entire process of mountaineering. I had developed a strategy for treating my knees gently until they built up strength. It began with a loaded pack and a ten-minute jog from our house. I followed the wide trail through wind-pruned heath on the edge of the sandstone plateau, until a short downhill slope brought me to where Jamison Creek plunged over Wentworth Falls. The 700-foot drop was interrupted halfway down by a broad rocky shelf. There are pools here big enough to swim in, but the largest pool is at the base of the lower falls, edged by rainforest. I climbed down the steep ladders and steps to the base of the lower falls, where I filled the plastic bottles with two gallons of water from the pool. Ascent is much gentler on the knees than is descent, which was why I wanted the extra twenty pounds of weight only for the climb back up. At the top of the falls, I poured the water into the creek, then headed down to repeat the cycle.

A year later, on the last Saturday of February 2007, I decided to revisit the falls. The wound where my big toe had been had taken a long time to heal properly, so I had only been able to manage walks on level ground, most of which I did with our dogs and either Dorje or Dylan. On this Saturday, I did not bother to take a pack with empty apple juice bottles. Although I was far from fit after months of convalescence, I no longer had a mountain that needed to be climbed. When I came to the lookout on the southern side of the amphitheater of cliffs, I watched the curtain of water pour over the upper cliff, much of it turning to spray. Where the spray caught the sun, there were flashes of rainbow—the full spectrum of colors but none of the bow.

From where I stood, my line of sight was directly down the edge of the second drop, which meant I could see the water pouring over the lip and vanishing. The only proof of its continuous fall was the ripples spreading across the big sunlit pool below. Unexpectedly, as I began to watch the water, I regretted that I had no way to collect any water from the bottom, no way to carry it up and pour it into the stream at the top of the falls. I remembered the satisfaction of fetching, carrying, and releasing the water—my own tiny water cycle at the edge of the thundering falls. The memory made me feel connected to this place again, where a year ago I had felt myself grow stronger. Pouring the fall's water back into itself was like tending a garden, a way of lending a hand to life. But, of course, the only life in this process was mine.

The year between those two Saturdays was an ongoing journey of recovery, combined with a search for meaning and understanding. Writing this book helped me to dig deep into myself, but the search is not over simply because I have finished writing. My brush with death may always remain an enigma, but I won't turn my back on it. Meditation has an extra purpose now.

My twenty-two-year relationship with Everest has reached a turning point. I vividly remember my few minutes alone on the summit, with the world beneath me. And I can still recall how daunted I felt on the day that I stepped onto the North Face for the first time back in 1984. Everest had an undeniable aura then, but at the time, I tried to tell myself that it was just another mountain. However, there is no denying the power of the ongoing accumulation of myths and legends, successes and tragedies—in fact, I had become a part of that accumulation myself.

Edmund Hillary's climbing partner, Tenzing Norgay, reached the summit of Mount Everest on his seventh attempt, in 1953. It took fifty-three-year-old Australian Mike Rheinberger seven attempts as well before he summited in 1994. Mike had declared that 1994 would be his last Everest expedition, and it was. Not far below the summit he died from exhaustion, perhaps boosted by edema. I had known Mike, of course, as there were very few Australian high-altitude mountaineers in those days. It is only now that I realize how his fate could so easily have also been mine.

It is the tragedies more than the triumphs that maintain Everest's aura. The mountain is a mirror, where climbers look to find themselves. They discover their frailty, take heart from their strengths, drink deep of the insights. But if the mountain was to have a perspective, it would be that humans are the dust on the surface of the mirror—readily wiped away by storms, hardly relevant in scale, ephemeral in the scope of the mountain's existence. Human hopes and ambitions are as independent of the mountain as my fetching and pouring water have been for the waterfall beside me.

Although my foot had almost recovered, it took me more than twenty minutes to walk back to our house that Saturday afternoon. I was happy to walk slowly. Thunder clouds were gathering to the south, which meant it was very likely we would enjoy not only lightning but also some rain. I had learned that some of the best sunsets happened when the clouds were moving eastward after a storm.

Often at home we sit outside and watch the sunset from the sandstone slab that slopes away from our doorstep. Dylan likes to take photographs of the best sunsets and regularly updates them as the desktop background to his computer screen. Sometimes all four of us sit and watch the colors change; sometimes it is just me and Barbara, often only me. At that time of day our two big dogs like to burn off the last of their energy, running in circles, biting each other's necks, legs, or tails. I love the dogs, I love my family. In particular, I love the two-way street of love, but I am a man so I'm not going to say that to anybody. I certainly do not have to tell Barbara. All that has to happen is for our eyes to meet.

These days I love to take in the sunset because every time I do so, I remember how lucky I am to be alive. That's a great relationship to have with the setting sun.

I SEE THE WORLD differently after Everest but not because my eyes are hazel now rather than the blue of the preceding fifty years. The difference is that I have a 360-degree view. The devil did not attach eyes to the back of my head before I leaped from his spade. All that has happened is that I am now very aware of what surrounds me. As I sit here at 2:00 A.M., typing these final words, I am aware of the mist swirling around our cozy home, of the cliffs to the west and the valley beyond, of the waterfall thundering in the dark beyond my hearing. I am aware that everyone else in the house is sleeping, not only Norbu on the rug beside me. It is not an assumption; I can feel the pervasiveness of sleep.

There are so many stimuli thrown at us through our lives and so many roads of perception down which we could travel. If we indulged ourselves in all of them, we would go mad, but instead most of us go to the other extreme and numb ourselves by developing habitual responses that allow us to slip into autopilot mode. We go to foreign countries but see everything in the form of postcards.

On the mountain, death had, in effect, begun to consume my consciousness, and the autopilot had been turned off. My habitual responses to everyday issues were deprogrammed. I found myself holding fewer opinions when I realized that they only created dichotomies, and the next step from there is judgment. Too often we judge when we have no need to do so, and just as often we ignore. My scrape with death had shaken me free of some of those restrictions. I now find myself in a space where judgments are fewer, where habits don't seem as necessary. I do not have any more answers than anyone else, or even more than I was accustomed to having. What I do have is a stronger feeling of the unity of which I am a part. There is no messiah complex here—unfortunately, I am just as fallible and imperfect as I have always been.

IN THIS NEW LIGHT I see that the best thing about having climbed Mount Everest is not so much having done it but more the fact that now I don't have to do it. No longer do I have that unfinished business, and I can move on.

7SUMMITS-CLUB
EVEREST EXPEDITION

April 10–June 10, 2006

Leader
Alexander Abramov (Russia)

Sirdar
Mingma Gelu Sherpa* (Nepal)

Guides

Sergey Chistyakov (Russia)

Sergey Kofanov (Russia)*

Ludmila Korobeshko (Russia)

Maxim Onipchenko (Russia)

Dr. Andrey Selivanov (Russia)

Igor Svergun* (Ukraine)

Nikolai Cherny (Russia)

Climbers

Vince Bousselaire†† (USA)

Johnny Brevik (Norway)

John Delaney (Ireland)

Michael Dillon (Australia)

Patrick Flynn (Ireland)

Giuseppe Gariano (Italy)

Petter Kragset (Norway)

Vladimir Lande* (Russia)

Lorenzo Gariano* (UK)

Noel Hanna* (UK)

Lincoln Hall* (Australia)

Christopher Harris (Australia)

Richard Harris (Australia)

Frode Høgset (Norway)

Vladimir Pushkarev (Russia)

Ilya Rozhkov (Russia)

David A. Lien (USA)

Ron Morrow (USA)

Ronald Muhl** (South Africa)

Henrik Olsen* (Denmark)

Torbjørn Orkelbog (Norway)

Igor Plyushkin† (Russia)

Arkadiy Ryzhenko* (Russia)

Slate Stern* (USA)

Barbara Tyler (USA)

William Tyler III** (USA)

Thomas Weber† (Germany)

Kirk Wheatley* (UK)

Sherpas

Dawa Tenzing Sherpa*

Dorje Sherpa*

Furba Kushang Sherpa*

Jangbu Sherpa*

Lakcha Sherpa*

Mingma Sherpa*

Nima Sherpa*

Pasang Sherpa

Passang Gyalgen Sherpa*

Passang Sherpa

Pemba Sherpa

Pemba Norbu Sherpa

Renjin Sherpa*

Cooks

Chandra Sherpa (chief cook)

Chandra Sherpa (assistant cook)

Dawa Sherpa

Tendi Sherpa

KEY

* Summited 2006

** Summited 2007

† Died

†† Died 2008, on Matterhorn

Notes on My Survival

I have been asked many questions about the physical factors that kept me alive during my ordeal. One thing I have learned over the years is that it is often impossible to separate interactions among the mental, the spiritual, and the physical. A good example from my experience is the spiritual practice of yogic breathing, which has the huge benefit—for high-altitude mountaineers, at least—of making everyday breathing more efficient, regardless of the purpose and motivation of the practitioner. The boundaries of the body-mind-spirit trinity are even more blurred for me after my night on Everest.

Some physical realities, on the other hand, are easier to outline. What follows is a list of items—food, clothing, and the like—that are a part of normal life on the mountain. Some of these, I feel, contributed greatly to my survival that night.

MOUNTAIN CLOTHING AND OTHER ESSENTIALS

The climate is uncomfortable at Base Camp and intimidating on the mountain. I knew what to expect from the weather, but the storms, winds, and sub-zero temperatures frightened me more than anything else because these elements were completely beyond my control. Survival on a big mountain begins with appropriate clothing.

Base Camp to North Col

Skin layer: Long-sleeved T-shirt of silk-wool mix, by Silkbody. Merino wool long johns, by Icebreaker.

Second layer: Long-sleeved zip-neck top of merino, by Icebreaker.

Third layer: Lhotse lightweight fleece jacket by Mountain Designs. During good weather this garment was rarely worn under the wind suit.

Outer layer: Gore-Tex wind suit, by Mountain Designs. A great solution for keeping out icy winds; worn with two or three layers underneath, depending on conditions.

Head: Fleece headband (covering ears), by Mountain Designs. Face scarf, to protect from wind and sun, by Buff.

Hands: Fleece gloves, or silk gloves inside fleece gloves, or Black Diamond ice climbing gauntlets, depending on conditions and terrain.

Feet: Scarpa Zero Gravity 10 leather boots with two pairs of woolen socks to 22,000 feet. Above 22,000 feet, La Sportiva Olympus Mons EVO double boots (insulated inner boot and an outer plastic shell with insulated integral gaiters).

In my pack for colder conditions: Lhotse lightweight fleece jacket with polypropylene panels providing stretch on insides of sleeves and sides, by Mountain Designs; Bee's Knees polypropylene long johns paneled with 100-weight fleece on thighs and buttocks, by Macpac; expedition down jacket, by Mountain Designs; woolen cap; Petzl microlamp (always in my pack for emergencies).

23,000 feet to 27,000 feet

Skin layer: Long-sleeved T-shirt and long johns of silk-wool mix, by Silkbody.

Second layer: Zip-zap long-sleeved zip-neck top of polypropylene with 100-weight fleece across shoulders, chest, and outside sleeves, by Macpac. Merino long johns, by Icebreaker.

Outer layer: Full-body down suit, by Mountain Designs.

Head: Home-knitted woolen balaclava; face scarf, to protect from wind and sun, by Buff; prescription glacier glasses.

Hands: My Black Diamond gauntlets proved to be warm enough all the way to High Camp. I used silk or fleece gloves for photography.

Feet: Bridgedale Trekker socks (70 percent merino wool) inside

Bridgedale Summit socks (merino/Coolmax). La Sportiva Olympus Mons EVO double boots.

In my pack: Lhotse lightweight fleece jacket; Bolle ski goggles; spare prescription glacier glasses; Princeton Tec headlamp; Petzl headlamp as backup; Petzl microlamp; Canon 30 SLR film camera; diary.

What I Took to the Summit

Skin layer: Long-sleeved T-shirt and long johns of silk-wool mix, by Silkbody.

Second layer: Zip-zap long-sleeved zip-neck top. Bee's Knees long johns, both by Macpac.

Third layer: Lhotse lightweight fleece jacket.

Outer layer: Full-body down suit, by Mountain Designs.

Head: Home-knitted woolen balaclava; face scarf, to protect from wind and sun, by Buff; Bolle ski goggles; oxygen mask.

Hands: I had expected to be wearing silk gloves inside fleece gloves inside down mitts during my climb from High Camp to the summit and back. Instead, my Black Diamond ice-climbing gauntlets proved warm enough for the rock-climbing sections of the Exit Cracks, and for the North Ridge, including the Second Step. When we rested at the Third Step, I switched to the silk gloves inside fleece gloves inside down mitts.

Feet: Two pairs Bridgedale merino socks, one sock inside another; La Sportiva Olympus Mons EVO double boots.

In my pockets: Spare gloves; chemical handwarmers; Diamox diuretic tablets (for treatment of edema); two carbohydrate nutritional gels; two small zip-lock bags with daily allocation of supplements.

Tucked inside my down suit: Small digital camera on neck strap; thermos of warm flavored water.

Pack: Pillar Climbing pack, 45 liter capacity, by Mountain Designs, containing: Poisk oxygen cylinder with regulator; handmade Australian flag; copy of *Teaspoon of Courage* by sponsor Bradley Trevor Greive; Princeton Tec headlamp; Petzl headlamp as spare; Petzl microlamp; extra carbohydrate nutritional gel.

Throughout the climb I had crampons for my boots, my ice axe, my harness, several carabiners, and descender and ascender for use on the fixed ropes. At Base Camp I kept a cozy fleece bib-and-brace and other comfort items.

NUTRITION

Earlier in the book I mentioned nutritional supplements, carefully chosen to fill vital gaps in the classic expedition diet and to help my metabolism deal with the great stress of extreme altitude. Although I was amazed at the extraordinary range of the foodstuffs that Alex brought to Base Camp, I knew that the lack of fresh food had major nutritional implications, particularly with the strenuous nature of high-altitude living.

Energy needs are enormous in the low-oxygen environment of high mountains, but appetite fails, nausea follows, and vomiting what little food you have eaten is not uncommon. Toward the end of a major expedition, the available foodstuffs are highly processed and loaded with preservatives. For this reason I make sure to have a comprehensive range of nutritional supplements specifically for my high-altitude needs; I have done so since 2001. I take one of the most comprehensive supplements available every day, as it provides optimal levels of important vitamins and minerals.

For lung function I take an extract of the *Cordyceps sinensis* fungus. For brain function and cerebral edema prevention I take a potent *Ginkgo biloba* leaf extract. Obviously, I suffered severe cerebral edema, but to my knowledge, I am the only person to have survived the fatal condition above 28,000 feet. I believe ginkgo may have had a positive influence on my cerebral edema. Some mountaineers use ginkgo instead of the drug Diamox as an altitude-sickness prophylactic. Ginkgo can also help limit cold injury by stimulating microcirculation.

Sore knees are a common complaint of long-term mountaineers. One reason is that mountaineering boots protect the ankles but limit ankle movement, so that the jolts and stresses are passed on to the knees. After several years with a sore left knee, for which I had acupuncture treatments, I found a product that kept my knees in good shape. The crucial ingredients are glucosamine sulfate, vitamin E (in two forms), and quercetin.

The reishi mushroom, also known as *ling zhi*, has long been hailed as an immune system modulator in traditional Chinese medicine. I have found it an excellent alternative to taking drugs when I am ill or when I sense illness coming on. It boosts the efficiency of the immune system, which often allows me to avoid taking pharmaceutical drugs.

Another boost to nutrition on Everest was home-dried fruit. Barbara and I used an Ezidri Snackmaker to dry a wide range of early-fall fruits—plums, kiwifruit, nectarines, and oranges—which we then vacuum-sealed in plastic bags. I also bought organic dried bananas and several kinds of nuts. A final item was a bottle of flaxseed oil, valuable for its omega fatty acids.

CLIMATE FACTORS

When the Sherpas declared me dead near Mushroom Rock, at 28,000 feet on Everest's Northeast Ridge, the weather was comparatively mild, that is, below freezing, with very little wind. It was estimated that the wind increased threefold to fifteen miles per hour and the temperature dropped to –13° Fahrenheit (–25° Celsius). I am not sure of the accuracy of these forecasts, or how they could be verified with no one to measure at that height on Everest. The effective temperature would have been reduced by the wind cooling my body. The power of the fifteen-mile-per-hour wind at –13°F (–25°C) would have given a windchill temperature of –36°F (–38°C). The snowfall during the night would have meant that the temperature had not fallen lower.

THE UNFINISHED STORY

Not surprisingly, the topic of my survival against all odds is of ongoing interest for me, and I will continue to explore it. Already I am finding this an exciting journey. My degree in biological sciences gives me a scientific base for my investigations of near-death experiences and the factors that allow certain people to survive where others die. *Dead Lucky* may be updated in future editions; meanwhile, I will be posting information on the Web. Besides more information about the psychological, emotional, and mental aspects of survival—among them attitude, yoga, meditation, and "deep training"—I will include my thoughts on quality supplements and effective physical training. Please visit: www .fit4everest.com.

Acknowledgments

WHEN I RETURNED from Everest, I was a mental and physical wreck and, as a consequence, *Dead Lucky* has been the most difficult of the eight books I have written. The book begins not with my own words but with those of Lachlan Murdoch—to whom I owe special thanks for the time, consideration, and insight he put into writing the foreword.

I would not have been able to make a start on the book at all without the help of my agent, Margaret Gee. Margaret understood that on this occasion I needed much more than most authors ask of their agents, and she gave that and more. Margaret's psychiatrist husband, Brent Waters, not only prompted the recall of memories but in the process also led me to develop the backbone of the story. Without Margaret and Brent I would have begun the writing like Chapter 3—behind the eight ball. Thanks also to Dee Spinks for her transcriptions.

The perfect publisher whom Margaret found for my book was Random House Australia, where Jeanne Ryckmans embraced the project. The greatest thanks that I would like to give to Jeanne is for her faith in my ability to deliver. I had a track record of other books with well-known publishers, but for all those I had at least been physically able to write! Vital to the success of the book was the offer by Jeanne of an editorial assistant. Barbara and I approached Margaret Hamilton, a friend who was also a semiretired publisher, for advice. Although vastly overqualified, Margaret was perfect for the job: very knowledgeable about everything to do with books, very patient and understanding of my erratic work habits, and uncomplaining about the many, many hours of transcribing interviews and other recordings. The book would have been much the poorer without her help. I would also like to thank our Seattle friend Salley Oberlin for her valuable comments on the manuscript.

Julian Welch, my editor at Random House, did an excellent job of gently convincing me that changes needed to be made. His work definitely improved the standard of the manuscript. By the end of the process, timing was very tight, and it was only due to Julian's flexibility and initiative that the book came out on time. I enjoyed working with Peta Levett on the publicity campaign.

Although the book is largely my personal story, there were many facts I needed to check. Medical distractions prompted me to ask outdoors enthusiast and journalist Alistair Paton to find the facts hidden within the rumors and hype that surrounded events on Everest that season. Alistair also directed me to Billi Bierling, who had also visited the north side of Everest and shared with me her understanding of several events that were important to my story. Jamie McGuinness was very supportive of me at Advance Base Camp and afterward provided Alistair with some good sources of information, including Michael Kodas, who gave me valuable background on ethics and robbery on Everest.

Thanks to Ken Beatty for his inspired illustrations and to Norbert Gilewsky for scanning my photos and for supplying me with "the devil's spade." Harry Kikstra and Mike Dillon have added to the book with some superb photographs, as have Andrew Brash, Jamie McGuinness, Robyn Leeder, and Lucas Trihey.

Also vital in making the story possible were, of course, Dan Mazur, Myles Osborne, Andrew Brash, and Jangbu Sherpa, whose care and attention gave me the opportunity to descend the mountain after my night out. Thanks are also due to the unsung hero of that morning, Phil Crampton, who was able to alert Alex's team to the fact that I was still alive. Jamie McGuinness, leader of the expedition, camped next to us at ABC, offered every support that he could to Alex.

The fact that I am alive today is due to the dedication of Lakcha Sherpa, Dorje Sherpa, Dawa Tenzing Sherpa, and Pemba Sherpa, who brought me down to Mushroom Rock, the launching pad for my escape from the mountain. Mingma Gelu and his team of Sherpas also worked hard on my behalf.

Essential to my well-being was the support offered by Richard Harris, Christopher Harris, and Michael Dillon. Alex Abramov provided all the medical necessities, including the services of Dr. Andrey Selivanov. Ludmila Korobeshko, Maxim Onipchenko, Sergey Kofanov, Milan Collin, and Harry Kikstra helped me at both Advance Base and Base camps. Kevin Augello told me that arranging the first phone call between Barbara and me was one of the most significant moments in his life, and Barbara and I are grateful for the care he showed us. Another key figure was Russell Brice, who advised Alex and his team when it seemed that I would die and subsequently helped me understand what had happened.

At the Tibetan border I was welcomed by the Australian ambassador, Graeme Lade, who made sure that Barbara, Mike, Simon, and I were well looked after during our stay in Kathmandu. Thanks to Christine Gee, Garry Weare, and Margie Hamilton (not to be confused with Margaret Hamilton) of the Australian Himalayan Foundation, and of course to Simon Balderstone for the many tasks and responsibilities he took on for us in Sydney, Kathmandu, and New York. Greg Mortimer and Margaret Werner gave us great support, as always.

After an Olympic relay of e-mail exchanges it was a great pleasure to visit the Penguin Group offices in New York and meet with the folks from Tarcher. Thanks to Joel Fotinos for his enthusiasm for the book and for putting his words into action by publishing it. I was particularly pleased to sit down with the three people charged with the task of bringing the book to North American readers: Sara Carder, who managed the project; Katherine Obertance, who had the demanding task of working on the manuscript via e-mail despite mutually exclusive time zones; and Shanta Small, who has organized an exciting nationwide publicity campaign that is sure to give the book wide exposure.

Writing the book was only possible because of the many people who tended to my health after my ordeal. Expedition doctor Andrey Selivanov began the process. I had total faith in his ability to do what was best for me, in difficult and initially dangerous circumstances. Dr. Pandey and Nurse Shanti took wonderful care of me at the CIWEC Clinic in Kathmandu. Back home, I give my heartfelt thanks to Dr. Ian Carr-Boyd, Dr. Stuart Myers, Dr. Ian Jacobson, and Dr. Adrian Walker. The surgery that Dr. Sean Nicklin performed on my hands was so good that I almost wished I had asked him to trim the tips of my fingers years ago.

For an amazing four weeks, I spent two hours a day, four days a week, at the hyperbaric chamber at Prince of Wales Hospital, thanks to Dr. Rob Turner and his team. I am particularly grateful to voice pathologist Rachelle Simpson for helping me deal with my paralyzed vocal cord, and to hand therapists Emilie Myers and James Storeman for training me to look after my modified fingers. Finally, on the health front, I would like to thank natural therapist and reflexologist Penny Henderson, acupuncturist Ruth Mayroz, and Arara Bhakti for boosting my healing with their knowledge, their skills, and their understanding of my needs.

I also thank my workmates at Emap and *Outdoor Australia*—David Kettle, Louise Southerden, Tony Nolan, and Derek Morrison. I would also like to thank Derek for the protective *hei matau* amulet of New Zealand greenstone, which I wore around my neck for the whole expedition. Other talismans that accompanied the *hei matau* were a holy thread given to me by Ang Karma Sherpa and blessed by the Rinpoche of Rongbuk Monastery, and a necklace of coral, turquoise, and malachite assembled for me by Barbara. Bradley Trevor Greive liked to think that his Rolex also performed the function of a talisman, and perhaps it did indeed. His support of our repatriation from Kathmandu was a very generous act. As a successful author, BTG's encouragement was invaluable in the early months of the book when I was having difficulty making progress.

Thanks to Ngakpa Karma Lhundup Rinpoche for the *puja* at our home that lifted our spirits and brought together so many of our friends.

I would also like to thank our expedition sponsors: Dick Smith Foods, BTG Studios, the Australian Geographic Society, Mountain Designs, Spinifex Interactive, WebCentral, TC Communications, Thai Airways, Ivany Investments, Hillmark Industries, Adventure Extreme, and Buff Downunder. My teammates and I are grateful for the individual support offered by Ian and Min Darling, Gretchen Dechert, and Andrew Rogers. I would like to applaud Dick Smith for being such a staunch supporter of adventurers over many years.

And last but not least, to my friends and family, who endured the unthinkable. The list is too long to mention here, but you know who you are.

Glossary

ACCLIMATIZATION
Changes in response to altitude that develop over weeks or months and allow climbers to tolerate increasingly lower levels of oxygen.

ANIMISM
The belief that spiritual components and qualities exist in animals, plants, and other material objects, implying a unification of matter and spirit.

ASCENDER
A metal clamp used for climbing fixed ropes. It can be slid up the rope, but as soon as weight is applied, it locks in position. Also known as a jumar.

AVALANCHE
The sliding away from a mountain of massive amounts of surface material, commonly snow but also ice, mud, and rocks.

BIVOUAC
A night spent on a mountain without a proper camp, i.e., no tents and often no sleeping bag.

BUTTRESS
A mass of rock bulging out of a mountainside.

CARABINER
A strong oval snap-link used to clip the climber or the rope to an anchor or a harness.

CEREBRAL EDEMA
Retention of fluid in the brain, an often fatal malfunction of the metabolism due to the lack of oxygen and low air pressure at high altitude. Can generally be avoided by careful, gradual acclimatization.

CHANGTSE
The north peak of Mount Everest, which is separated from the main peak by the North Col. At 25,870 feet, it is an impressive mountain, offering challenging climbing, but it is overshadowed by Everest and practically ignored by climbers.

CHO OYU
The world's sixth-highest mountain (26,906 feet). It lies on the border between Nepal and Tibet, west of Mount Everest, with ascents invariably made from the Tibetan side of the mountain.

CHORTEN
A small wayside Buddhist shrine constructed of stones.

COL
A high pass.

CORNICE
An overhanging lip of ice, formed by wind on the crest of a ridge.

COULOIR
A major mountain gully, usually with a base of snow or ice and often providing the easiest route through steep rock, but also subject to rock- and ice-fall.

CRAMPONS
Lightweight alloy frames with twelve spikes that are strapped or clipped to mountaineering boots to enable the boots to grip on ice. Two points protruding horizontally from the front of the boot make climbing steep ice possible.

CREVASSE

A fissure or deep cleft in the ice of a glacier, frequently hidden beneath a surface crust of snow, forming a considerable hazard.

CWM

A Welsh word (pronounced *coomb*) meaning "high valley."

DESCENDER

A small metal device for rappeling. The descender regulates the speed of the slide by increasing the friction between the climber and the rope.

DIURETIC

A substance, either natural or synthetic, that increases the formation of urine. Used at high altitude to regulate fluid retention.

EDEMA

See CEREBRAL EDEMA and PULMONARY EDEMA.

EIGHT-THOUSANDERS/8000ers

There are fourteen peaks in the world that are over 8,000 meters (26,247 feet) above sea level. Climbing all fourteen is far more challenging than the Seven Summits.

FIXED ROPE

Fixing rope on a mountain can be compared to building a railway line. It permits quick and safe ascents and descents between camps on the mountain. The different sections of the route need only be climbed once—after that they are surmounted by ascending the fixed rope. Rope-fixing is a laborious and expensive procedure, so the method is usually restricted to big mountains—mainly those of the Himalaya.

FROSTBITE

Extreme cold causes the minor blood vessels to constrict and, at the same time, ice crystals to form between cells. This leads to a reduction in the oxygen supply to the cells and their consequent deterioration. It particularly affects extremities—fingers, toes, ears, nose, lips. Badly frostbitten members may have to be amputated.

HARNESS

In the event of a fall, a waist harness with leg loops (to which the climbing rope is tied) is much safer and more comfortable than a rope around the waist. Harnesses are used for rappeling and ascending fixed ropes.

HIMALAYA

A series of mountain ranges running from Bhutan in the east, through the Indian province of Sikkim, westward along the northern border of Nepal, into the Indian provinces of Garhwal and Uttar Pradesh, then tapering into the alpine ranges of Kashmir.

HYPOTHERMIA

Subnormal body temperature. When exposed to extreme cold, the human body cannot maintain a constant core temperature. The hypothermia which occurs is fatal unless the person is rapidly rewarmed.

HYPOXIA

Lack of oxygen; the state of being deprived of oxygen.

ICE AXE

The essential mountaineering tool, used for climbing and belaying, and as a brake when a climber slips.

ICEFALL

The enormous crevasses and pinnacles formed when a glacier falls over a steep declivity and the ice fractures. Because of the downward movement of the glacier, an icefall is unstable and consequently dangerous.

KANCHENJUNGA

The third-highest mountain in the world at 28,169 feet, it lies on the border of Nepal and the Indian province of Sikkim.

KARAKORAM

The great Central Asian mountain range, this northwestern sister of the Himalaya extends from India, through Pakistan to Afghanistan, and is bordered by Chinese territory on its north.

LAMA

A Tibetan Buddhist monk.

LHOTSE

The western peak of Everest, separated from the main summit by the South Col and, at 27,940 feet, the fourth-highest peak in the world.

MAKALU

The fifth-highest peak in the world at 27,765 feet, located fifteen miles east of Everest.

MANASLU

At 26,781 feet, Manaslu is the world's eighth-highest peak. It is situated in central Nepal.

MISÈRE

A hand which contains no winning card but which, in the card game of Five Hundred, allows the misère player to win.

MORAINE

The mass of boulders, gravel, sand, and clay carried on or deposited by a glacier.

MOUNTAINEERING BOOTS

For extremely cold conditions, a light felt or synthetic boot is worn inside a large outer boot, usually with an insulated gaiter attached externally.

NÉVÉ

An area of accumulated snow at the head of a glacier.

NORTH COL

At 23,200 feet, the North Col forms the low point on the ridge between Changtse and Everest. This is where expeditions climbing Everest's Northeast Ridge set their first camp on the mountain proper (as opposed to Advance Base Camp and Intermediate Camp, which are on the East Rongbuk Glacier).

OXYGEN EQUIPMENT

A cylinder of oxygen gas equipped with regulators and a face mask for counteracting oxygen deficiency at high altitude.

PICKET

A piece of angular aluminum, about two feet in length, which is hammered into hard snow to provide an anchor for ropes.

PUJA

The act of showing reverence to a god, a spirit, or another aspect of the divine through invocations, prayers, songs, and rituals.

PULMONARY EDEMA

An acute form of altitude sickness in which water accumulates on the linings of the lungs. Retreat to lower altitudes usually results in complete recovery, but failure to descend is generally fatal.

RAPPEL

Method of descent by sliding down a rope. The amount of friction between the climber and the rope determines the speed of descent. If the rope is doubled, it can be retrieved after the rappel by pulling one of the ends. A descender is a small metal device clipped to a climber's harness that provides the same degree of friction in a more secure and easily controllable fashion. Descenders are generally used when descending fixed ropes.

ROPE

Climbing rope is used most frequently in lengths of 165 feet. Modern rope is designed to stretch, in order to absorb the force generated by a falling climber. Ropes used for rappeling and ascending are called static ropes and have less stretch.

SCREE

A steep mass of broken rock on the side of a mountain.

SERAC

An isolated block of ice formed where the glacier surface is fractured. Seracs pose a threat to climbers because they are sometimes unstable and can topple over at any time. Falling seracs on steep glaciers can trigger avalanches.

SHERPA

A race of people, Tibetan in origin, which settled in the Solu Khumbu area near Everest and other high valleys in Nepal, though many Sherpas now live in Darjeeling, Kathmandu, and North America.

SIRDAR

A Nepali word meaning "boss," applied to the foreman, guide, and employer of a group of porters.

SLEEPING MATS

Used as insulation when camping on snow. There are two basic types: closed-cell foam and thin self-inflating mats such as Thermarest®. They are warmer and lighter than airbeds.

SNOW BLINDNESS

Temporary blindness caused in a matter of hours by the glare from a glacier or snow field. The condition is very painful and recovery can take days. Goggles and sunglasses are worn to prevent snow blindness.

STUPA

A Buddhist shrine, generally with a solid dome as a base and a rectangular tower on top.

TALUS

A sloping mass of rocky fragments at the base of a cliff. Common usage classifies the talus rock fragments as being larger than those of scree.

TIBETAN BUDDHISM

Tibetan Buddhism is a form of Mahayana Buddhism, with an element of animism, that is practiced in Tibet, Ladakh, Nepal, Sikkim, Bhutan, and Mongolia, and is derived from the confluence of Buddhism and yoga.

TIBETAN MOUNTAINEERING ASSOCIATION (TMA)

An organization that appoints Liaison Officers to monitor the behavior of expeditions and travelers in politically sensitive areas. Usually, two or more Liaison Officers are stationed at Everest Base Camp during the climbing seasons.

YAKPA

A person who herds yaks or uses them for transport.

Index

A Conversation with Barbara Scanlan

Many readers of *Dead Lucky* have been intrigued by the experience of Barbara Scanlan, Lincoln's wife. Was she frightened when he announced that he would be returning to Everest at the age of fifty? And what must it have been like for her to have thought she had lost her husband only to discover he was still alive? In this fascinating interview, she answers these questions and more.

Q: Even though Lincoln is a veteran mountain climber, did you have any concerns about him taking on Everest? If so, what were they?
When Lincoln first mentioned going back to Everest as a cameraman I had a few reservations, mainly about his age and related fitness. I certainly knew he had experience and good judgment on his side. As things turned out he quickly acquired the level of fitness he needed, almost as though his body remembered how to adapt to the changes associated with altitude.

Q: You visited Everest prior to Lincoln's expedition. Did that visit help you understand your husband's desire to climb Everest or did it awaken fears in you about the attempt?
I had been to Nepal twice before, once when Dylan was a baby and

*again when Dorje was a baby, and when I met Lincoln's friends there
I understood why he enjoyed spending time in the mountains with the
local people. As for Lincoln's climbing, I already understood his love
for mountains and mountaineering, and his particular attachment for
the Himalaya. Mountaineering in those amazing ranges has shaped and
honed many of Lincoln's values. Visiting Everest Base Camp with my
family helped to set the scene a little more clearly in my mind's eye.*

Q: How did you cope with the stress and anxiety while he was away?
*When Lincoln is away our family finds a different rhythm. We were all
very busy: Dylan was in his final year of high school, studying for his
final examinations; Dorje was busy with school, sport, and music; and
I had work commitments as well as running the home and supporting
the boys in all their endeavors. I also knew that the dangerous part of
the climb was at the very end in the last day or so. So I wasn't feeling
stressed and anxious most of the time. Dylan's eighteenth birthday was
May 24, but because Lincoln was away we had decided to wait until
he returned before having a big celebration. Instead we went out for
a quiet dinner. When we returned home there was a message on the
answering machine from Lincoln saying he was going for the summit
the next morning. He described ideal conditions, but that was actually
when I began to feel anxious.*

Q: During Lincoln's Everest climb, you mention having the sensation
that something wasn't right, that he might be in danger. Describe what
made you feel that way.
*I was at work on the afternoon of May 25 when a call came through
from a friend who announced jubilantly that Lincoln had reached
the summit that morning. I didn't feel jubilant at all because I hadn't
wanted to hear that news except from Lincoln himself when he was
back at a safe camp. I knew that the descent was more dangerous due
to fatigue. I had a very long train ride home that evening and although
I thought about calling everyone, I eventually decided only to call two
people, Lincoln's father and the outdoor magazine Lincoln edited at*

that time. It didn't feel quite right. I hoped that there would be another message from Lincoln when I arrived home as he would have had plenty of time to reach camp by then. There wasn't any message and so that's when I began to sense that something had gone wrong. When I finally heard that he was still close to the summit, seven or eight hours after reaching it, I was stunned as there was no explanation, at that stage, of what had happened to him and I knew that the chances of him getting down were shrinking rapidly.

Q: The night you went to sleep, believing your husband to be dead, you had a dream that gave you hope. Do you remember what that dream was?

I had a very restless night. It was very cold, and even though I turned on the electric blanket to full I just couldn't get warm. Eventually I was woken by a vivid dream. I could see Lincoln very clearly. He was wearing one of his favorite fleece jackets from a much earlier expedition. I was waiting for him as he strode with his very distinctive gait, smiling. I awoke feeling a surge of happiness that was immediately replaced by a feeling of hollowness. But I couldn't forget the dream and as I was making coffee, Dorje came into the kitchen. I told him about the dream and we just looked at each other, feeling rather hopeless. When we heard much later that day that Lincoln was alive, Dorje immediately reminded me about my dream and we just hugged each other very tightly. Some weeks later, Lincoln and I were talking about the dream and worked out that it occurred roughly at the time that Lincoln felt he was "returning the cloak." It was shortly after this hallucination that he regained consciousness and realized where he actually was and knew it would take everything he had to return to us.

Q: When you were finally reunited with Lincoln in Nepal, what went through your mind? Did you have the sense that you were "out of the woods" danger wise?

When I was first reunited with Lincoln in Kathmandu, I could see that there was something very different about him. We were only able to spend a few moments together that afternoon and so it wasn't until later that night that I noticed that his eyes had changed color! I knew then that the road to recovery was going to be long, but I had complete faith in his strength and ultimately his resilience. I had been concerned that he might have changed in character, but his rather left-field sense of humor was completely intact. So I knew that the old Lincoln had come back, for which I was, and still am, immensely grateful.

Q: Have any of your children expressed a desire to get into mountain climbing—and possibly scale Everest some day? If so, how do you feel about that?

Although both our sons are very competent in the outdoors, neither have expressed a strong desire to become mountaineers. However, when we were trekking to Everest Base Camp in 2004, our oldest son Dylan spent a morning jogging to Ama Dablam Base Camp with one of the Sherpas accompanying us. Dorje needed a rest day as he had had a terrible gastric infection, from which he was recovering with antibiotics. We had thought that it would take Dylan the whole day but he was back by lunch. He was totally inspired and thought at that time he would like to do more. He does seem to have the same natural physical aptitude for mountaineering as Lincoln and so perhaps one day he will do more. Dorje is similarly built. Five thousand meters slows me down significantly but they barely notice it! I have no doubt that if either of them wanted to seriously take up mountaineering they would do so with a much deeper understanding of the dangers involved than other young men.

Lincoln Hall is one of Australia's best-known mountaineers, with a climbing career that spans three decades, most notably in the Himalaya, Antarctica, and the Andes. He had a key role in the first Australian ascent of Mount Everest in 1984, and his account of that expedition, *White Limbo*, became a bestseller. Hall's second book, *The Loneliest Mountain*, recounted a journey to Antarctica in a small yacht and the first ascent of Mount Minto. *Fear No Boundary* is Hall's biography of his friend Sue Fear, who died mountaineering in the Himalaya while Hall was on Mount Everest in 2006. He has published one work of fiction, *Blood on the Lotus*, a historical novel set in Nepal and Tibet.

Hall, who has worked as a trekking guide and edited adventure magazines, is a director of the Australian Himalayan Foundation. He was awarded the Medal of the Order of Australia in 1987 for his services to mountaineering. He lives with his wife, Barbara Scanlan, and their two sons, Dylan and Dorje, in Wentworth Falls in the Blue Mountains, New South Wales. His website address is www.lincolnhall.net.